Writing Philosophy Papers

This sixth edition of *Writing Philosophy Papers* updates and expands one of the most popular guides to philosophical writing assignments for undergraduate students. Written in a clear, straightforward style, the book covers everything from time management to the difference between "i.e." and "e.g."

The heart of the book is devoted to how to write a thesis-defense paper, with chapters on the structure of a strong paper, the process of writing and revising, matters of style and usage, and scholarly citation. This advice is illustrated with concrete examples throughout, including a complete thesis-defense paper written and formatted according to the book's recommendations.

The book also covers how to take good notes from various kinds of philosophical sources, how to write other commonly assigned kinds of papers, and how to study for and take a philosophy exam. A chapter on doing philosophical research contains practical advice on how to discover and access the most helpful sources for a philosophical research paper or annotated bibliography. Because virtually every philosophy assignment requires a basic grasp of arguments, the book ends with a chapter introducing some basic concepts and skills for reasoning well.

The heart of the sixth edition has been revised and restructured to lead students even more clearly through the process of drafting, revising, and formatting a thesis-defense paper. This new edition also includes:

- an updated, completely revised, and expanded chapter on citing sources, giving equal consideration to print and online sources;
- an updated, completely revised, and expanded chapter on doing philosophical research, focused on how to find the most helpful sources for completing a philosophical research paper or annotated bibliography;
- updated, revised, and greatly expanded advice on writing style and usage;
- a completely revised and expanded treatment of good reasoning, with a new discussion of inductive and abductive reasoning; and
- new advice on how to take good notes and how to study for and take philosophy exams.

Zachary Seech is Professor of Philosophy at Palomar College and is the sole author of *Logic in Everyday Life* (1987), *Open Minds and Everyday Reasoning* (2nd Edition, 2004), and the first five editions of *Writing Philosophy Papers*. He was the Founder and Director of the Lincoln Critical Thinking Project.

Andrew Kania is Professor of Philosophy at Trinity University. He works primarily in philosophy of the arts and is the author of *Philosophy of Western Music: A Contemporary Introduction* (2020), co-editor (with Theodore Gracyk) of *The Routledge Companion to Philosophy and Music* (2011), and editor of *Memento* (Routledge "Philosophers on Film" series, 2009).

Writing Philosophy Papers

Sixth Edition

Zachary Seech and Andrew Kania

Routledge
Taylor & Francis Group
NEW YORK AND LONDON

Designed cover image: Cover photograph by Andrew Kania.

Sixth edition published 2025
by Routledge
605 Third Avenue, New York, NY 10158

and by Routledge
4 Park Square, Milton Park, Abingdon, Oxon, OX14 4RN

Routledge is an imprint of the Taylor & Francis Group, an informa business

First edition published by Cengage 1993
Fifth edition published by Cengage 2009

ISBN: 978-1-032-84343-8 (hbk)
ISBN: 978-1-032-84337-7 (pbk)
ISBN: 978-1-003-51231-8 (ebk)

DOI: 10.4324/9781003512318

Typeset in Sabon
by SPi Technologies Private Limited, India (Straive)

To the young ones:
Madeline
Thomas
Cole
– Z. S.

To my former students, and
to Zack—*il miglior fabbro*
– A. K.

Contents

Figures

Preface to the Sixth Edition

There are many books that provide general writing instruction; this book focuses on how to write *college-level philosophy papers*. Although the details of assignments vary from course to course and instructor to instructor, we provide advice and information that should be useful to any philosophy student tackling a writing assignment. Whether it's a question about organization, citation, research, or writing style, the student will now have the answer *before* submitting a paper to the instructor. This should be a relief both to the student, who can hardly do a good job of writing a paper if she is unsure how to proceed, and to the instructor, who must read the resulting paper.

Those familiar with earlier editions may be interested to know what has changed. On the one hand, *Writing Philosophy Papers* has proved its value through the success of five previous editions. On the other hand, with 15 years having passed since the fifth edition, and with the addition of a co-author, we have taken the opportunity to revisit the book with fresh eyes. We hope that we have preserved the same straightforward, accessible style while improving the clarity of the structure of the book and adding much new helpful material. (This sixth edition is roughly twice as long as the fifth.)

The material on the use of language has seen the greatest increase. What was a single chapter in the fifth edition has been expanded into two chapters: one on more general stylistic matters and the other on more detailed aspects of usage. The chapter on philosophical research has been reorganized, updated, and expanded. In the chapter on good reasoning, we now cover deductive reasoning in more detail and also consider nondeductive reasoning. (This material has also been promoted, as befits its length, from an appendix to a chapter proper.)

We have chosen to cover only one system of scholarly citation in Chapter 7: MLA-style in-text citations with a list of works cited. We chose this system because in-text citation seems to be in the ascendant in philosophical scholarship, and the MLA system is arguably a little simpler than its main rival, the Chicago system. We hope that we have given enough detail to enable students to cite almost any source they use. If more information is needed, or if instructors prefer their students to use another system, students should consult the relevant handbook or manual.

Appendixes A and B still offer illustrative marked-up drafts and a sample complete thesis-defense paper, but they have been revised to cover a wider range of writing issues and cited sources. Appendix C—offering some general advice on studying for, and taking, philosophy exams—is entirely new.

During the year in which we were drafting this edition, the academic world was convulsed by the release of ChatGPT. We say nothing in this book about the use of generative-AI tools in writing a philosophy paper. This is partly because it would be foolish to prophesy the norms of its use in student writing that will surely develop over time. But we also believe that, whatever those norms turn out to be, students will continue to be required to write philosophy papers, and that the skills we discuss in this book will continue to be essential to students who want to write good philosophy papers, whatever tools they use.

Acknowledgments

We would like to thank Andy Beck for his support of this project from its inception. We also thank two anonymous readers of the proposal and a complete draft, who gave us much food for thought. Melissa Brown Levine did an excellent job of copy-editing the text, Aishwariya Shankar and Britto Fleming Joe dealt with some complex typesetting challenges, and Alf Symons assisted us at a crucial point. Lindsey Esplin oversaw the book's production with reassuring professionalism.

– Z. S. & A. K.

I would like to thank the friendly crew at TERI Common Grounds Café and Coffee Bar for providing a pleasant setting for so many of my hours of manuscript preparation, and Matt Parsons for his warmly welcoming presence at TERI. I would also like to acknowledge my colleagues at Palomar College, and especially Mike Lockett, who received a number of surprise calls from me as I sat in reflection at the keyboard. I offer a special thanks to co-author Andrew for his spirited resolution to give new life to *Writing Philosophy Papers* and to Julie Post for helping us all along the way. Andrew has been easy to work with, gracious, and ever so hardworking on this, our shared project. Thank you, Andrew, for this collaboration that has taught me much. Finally, I gratefully offer grand hugs to all of my dear family.

– Z. S.

I had used the fifth edition of Zachary Seech's *Writing Philosophy Papers* in every one of my courses for over a decade when a student informed me in January 2022 that it had gone out of print. I immediately wrote to Dr. Seech, asking anxiously if he was planning a new edition. It was dismaying to imagine teaching my students how to write philosophy papers without the help of this excellent book. I was thus honored and delighted when (to cut a long story short) Zack and I agreed to collaborate on a new edition. I thank him for this opportunity and the wonderful experience of collaborating with such a wise writer, thinker, and teacher. I hope that the spirit of the book has survived my interventions.

I thank Julie Post for reading the entire manuscript and making numerous helpful suggestions. Thanks to Curtis Brown for generous and substantial help with my contributions to the chapter on good reasoning. Curtis Brown, Joe Bullock, and Chris Martin all helped with a small but intriguing question of logical history. Ronni Gura Sadovsky generously applied her equally sharp aesthetic and critical judgment to potential cover images. I thank Trinity University's Office of Academic Affairs for the academic leave that enabled me to work on the book in New Zealand and Jane Costanza, Lacey Brooks-Canales, and Alaynna Marttala at Trinity's Coates Library, who all helped me from afar. Benjamin Harris and Michael Hughes have worked with me on philosophical research assignments in my courses over many years. Much of the value of my contributions to Chapter 9 is due to them. Thanks, finally, to all the family and friends—too numerous to mention individually—who made my New Zealand sabbatical so easy and enjoyable.

– A. K.

Introduction

In daily life, people often toss ideas around—voicing their own opinions and criticizing others' on the basis of scant information gleaned from newspapers, magazines, and social media. But rarely do we take the time to develop our thoughts fully on a single topic. Half-baked ideas are sometimes the only items on our daily menus. In college, instructors require students to *write papers* to show how well they understand and express ideas, think critically about arguments, and do their own research. These same instructors research, write, and publish papers of their own for the benefit of other thinkers around the world.

A paper assignment is an opportunity to develop your ideas on a topic in a thorough and precise way. Unfortunately, much of what students need to know to take full advantage of this opportunity often goes unsaid. Instructors are so concerned with ensuring that their students understand a course's content that writing instruction is sometimes neglected. Students' resulting uncertainty and confusion are evident in common complaints and laments:

- The paper is due tomorrow, and I haven't even started it yet.
- I have no idea what the professor is looking for in this paper.
- What does she mean by "argue for"?
- I'm on the last page of my paper, and now I see that I can't prove what I said I would on the first page. What can I do?

Writing Philosophy Papers is designed to help students in philosophy courses make full use of the opportunity to write a paper. The first seven chapters are devoted to explaining how to go about what we take to be the paradigmatic college-level philosophy assignment: writing a thesis-defense paper. We begin, in Chapters 1 and 2, by explaining the basics of this kind of assignment and how to get started. In Chapters 3 and 4, we explain how you can create your own thesis-defense paper, covering everything from the charitable consideration of opposing viewpoints to how to format the paper. Chapters 5 and 6 are devoted to issues of language use, ranging again from the high-level (e.g., emotional tone) to the nitty-gritty (e.g., how to use apostrophes). In Chapter 7, we cover how to acknowledge the work of others, both formally—by giving citations in MLA style—and in other, less formal ways. Two of the appendixes give illustrative examples: Appendix A shows draft material marked up by a helpful reader and the same material revised in light of the reader's comments, while Appendix B provides a complete thesis-defense paper written and formatted according to the advice we give in the first seven chapters.

The rest of the book covers topics that go beyond the paradigmatic thesis-defense paper in some way. In Chapter 8, we explain how to take notes from various kinds of philosophical sources. We then discuss some kinds of papers that are typically shorter than standard thesis-defense papers, showing how they are related to, yet different from, both notes and a thesis-defense paper. In Chapter 9, we discuss two common philosophical research assignments—the annotated bibliography and the research paper—including how each is related to the kinds of assignments discussed earlier in the book. We also discuss how to do research on philosophical topics, explaining what a scholarly philosophical source is and how to find sources that will be helpful for completing a research assignment. Because virtually every philosophy assignment requires a basic grasp of arguments, Chapter 10 introduces some basic concepts and skills for reasoning well. Finally, though there is more variety in philosophy exams than in paper assignments, many philosophy exams require something like an argumentative essay. So, in Appendix C, we discuss how to succeed in another common kind of assessment in college philosophy courses: philosophy exams.

Even with all the help in the world, writing your own philosophy paper can be hard work. If you make the effort, though, we believe that the experience can be extremely rewarding. We wish you good luck!

1 First Things First

You have to write a paper for a philosophy course. Here is your first advice:

Start right away.

Whether the paper is due this week, next month, or two months from now, do something about it today. You may not be able to start the heaviest phase of your work, but doing *something* will ease your mind and start you thinking about the project. Putting off getting started often results in a late paper, a poorly written paper, or both. At the very least, you can schedule time tomorrow to work on the paper. (Yes, this counts as doing something!)

1.1 Know the Assignment

You should start by getting as clear as possible on what the assignment requires. Writing a good philosophy paper is hard enough when you know exactly what must be done. If you are unsure what is required, it will be even harder. The requirements of the assignment will affect how you schedule your time, what sort of work you do, and even how you continue to think about the topic at hand. If you begin work without understanding the assignment, you may waste precious time and effort.

You can't expect to write the kind of paper your instructor has in mind if you don't understand what the requirements are. Read the instructions carefully, marking the most important parts and anything that is unclear. Reread them. If anything is still unclear, ask your instructor about it as soon as possible.

Once you understand the instructions, make sure you follow them. If the assignment requires a formal introduction (see § 2.2.3), you must include one; if the assignment says you should not include a cover page, don't include one—even if you usually do. Your instructor will have reasons for such requirements (and is probably happy to discuss them with you) even if they're not obvious to you. Some requirements (e.g., "argue for your view") will be relevant throughout your work on the paper. Others (e.g., "double-space your text") can be relegated to a checklist you go through soon before submitting the paper. Make sure you don't lose track of any requirements.

If you missed a class or were late even once, find out whether you missed any oral or written instructions about the paper. If you missed written instructions, obtain a copy. If you missed oral instructions, copy them from a student who took good notes or ask the instructor.

DOI: 10.4324/9781003512318-1

1.2 Kinds of Philosophy Papers

The most common kind of paper assigned in philosophy courses is the **thesis-defense paper**, in which you defend a claim (your *thesis*) by giving reasons for believing it is true—that is, by *arguing* for it. In everyday discourse, people commonly use the word "argue" to mean *fight with words* or *emotively disagree*. In philosophy and other academic disciplines, however, to "argue" simply means to *provide reasons that are intended to establish the truth* of some claim. Strong reasoning and consideration of alternative positions are at the heart of a good thesis-defense paper. We explain the structure and elements of a thesis-defense paper in Chapter 2.

Other kinds of papers are commonly assigned. In a **summary paper**, you explain someone else's views in your own words. A **response paper** goes beyond summary to provide your own critical response to the arguments of a text. "Critical" here means *thoughtfully evaluative*; critical responses can be positive, negative, or a mixture of both. The purpose of a **compare-and-contrast paper** is to show how two views, books, articles, or philosophies are alike and how they differ. A **research paper** is a thesis-defense paper that requires you to investigate published work on your topic that has not been assigned for your course. We discuss these kinds of papers in detail in Chapters 8 and 9.

If you are asked to write an essay for an in-class or take-home exam, it will often be in the form of a thesis-defense, summary, or compare-and-contrast paper. So even if you are not required to write papers of these kinds, you may benefit from reading the parts of this book that address them. We give more advice about studying for, and taking, philosophy exams in Appendix C.

1.3 Common Criteria for Evaluation

Be sure you understand as well as possible how your work will be evaluated and graded *before* you do substantial work on the paper. You should consider the instructions in the assignment to be *part* of the criteria on which your paper will be evaluated. Your instructor may also give you a grading rubric, which makes certain criteria explicit. But there may be unstated criteria. What follows is an overview of common criteria for evaluating student papers in philosophy, each of which we revisit in detail later in the book.

Your instructor may use some of these criteria or all of them. Your instructor may also use other criteria. And your instructor will doubtless consider some criteria more important than others. In some cases, a glaring weakness with respect to only one of these criteria will be enough to drop your paper's grade below passing. For example, if you do not accurately explain a view or argument that has been discussed in class, you may not receive a passing grade, no matter how well you accomplish some of the other tasks.

We have, of necessity, formulated these criteria vaguely. What counts as too broad a topic, for instance, will vary from course to course and instructor to instructor. But you should keep all these criteria in mind, and do your best to figure out how your instructor will apply them when grading your paper.

Content

<u>Strength of argumentation:</u> When arguing for a claim, offer reasons that an unbiased, clear-thinking person would find persuasive. (See § 2.1 and Chapters 4 and 10.)

Accuracy: When presenting information or someone's views (including your own!), be careful not to misrepresent them. Careless wording can skew ideas in ways that make a big difference in philosophy. (See § 2.3.2–2.3.4, § 4.7 on the straw-man fallacy, and Chapter 5.)

Consideration of alternatives: When arguing for a view, your position is strengthened rather than weakened by discussing alternative views on the issue and explaining why you think it is reasonable to prefer your own. (See §§ 2.3.3–2.3.4 & 4.1.)

Choice of topic or thesis: Your topic or thesis should not be too broad to be addressed sufficiently in the space available to you. If you are defending a thesis, it should not be so uncontentious that no reasonable person would disagree or so far-fetched that no argument could make it seem plausible. Of course, what counts as reasonable disagreement or plausibility can be quite different in philosophy than in everyday life! You should be guided here by your experience in the course. (See §§ 3.3–3.4.)

Originality of ideas: A plausible, wholly original argument for a contentious claim is highly valued in philosophy. It's also extremely difficult to achieve on traditional philosophical topics since they have been discussed for so long by so many people. If your instructor asks for an original argument, she probably means either one that hasn't been discussed in class (rather than one that's never been offered by anyone) or one that is a novel application of an existing argument. (See § 3.1.)

Clarity

Organization: Unless the paper is very short (say, under 3 pages or 1,000 words), the opening paragraph should usually motivate and explain the task you are undertaking and preview the main parts of the paper. Transitions from each paragraph to the next should be clear and smooth. The specific structure of the paper will depend on the particular assignment. (See §§ 2.2 & 3.5–3.7.)

Consistency: Consistency is important at all levels of your paper. At the level of vocabulary, be sure to use the same word to mean the same thing throughout your paper. At the level of structure, make sure that you express and defend exactly the same thesis throughout your paper. Differences in wording that would be negligible in other contexts may be very confusing in a philosophy paper. (See §§ 3.4 & 4.5.)

Technical terms: You should define any technical term the first time you use it in your paper. A good rule of thumb is that a term counts as technical if a reader who has never studied the discipline to which it belongs could not be expected to know what it means. (See §§ 3.2, 4.5, 5.7.2, & 6.7 on "Technical Terms.")

Use of language: Correct spelling, grammar, and punctuation are, at the very least, appreciated by most instructors. Even those who do not directly penalize errors in such matters may less quickly or easily grasp what you are trying to say if you make such errors. (See § 3.9 and Chapter 6.)

Conventions

Tone: Most philosophy papers (like academic papers in general) call for an *objective* tone—that is, the tone of someone who may have a personal opinion but can still see the merits of opposing views. This tone can be undermined by inflammatory or indignant language. If you find yourself characterizing an opposing view as idiotic, it is likely that either you have misunderstood it or it is not worth considering in your paper. You should also aim for a *moderately formal* tone. You err on the side of informality when you use slang terms; you err on the side of excessive formality when you use unnecessarily long or complex words or sentences. Aim for the kind of language you would hope to find in a textbook assigned for your course. (See § 3.2, § 6.7 on "I, you," and Chapter 5.)

Format: If your instructor provides requirements for formatting the paper or your references (e.g., a certain font size or MLA style), follow them. If there are no such requirements, follow the widely accepted guidelines we provide later in the book. (See § 3.10 and Chapter 7.)

Using Others' Work

Acknowledgment of others' work: If there are academic sins, plagiarism is among the most damning. You plagiarize when you use another author's ideas or words in such a way that a reader would reasonably conclude that those ideas or words originated with you. Always indicate the source of any ideas or wording that you have borrowed for use in your paper. (See §§ 3.11, 4.3, & 6.8.6, and Chapter 7.)

Originality of expression: The way in which you express ideas and arguments—how you choose to structure your paper, paragraphs, and sentences—should mostly be original to you. Use quotations sparingly, if at all. Where you use someone else's way of expressing something, just as when you use someone else's idea, you must explicitly and clearly acknowledge it. Failure to do so is plagiarism. (See § 3.1 in addition to the cross-references in the preceding paragraph.)

Charity: You should present the views and arguments of others in their strongest form. It's easy—and tempting—to present views and arguments one disagrees with in a way that highlights their weaknesses. But that can give your audience the impression that a stronger version of the argument might avoid your criticisms. (See §§ 2.3.1–2.3.4 & 4.1.)

Quality of sources: Use only credible, relevant sources in your paper (and acknowledge them appropriately). Any source assigned for your course is likely credible. If you do original research for your paper, remember that the primary purpose of philosophical research is to learn what other people have argued with respect to your topic. Even the most thorough research does not absolve you of the obligation to compose your own paper on the topic. (See Chapter 9.)

1.4 Schedule Your Time

Once you are confident that you understand the assignment and how it will be evaluated, you should break the project down into specific tasks and set a deadline for each of them. This will enable you to work at an effective pace and submit the paper on time.

Some of your tasks might be delayed by circumstances that are beyond your control yet predictable. Get to those things as early as possible. For instance, as you probably already know, understanding some philosophical texts takes repeated, slow reading—and thus a lot of time. So start reading as soon as possible anything you'll need to read to complete your paper. If you want to meet with your instructor, she may only be available later than you had hoped. So get in touch now. You can submit interlibrary loan requests (see § 9.4.1) only once you've done sufficient research to know what you want to request—and even then, books may take weeks to arrive from other libraries. So get started early.

As you create your schedule, take into consideration your other school and nonschool obligations; the availability of resources such as books, journal articles, or a quiet place to work; and the deadlines of the paper and any preliminary submissions you are required to make. Don't schedule your tasks so tightly that unforeseen personal emergencies will prevent you from completing the paper on time.

You should start your schedule with the final deadline for your paper and schedule *backward* from there:

1a. First, if your paper will be submitted electronically, start with a time—at least one hour before the paper is due—when you will submit it. That should give you enough time to deal with a dropped Wi-Fi signal, website glitches, and so on. In the worst-case scenario, it should leave you enough time to contact your instructor *before* the deadline to explain the technical difficulties preventing you from submitting your paper on time.

1b. If, instead, you will submit a hard copy of your paper, start with the time you will print and staple the final version for submission. Pick a time—at least one hour before the submission deadline—that will give you enough time to find another printer if the one you were planning to use is broken or out of ink or paper. Make sure you know where to find a stapler you can use to staple the pages together.

2. Next, set a deadline—at least two hours before the previous deadline—for proofreading the final version of your paper and going through your checklist of formatting requirements.
3. At this point, things get more difficult (for us) to specify since your schedule will depend on your particular assignment, abilities, commitments, and so on. But ask yourself how many days you *may well* need—not the minimum you'll need if all goes perfectly—to revise a complete rough draft into a final version for submission. Count back from the previous deadline, and put this date in your schedule as the deadline for your rough draft.
4. Continue scheduling backward. Create deadlines for the following sorts of things: a first draft of each major part of the paper, a revised outline, completion of any necessary research, a first outline, selecting a topic, and so on.

As you draft your schedule, you may find that you do not have as much time as you want—or even need. There is usually no alternative to compressing your schedule. Even when you are working under severe time constraints, knowing you have a schedule that will allow you to complete the paper on time may bring some peace of mind.

If, because of circumstances beyond your control, you have significantly less time to write your paper than most students do, you can always explain your situation to your instructor and ask for an extension. Even if your request is reasonable, however, you should be prepared for it to be denied.

If you feel that you have so much to do that you don't even have time to make a schedule for your philosophy paper, the solution may ironically be *more scheduling!* If you can take a few hours to schedule your regular commitments for the remainder of the semester—regular classes, reading, homework, sports practice, music rehearsals, and so on—then you can (honestly!) tell yourself that you don't need to worry about all your other activities while you participate in one of them. This can take a huge psychological weight off your shoulders. Nonetheless, if this seems too daunting right now, consider scheduling time (!) at the beginning of your *next* semester to create this kind of mega-schedule.

Here is a sample schedule for a paper requiring no independent research:

Thursday, October 7:	Review assignment; pick topic.
Sunday, October 10:	Draft outline.
October 11–31:	Work on paper 2:30–3:30 p.m. every Monday, Wednesday, and Friday.
Sunday, October 31:	Rough draft completed (before Halloween party!).
November 1–7:	Revise paper 2:30–3:30 p.m. on Monday, Wednesday, and Friday; 1–3 p.m. Sunday (final version completed).
Monday, November 8:	Proofread and check formatting requirements.
Tuesday, November 9:	10:30 a.m.: Print final version at the library. (Take stapler!) 2:10 p.m.: Hard copy due at the beginning of class.

Here is a sample schedule for a project with several different requirements.

Saturday, March 21:	Reread assignment; pick research topic.
Sunday, March 22:	Complete research-topic worksheet (including paper outline).
Noon, Monday, March 23:	Research-topic worksheet due *by email to instructor*.
Tuesday, March 24:	After class, submit interloan requests for any research materials not in the school library.
March 25 to April 12:	Read and annotate *two sources per week*. (I need five total.)
April 13 and 14:	Draft paper proposal.
April 16:	Revise paper proposal, proofread, and check formatting requirements.
4:00 p.m., Friday, April 17:	Submit annotated bibliography and paper proposal through Canvas. (They're due at 5:00.)
April 18 to May 1:	Work on paper 7:30–9:00 p.m. every Tuesday and Thursday; 9:30–11:30 a.m. every Sunday.
Sunday, May 1:	Rough draft completed (before May Day party!).
May 2 to May 9:	Revise paper 7:30–9:00 p.m. on Tuesday and Thursday; 9:30–11:30 on Sunday (final version completed).
Monday, May 11:	Proofread and check formatting requirements.
Tuesday, May 12:	4:00 p.m.: Submit final version through Canvas (to be on the safe side). 5:00 p.m.: Research paper due electronically through Canvas.

Keep your schedule where you will see it every day. For some people, this means printing it out and posting it over your desk or bed; for others, it means integrating it into your online calendar or setting alerts. As your work progresses, record the *actual* completion date for each task in your schedule. If you fall behind by more than a few days, you may have to revise your schedule. This is also useful information for the next assignment schedule you create.

1.5 First Things Once More

We wish you good luck with your paper. Be sure you *make* most of that luck by taking the advice in this chapter, and throughout this book, seriously—not least the advice we opened with:

Start right away.

2 Thesis-Defense Papers

The thesis-defense paper, sometimes called an "argumentative paper," is the kind most often assigned in college philosophy classes. In a thesis-defense paper, you make a claim—your thesis—and defend it by arguing that better reasons exist for accepting it than for rejecting it. You may not be able to prove beyond all doubt that your thesis is true, but you should try to show that an unbiased, clear-thinking person would have good reason to accept it *over the other available options*.

We emphasize the last point because it's important to remember that a thesis-defense paper is essentially *comparative*. If there is no plausible alternative to your thesis, then there is no point in writing a paper defending it. (What, or whom, would you be defending it against?) But if there *are* plausible alternatives, then there must be *some* or at least *apparently* good reasons to reject your thesis. (That's what it means for the alternatives to be plausible.) In fact, in philosophy, we often seem to be faced with a choice between unappealing alternatives: Either we have no free will, or the world is fundamentally different from what science tells us. Either human lives are expendable for the good of others, or we cannot morally seek only the greatest good for the greatest number. Either we can know something without being certain it is true, or we can know almost nothing. The best we can often hope for is to show that there are slightly better reasons to prefer one alternative over the others. To put it more positively: It is a significant achievement to convince an unbiased, clear-thinking person that she has better reason to accept your thesis than the alternatives.

In this chapter, we explain the structure and common elements of a thesis-defense paper. In the following five chapters, we discuss in detail how to go about writing your own thesis-defense paper.

2.1 The Thesis and the Defense

Your **thesis** is the stand or position you take on an issue. The term "thesis" comes from an ancient Greek word that means *stand* or *position*. (The plural is "theses," pronounced *THEE-sees*, with a soft "th".) In a thesis-defense paper, you state your thesis at the beginning of the paper and spend the rest of the paper showing why that position is correct—or

DOI: 10.4324/9781003512318-2

at least preferable to the alternatives.[1] Avoid the temptation to withhold your thesis from the reader in order to make your paper more exciting; this will only make your paper more confusing. Your paper will be much easier to follow if your reader knows where it is headed.

A topic (for instance, *abortion*) is not a thesis. A thesis is always a position taken on a topic. It answers a question or solves a problem. If you can ask, "What do you think about X?," then X is a topic, not a thesis. An *answer* to such a question would be a thesis, for instance: *Abortion is morally wrong in all cases, except when the mother's life can only be saved by aborting a nonviable fetus.* Here is an alternative thesis on the same topic: *Abortion of a fetus in the first trimester of pregnancy is always morally permissible.* Notice that these theses (unlike the topic *abortion*) are expressed in complete grammatical sentences. You must be able to express your thesis in a complete sentence. If you can't, what you're trying to express is not a thesis. (We discuss how to develop a thesis for your paper in §3.4. For a refresher on grammar, see §6.4.)

In a thesis-defense paper, you **defend** your thesis by *arguing* that it is correct or at least preferable to the alternatives. It's important to note that "preferable" here means *rationally* preferable—that is, preferable on the basis of *reasons*, as opposed to what would be, say, convenient or comfortable to believe. As we said in Chapter 1, in everyday discourse, people commonly use the word "argue" to mean *fight with words* or *emotively disagree*. In philosophy and other academic disciplines, however, to "argue" means to provide reasons that are intended to establish the truth of some claim. The hope is that if you can show your reader the reasons that have led you to your view on the topic at hand (your thesis), she—being a similarly clear-thinking, unbiased person—will be led to the same view.

When you argue for a claim, then, you provide reasons—often called *premises*—for thinking that the claim—often called a *conclusion*—is true. Clearly, the thesis of your paper is a conclusion. You will probably have other conclusions in your paper, though. If you make several main points that together are meant to demonstrate the truth of your thesis, some of them will likely be supported by further reasoning. Thus, the statements that directly support the thesis are both premises (with respect to the thesis) and conclusions (with respect to the reasoning presented for them). You can think of your thesis as the *ultimate conclusion*, which is supported by premises that are themselves *transitional conclusions* supported by their own premises. We might call the move from the transitional conclusions to the ultimate conclusion (i.e., your thesis), the *primary* argument of your paper, and the reasons for those transitional conclusions *secondary* arguments.

Consider, for example, a paper defending the thesis that *animal experimentation is necessary in the search for cures for human diseases, even though it sometimes causes pain and even death to the animals*. The author might provide several points in favor of this thesis. Some, such as the claim that *humans and other animals have different cognitive capacities*, may simply be assumed and thus do not require argument. But others,

1 We should acknowledge that there is a different, common use of the word "thesis" in philosophy, meaning something like "single element of a theory or paradox." For instance, someone might explain the *paradox of fiction* as the following three inconsistent *theses*:

1 We feel emotions for fictional characters.
2 We feel emotions only for things that we believe exist.
3 We know that fictional characters don't exist.

such as the claim that *we have a greater obligation to prevent harm to humans than to other animals*, will be contentious, and thus require argument, making them transitional conclusions.

In addition to direct arguments in favor of your thesis, there are two common kinds of indirect arguments for your thesis. First, you might argue *against alternative views*. If you can show that every alternative to your view on a topic is false, then you will have shown, by a process of elimination, that your view must be true. Considering *every* alternative would usually take too much space, so philosophers typically limit themselves to showing that the *best* alternatives to their own views are false.

Second, you might consider *objections* to your thesis or to your arguments for it and show that those objections fail. Once more, it will likely be impossible to consider every possible objection to your thesis and arguments so, again, philosophers typically limit themselves to rejecting the *best* objections to their thesis or arguments.

2.2 Showing the Structure of a Thesis-Defense Paper

You will do a variety of things in your paper: You might present arguments, consider objections, explain theories, and so on. We discuss a few of the most common such tasks in Section 2.3. In addition to *doing* these things, however, you must clearly *indicate* to your reader what you are doing throughout your paper so that she can easily follow the case you are making for your thesis. We discuss how to do that in this section.

2.2.1 Body Paragraphs

The **body** of the paper is everything between the opening and closing paragraphs (discussed below). It is divided into **paragraphs**. Each paragraph should have a single, clear function—the paragraph is the unit of thought in a thesis-defense paper. Starting a new paragraph differentiates one task from another in your paper and thus in your reader's mind. So, if you are shifting from explaining a theory to critically discussing it, you should start a new paragraph. If you have finished explaining an objection to your thesis and are about to reply to it, you should start a new paragraph—and so on for each distinct task you attempt in your paper.

When students are first taught to write essays in high school, some of the advice they are given is like bicycle training wheels: helpful when starting out, but better abandoned as one's skills improve. Some students have been told that a paper should always include five paragraphs. Some have been told that all their paragraphs should be roughly the same length. Others have been told that they should vary the length of their paragraphs to keep the reader engaged. As you begin writing college-level, thesis-defense papers—at least in philosophy, and unless your instructor tells you otherwise—you should ignore all this advice. (It wouldn't hurt to check with your philosophy instructor about any other such advice you regularly follow when writing papers.)

The number of paragraphs in your paper should be dictated simply by how many individual tasks you attempt in the paper (explaining a theory, explaining an argument for the theory, explaining an objection to the argument, and so on). When students are taught to write five-paragraph papers, it is usually an attempt to show them that each paragraph should have a single, clear function, distinct from that of the paragraphs surrounding it. In a college paper, there is simply no reason to aim for a certain number of paragraphs (unless, of course, your instructor requires it).

The length of a paragraph should be dictated by how many words it takes to do the single, clear job of that paragraph accurately, completely, and concisely (given all the other constraints on your paper, such as the maximum length). That may mean that some paragraphs end up being rather short and others rather long. If you end up with a paragraph longer than a page, you run the risk of your reader losing the thread. Such paragraphs can almost always be divided into at least two shorter paragraphs—not arbitrarily, but because you are really trying to do more than one thing in the paragraph. (If this isn't the case, you can likely be considerably more concise—that is, cut the single paragraph down.)

2.2.2 Signposts

Your reader should know what you are trying to do in each part of the paper. You may already have had the frustrating experience of reading a philosophical text and wondering, "What is going on here? What is the author trying to do at this point? Where are we in relation to the main conclusion of this piece?" These thoughts obviously distract you from the author's defense of his thesis, and if you can't answer them, you may completely miss part of that defense. You don't want that to happen to the reader of *your* paper.

A paragraph break tells your reader that you have completed one task and are embarking on another. But it doesn't tell your reader anything about what those tasks are. You should thus use *signposts* (often called *transitions* or *topic sentences*) to guide your reader through your paper. Consider the following sentence, taken from the beginning of a paragraph in a thesis-defense paper:

> Having explained the metaphysical problem of race, I will now explain the best solution to the problem: eliminativism.

What do you imagine was covered in the previous paragraph of this paper? What do you think the author will do next? Even if you have no idea what "the metaphysical problem of race" and "eliminativism" are, it is obvious that the author thinks the first is a problem she has just finished explaining, and the second is a solution to that problem that she is about to embark on explaining. That means that as you read the paper, you don't need to worry about figuring out the *structure* of the author's primary argument. You can focus on the content since each time there is a change in what's happening, you are reminded of where you are in the grand scheme of things.

Here are some further examples of signposts:

> Let's consider the most serious objection to this theory.
> The compatibilist's best response to this objection is that ....

A more substantial turning point in your paper warrants a more substantial signpost. For example:

> I have now considered the evidence for the first of the three main points I offer in support of my thesis that private individuals should not be allowed to possess semiautomatic weapons. Let me move on to the second point.

(We discuss signposts further in §5.4)

Headings are a higher-level type of signpost but are usually only appropriate in papers longer than 10 pages (around 3,000 words). Headings may be numbered or not, but bear in mind that numbering your headings can only *increase* the ease with which your reader navigates your paper. Using numbers *without* headings to break a longer paper into sections may be better than nothing, but why not tell your reader what's in each section with a descriptive heading? (Perhaps, like us, you've had the experience of reading a philosophical text divided into numbered sections and wishing that the author had also provided headings.)

2.2.3 Opening and Closing Paragraphs

Unless your instructor directs you otherwise, your thesis-defense paper should have an opening paragraph and a closing paragraph. (These are sometimes called an "introduction" and "conclusion," though those names can mislead.) The **opening paragraph** typically serves four functions: (1) to *motivate* and (2) *explain* the question your thesis answers or the problem it solves, (3) to state your thesis, and (4) to give your reader a preview of the structure of the paper.

You "motivate" a question or problem when you explain why it is *worth* solving or answering. You can think of the task of motivation as that of connecting the topic of your paper to your reader's everyday life. One way to do this is with a striking example. In papers on ethics or political philosophy, it's usually not hard to think of an actual or imaginary example that will help your reader see the importance of the topic at hand. For less obviously practical topics (e.g., in metaphysics or epistemology), you might start with a science-fiction example (e.g., *How do you know you're not in the Matrix?*) or with how our ordinary thinking on a topic can generate a puzzle (e.g., *We might say that two dresses are "identical," but if they are* two different *things, how can they literally be* the same*?*). (We discuss the effective use of examples further in §4.6.)

If possible, you should avoid motivating your topic by pointing out that philosophers have disagreed about it. Your job is to motivate the topic to someone not already invested in the disputes of philosophers. Even if your topic seems to be an arcane matter of, say, the interpretation of an ancient philosophical text, disagreement over that interpretation is ultimately grounded in the interest of the subject of the text (e.g., the limits of the government's authority or the value of art). Consider starting with that subject and then discussing the text's relationship to it (e.g., its historical importance in discussions of that subject or insights it provides that have not been fully appreciated).

You *explain* the question or problem that your thesis addresses when you not only articulate it clearly but also show your reader why the answer or solution to it is not obvious. Giving brief reasons for or against at least two mutually exclusive answers or solutions is one effective way to do this. You should make sure in motivating and explaining your question or problem that you do not "beg the question" in favor of one answer or solution. That is, you should take care not to imply that one answer or solution is obviously correct. (See also §4.7 on begging the question and §10.2.3.)

Previewing the structure of your paper is simply a matter of telling your reader what you're going to do and the order in which you'll do it. This should include a clear statement of your thesis. If your paper is well signposted, generating a structural preview should be easy. You can start by copying all your signposts and pasting them into a single paragraph. This should be a fair, if rough, representation of the structure of your paper. If it isn't, that's a sign that the body of the paper needs more revision. This might be a matter of drafting new material or moving things around, or it might simply be a matter of supplying more signposts. Copying and pasting is just a start, however. This paragraph will require revising and rewriting—for instance, you will not want to give equal space in your structural preview to the role of every paragraph in your paper.

It's important in your structural preview to provide a sense of not only the *form* but also the *content* of your paper. Though it's better than nothing, your reader won't get much sense of what's coming up in your paper from sentences like this: *I make three basic points to defend my conclusion and then consider two objections to my argument.* That's a bit like a road sign that, instead of saying *Chicago: 130 miles*, says merely *City Ahead.* Perhaps the latter sign is better than nothing—but it's not nearly as helpful as it easily could be.

Here is an example of an opening paragraph from a thesis-defense paper:

> Non-human animals feel pleasure and pain, just like humans. Their lives can be better or worse, including by being longer or shorter. Is it morally acceptable to cause non-human animals pain and suffering if it helps us improve human lives? On the one hand, causing pain to any sentient being seems *prima facie* wrong. On the other hand, we often think that people have greater moral standing than animals. In this paper, I argue that animal experimentation is morally acceptable in the search for cures for human diseases, even when it causes the animals involved to suffer or die. I make three basic points to defend this conclusion. First, humans generally have a greater obligation to preserve human life than to preserve animal life. Second, some cures cannot be discovered in any other way. Third, some experiments give us information about an animal species that is ultimately used to protect that species or individual members of it. I end by briefly replying to the objection that my view fails to respect the dignity of the animals experimented upon.

The first two sentences motivate the problem the author is addressing, which is explained in sentences three through five. The next sentence states the author's thesis, and the rest of the paragraph is devoted to a structural preview of the paper.

Variations on the opening paragraph are possible. In a longer paper, the motivation, explanation, and structural preview may stretch over two or three paragraphs total. In a *formal* opening paragraph, one gives only the structural preview and omits the motivation. (It's "formal" in the sense of form or shape, not the opposite of "informal.") If the above example began at "In this paper …," it would be a formal opening paragraph. A *rhetorical* opening paragraph, by contrast, is dedicated exclusively to motivating the reader's interest by explaining the interest and importance of the topic at the expense of a clear structural preview. If you can't do both (because of space constraints, for instance), and if the choice is up to you, we strongly recommend that you provide a structural preview of your paper rather than rhetorical motivation since this will be much more helpful to your reader in following your paper. Most importantly, *it should be crystal clear to your reader what your thesis is.*

Your **closing paragraph** should provide a review of the structure of your paper. This can be very similar to the structural preview in your opening paragraph. For example:

> I have argued that we have a greater obligation to preserve human life than other animal life, that some cures cannot be developed by other means, and that the animal species involved can benefit from some of this research. Since I have also shown that

> this position does not disrespect the animals involved, we can conclude that animal experimentation is necessary in the search for cures for human diseases, despite the animal pain and death sometimes involved.

A closing paragraph often does one or two additional things: (1) It may include a mirror image of the opening paragraph's motivation, reminding the reader of the relevance of the paper's topic to the reader's everyday life. (2) It may indicate further work that needs to be done on the topic or other applications of the reasoning in the paper. For instance, the following material might be added to the beginning or end of the previous example:

> The question of non-human animals' precise moral standing deserves more attention than I have been able to give it here. But we need not wait for that to determine the morality of animal experimentation. Public funding of such research should not be constantly imperiled because of the sensitive character of the issue. Scientists in this field deserve to be recognized as socially responsible researchers, rather than accused of being moral outlaws.

As with the opening paragraph, in a longer paper there may be more than one closing paragraph, each with a different function.

2.3 Common Elements of a Thesis-Defense Paper

In the next chapter, we discuss how to develop a thesis, create an outline, and map your arguments. In this final section of this chapter, we discuss a few tasks that students often find themselves doing in thesis-defense papers. There is no formula for what to include in your thesis-defense paper, but we hope that our discussion may help you to clarify what you are trying to do in a given paragraph or section of your paper and thus enable you to signal more clearly to your reader what you are doing at each point in the defense of your thesis.

2.3.1 Explanation of Theories

A **theory** is a structured collection of claims intended to describe or explain a range of phenomena. For example, *quantum mechanics* (or "quantum theory") is a collection of claims intended to describe and explain what the fundamental parts of the physical universe are and how they behave. *Freudian theory* is a collection of claims intended to explain human behavior. These are not philosophical theories, though they may well play a role in a philosophical paper. But there are philosophical theories, too, such as *compatibilism* (a theory about the relationship between causal processes and free will), *skepticism* (a theory about what we can know), and *utilitarianism* (a theory about how we ought to act). Explaining a theory is simply a matter of explaining each part of the theory, how those parts relate to one another, and what the theory is supposed to describe or explain.

It is easy to confuse the notion of a theory with that of a thesis. One reason may be that many theses take a stand on a theory. For instance, you may be defending the thesis that *utilitarianism is false* or the thesis that *compatibilism is the best solution to the problem of freedom*. Another reason is that some theories can be summed up in a single sentence (even though this often conceals complexity that would be revealed in a fuller explanation). But remember that a thesis is a single claim that expresses a position taken on some topic and is the primary conclusion of a thesis-defense paper. (See §2.1.)

If a theory plays some role in your paper, whether you are simply assuming it for the sake of argument or arguing for or against it, it is important to be able to explain it *charitably* and *neutrally*—that is, in as strong a form as possible (this is "charity") and without taking a stand on whether the theory is correct (this is "neutrality"). This can be difficult. If the whole point of your paper is to argue that utilitarianism is false, then it is tempting to display its shortcomings whenever you have the chance. But, perhaps surprisingly, you will more easily convince a clear-thinking, unbiased reader of your view if you present opposing views charitably and neutrally before pointing out their flaws.

A different problem can arise when you explain a theory that you are defending. It is surprisingly easy to fall into the trap of explaining a complex theory and then thinking that you have thereby *argued for* that theory. This is a serious error. I can explain *Pastafarianism* to you in great and accurate detail—who the Flying Spaghetti Monster is, why he created the universe as he did, the role of pirates in climate change, and so on. But when I've finished, though you may *understand* the theory perfectly, you would have no reason to *believe* it. If I want you to *believe* a theory, I need not only to *explain* it but also—crucially—to *argue* for it. And argument is very different from explanation.

2.3.2 Explanation of Arguments

We have described the sense in which your entire thesis-defense paper is a kind of argument, but we've also said that your paper will likely include discussion of other arguments—for example, arguments for or against a theory or arguments objecting to your thesis. You will endorse, reject, or otherwise assess each of these arguments, and you will want your clear-thinking, unbiased reader to follow you in these assessments. As with theories, then, it is crucial that you explain arguments *charitably* and *neutrally*.

This is essentially the same task as explaining a theory charitably and neutrally; you just have to remember that an argument is a different kind of thing from a theory. While a theory describes or explains something, an argument attempts to convince someone of something (the conclusion). So when you explain an argument, you'll have to make clear which claims are the premises and which claim is the conclusion, as well as how the premises are supposed to show that the conclusion is true. (We discuss different aspects and kinds of arguments in §3.6 and Chapters 4 and 10.)

As with explaining theories you disagree with, when you explain an argument that doesn't convince you, it is tempting to put its weakness on display. But, again, you will more easily convince your reader of the failure of an argument if you *first* present it neutrally in as strong a form as possible and only *then*—separately—present your criticisms of it.

2.3.3 Critical Discussion of Theories and Arguments

As we mentioned in Chapter 1, "critical" discussion of a theory or argument is thoughtfully evaluative discussion of it, which may be positive, negative, or a mixture of both. A *theory* is a structured collection of claims. Positive critical discussion of a theory (i.e., endorsing a theory) amounts to giving an argument for that theory. Negative critical discussion of a theory takes two main forms: (1) You can show that one of the claims that constitutes the theory is false or at least questionable. Alternatively, (2) you can show that *if* the theory were true, it would imply something false or questionable. That's enough to show that there must be something wrong with the theory, though it may not show what.

An *argument* is a set of premises that are intended to support a conclusion. Positive critical discussion of an argument thus usually involves one or more of the following: (1) showing that the premises are true, (2) showing that the premises (if true) would support the conclusion, and (3) responding to objections to the argument (which we discuss in the next section). Negative critical discussion of an argument usually involves (1) showing that one or more of the premises are false or at least questionable, or (2) showing that even if the premises are (or were) true, they do not (or would not) support the conclusion. (Again, we say much more about arguments in §3.6 and Chapters 4 and 10.)

In a sense, there is a third way to criticize an argument: You could show that its conclusion is false. If the conclusion is false, then it cannot be true on the basis of the premises presented. But in another sense, this isn't a criticism of the *argument* for that conclusion because it doesn't show what is wrong with the reasoning for the conclusion. It is a kind of indirect criticism of the argument. If you haven't provided a direct criticism of the argument, this may leave your reader stranded between two arguments: She sees no reason to reject the first argument (in favor of the conclusion you deny) but also no reason to reject your argument that that first conclusion is false. She won't know what to believe. (Are you sure you do?) It's thus better to avoid this strategy if possible.

2.3.4 Objections to Your Thesis and Arguments

Thesis-defense papers typically consider *objections*—that is, reasoning that goes against the point of view expressed in the thesis of the paper. There are two kinds of objections. Some objections are leveled directly at your thesis, independent of the specific arguments you offer in support of it. Other objections aim to discredit one of the specific arguments with which you have supported your thesis.

Why would you bring up objections to your thesis or your reasoning for it? After all, the purpose of the thesis-defense paper is to present the strongest case *for* your thesis. As with presenting theories and arguments, the perhaps surprising answer is that you *strengthen* your case by giving voice to objections—provided you can convincingly respond to them. By demonstrating that you have anticipated the concerns of people who would critique your views, you can avoid giving your reader the sense that you are closed-minded or smugly self-assured. If you fail to bring up a likely objection to your position or reasoning, then a clear-thinking, unbiased reader may conclude that you are unaware of the objection or even of other perspectives on the topic at hand. Worse, she may suspect that you *are* aware of the objection but do not have a good response to it. A good response can neutralize that objection in your reader's mind, allowing your positive arguments to persuade her of your thesis.

3 Writing and Revising

In the previous chapter, we discussed the elements and structure of a thesis-defense paper. In this chapter, we discuss how to go about creating your own such paper (though you may have noticed us sneaking in some suggestions in the previous chapter!). Our most important advice bears repeating:

Start right away.

In Chapter 1, we said that you should make sure you understand the assignment and criteria for evaluation, and also make a schedule to ensure that you can complete the paper by the deadline. In this chapter, we explain how to choose a topic, develop a thesis, and prepare an initial outline of your paper. This is all good advice. But don't slip into self-deception by spending time on these preparatory activities while putting off the actual writing until the last minute. It is very common to postpone writing with the belief (or rationalization) that, even halfway to the deadline for the paper, you are "just not ready to start writing yet." You should consider our initial advice—*start right away*—to apply also to writing the body of the paper.

You should be writing *something* on the topic of your paper within a few days of receiving the assignment—earlier if the deadline is less than a couple of weeks away. The resulting, off-the-top-of-your-head prose might be very rough, but it's better to start writing *something*, even if it's only one paragraph or sentence, than to wait until you think you can write something longer or better. *Give yourself permission to write poorly*. You don't need to show what you write to anyone else. Perhaps you won't use these early musings in the final version of your paper, but writing will help you sharpen your thinking on the topic, and you will probably end up with ideas to keep and develop, as well as material to discard. If nothing else, you will learn about some dead ends, and this will leave you with a better sense of how to approach the subject differently. This initial drafting may also clarify what you are already capable of doing in the paper and what you will need to spend more time working on.

If you have a serious psychological block to starting to write, try giving yourself five minutes (set a timer!) to write just *one sentence* on the topic. It doesn't have to be a thesis statement, let alone a profound argument; the point is just to get some words related to your topic down on the page. If even this doesn't work, try telling a friend something about the topic (again, just one sentence is a great start), and then write down what you've said.

A word about the organization of this chapter: In Section 3.3, we begin discussing different tasks involved in writing a thesis-defense paper (developing a thesis, creating an

DOI: 10.4324/9781003512318-3

outline, etc.), and we discuss them in a particular order. We should emphasize that not everyone finds it helpful to do all these things—or even any of them—before beginning to draft the body of the paper. And some people prefer to do these things in a different order. That's perfectly fine. If you're one of those people, however, you should still read all the following sections. Even if, for example, you develop your thesis as you draft the body of your paper, our section on developing a thesis still contains valuable information about what that thesis should end up looking like.

3.1 Originality

Some students hesitate to start writing because they think they are expected to come up with a completely original thesis or argument—something that no one has ever thought of before. As we noted in Section 1.3, it is highly unlikely that your instructor expects that of you in an undergraduate philosophy course. Plausible original positions and arguments are just too hard to come by. If you have been required to read contemporary philosophical texts, you may have noticed that they contain substantial discussion of the work of others. The originality of such texts is in how they present and build on the previous work of others. Historical texts are like this, too, though their relationship to previous scholarship is often less explicit. (It might also help to know that only when you're writing a *doctoral dissertation* does "making an original contribution to philosophical scholarship" first appear as an evaluative criterion.) If your instructor does ask for an original argument, check to see what this means. It may mean either an argument that hasn't been discussed in class (rather than one that's never been offered by anyone) or a novel application of an existing argument. If your instructor really does want a wholly original philosophical argument, we can only wish you good luck!

At the undergraduate level, most instructors want to see that you've understood the material you discuss in your paper—the problems and solutions presented in the texts and lectures you've encountered as part of the class—well enough to articulate the problem of your chosen topic and make a plausible case for a particular solution to that problem in your own words. Your instructor *will* want to read an original paper in the sense that the paper is *yours*, that it *originates* with you. But if you have digested the material well enough to achieve the goals just mentioned, you will inevitably produce an original paper in this sense. Writing comes from the mind and often the heart. Neither of these is the same in any two people. So what you write will be different from what another person would write on the same subject. It will be original. (We approach this topic from a different angle in the final section of this chapter.)

3.2 Level and Tone

Chapters 5 and 6 are devoted to the use of language in philosophy papers. But since we are beginning to talk about writing the paper, we should say something about the level and tone you should be aiming for. This is something you will work on throughout the process of writing your paper (and throughout your writing life), but the level and tone you adopt will affect the content of your paper, making it difficult to revise *just* those features of your paper once you've done substantial work on it. So it is good to have some sense of these matters from the beginning.

When you write a philosophy paper in college, the primary (and often only) reader is the instructor of the course for which the paper is written. It is thus difficult—but important—to remember that your instructor is *not* the audience for whom you should write. Your instructor is obviously not asking you to write a paper on, say, the problem of freedom because she doesn't understand it. After all, she's just spent several classes trying to help *you* understand it. The reason that the thesis-defense paper is such a popular assessment tool in philosophy courses is that if you can write a paper that both clearly explains a philosophical problem and makes a compelling case for a particular solution to it—in such a way that someone unfamiliar with the problem would both come to understand the problem and be persuaded to adopt your solution to it—then you must truly understand the topic yourself.

So, in a paper for an introductory philosophy course, *you should write as if your reader were a clear-thinking, unbiased, intelligent undergraduate with no background in philosophy*. Imagine yourself writing for a biology, theater, or business major. You can assume that this reader has a good stock of general knowledge and is a competent user of the English language, but you should assume that she knows nothing about philosophy. Throughout this book, when we talk of the *reader* or *audience* of your paper, we are referring to this ideal, imagined reader. (When we talk about any *actual* reader, such as your instructor, we will make that explicit.)

In more advanced philosophy courses, your imagined reader may be different. In papers for these courses, you can often use basic philosophical terms such as "epistemology" and "metaphysics," and perhaps even make references to other philosophers, theories, or movements, without explanation. In such cases, your reader is an intelligent undergraduate who has a basic philosophical education but knows nothing about the topic of the course for which you are writing the paper. In general, however, err on the side of explaining a philosophical term or view rather than assuming that your reader is familiar with it. If in doubt about a particular example, ask your instructor.

The previous three paragraphs are about the *level* at which you should pitch your writing. Another important aspect of your writing is its *tone*. This is a matter of the formality of your writing. One way to think about the tone you're aiming for is to imagine you've been commissioned to write a chapter in a textbook introducing students to your topic and defending a particular stand on it. What kind of writing would you hope to encounter in such a textbook? We bet you would *not* want to read something by an author who is clearly trying to impress or intimidate you with obscure philosophical terminology and sentences so complicated that you have to read them three times to understand them. So don't put your reader through that unpleasant experience.

Some students fall into the trap of excessive formality because the texts they read in class (and maybe their instructor's lectures) seem full of fancy words and complicated sentences. But the authors of those texts are not writing in that way to sound impressive or to confuse their readers. In some cases, they are writing for a different audience, as when a work written centuries ago or for other professional philosophers is assigned in an introductory course because of its importance. In other cases, the author may simply have misjudged what an intelligent undergraduate with no experience in philosophy would find easy to understand. Writing clearly and simply is hard!

Another reason students sometimes adopt an overly formal tone is that they do not feel confident that they understand what they are explaining, and they (consciously or unconsciously) take refuge in obscure terminology and complex sentences. This will not help convince your reader of your thesis. If you don't understand something you are writing about, get clear on it first by rereading your notes or the relevant text, looking it up in a trustworthy source, or talking to someone who knows about it. If there's no time for that, be open in your paper about your uncertainty. That can help build your reader's trust. Sometimes it can even be a source of philosophical insight since it forces you to articulate something that requires further consideration.

If you find yourself falling into the trap of an overly formal tone, try to say out loud what you're trying to communicate, and then write that version down. (Recording yourself or using voice-recognition software might be helpful.) Perhaps you will have to revise what you end up with to make it grammatical or more precise, but it is likely to be easier to understand than something overly formal.

The other pitfall to avoid is an overly *informal* tone. You probably wouldn't want to read something by an author who addresses you as "dude" or drops f-bombs into every sentence. That tone can be fine for a late-night philosophical jam session, but on the page it comes across (at best) as the voice of an author trying too hard to sound hip or to ingratiate himself with his reader.

Note that in philosophy papers, as opposed to those in some other disciplines, it is usually perfectly acceptable to use the first-person pronoun: *I*. For example, *I will now argue that premise two is false.* (As always, there may be assignments or instructors that overrule this advice. For more on this issue, see §6.7 on "I, you.")

In sum, you should write for an intelligent undergraduate with no experience in philosophy, in language that does not distract her from what you are trying to say and that you genuinely hope will be easy to understand, dude.

3.3 Choosing a Topic

If a single paper topic has been assigned, stick with it. If you are unsure whether what you are writing is on topic, ask your instructor. If you would like to do something a little ... *out there*, such as writing a dialogue or producing a film instead of writing the thesis-defense paper required by the assignment, discuss it with your instructor as soon as possible. If your instructor is on board, you may have lost the element of surprise, but you will have spurred some anticipation and may receive some helpful advice. If your instructor is *not* on board, it's better to find out in time to change course than when your assignment is returned with a disappointing grade.

If you are given a list of options, pick the topic that genuinely interests you the most. One pitfall here is picking the topic that you think will be *easiest* to write on, even if it doesn't interest you. People tend to write better papers when their enthusiasm amplifies their energies and sharpens their thinking. Even when the topic is one you are excited about, having to be thorough and precise is demanding. You set yourself up for mediocrity if you select a topic that bores you before you start writing.

If no specific topics are assigned, generate a list yourself by formulating questions that articulate the issues that a good bit of class time has been devoted to discussing. (We give further advice on how to do this in §3.4.) Then follow our earlier advice to pick the topic that interests you most.

If you must choose your own topic, one pitfall to avoid is choosing a *nonphilosophical* topic. The most common way to commit this error is to choose an *empirical* topic—that is, one that should be answered by conducting a survey or doing an experiment. This is not to say that empirical facts are irrelevant to philosophical questions. But they typically play a supporting role in a philosophical paper and are simply stated rather than argued for. When you make an empirical assumption that is not common knowledge, you should cite a source in which that claim is defended, such as a reputable reference work in physics or sociology. If you're not sure whether it's common knowledge, cite a source or ask your instructor. (See §4.3 for more on this kind of "argument by proxy" and Chapter 7 on how to cite a source appropriately.)

3.4 Developing a Thesis

Recall that a thesis is a position taken on a topic, expressed in a complete grammatical sentence. (See §2.1.) You want your thesis to be worth defending—to take a position on a worthwhile topic. But when you are new to philosophy, it can be hard to figure out what counts as a worthwhile topic or thesis. One way to overcome this difficulty is to think about what topics have been the focus of lectures and class discussion, and to formulate questions that throw these topics into sharp relief. The answer to such a question can be the thesis of your paper.

In the previous chapter, we saw the following sample theses:

> Abortion is morally wrong in all cases, except when the mother's life can only be saved by aborting a nonviable fetus.
> Abortion of a fetus in the first trimester of pregnancy is always morally permissible.

The question these theses would answer is something like the following:

> In what situations, if any, is abortion morally permissible?

It can be very helpful, throughout the process of writing your paper, to return to the exercise of formulating the particular thesis you are defending and the particular question it answers. (At the end of this section, we discuss what to do when your thesis changes.)

Theses can be more or less specific. Here are some sample theses of increasing specificity, followed by the question each thesis answers:

1. God's existence cannot be proved.
   (Can the existence of God be proved?)
2. Teleological arguments cannot establish that God exists.
   (Can a teleological argument establish that God exists?)
3. William Paley's teleological argument does not establish that God exists.
   (Does William Paley's teleological argument establish that God exists?)

As the theses get more specific, they get more complicated and thus take more words to express. But it is *easier to defend* a more specific thesis. Think about what would be required to defend our first sample thesis. You would have to (i) consider *every possible* proof of God's existence (or all the different kinds of such proofs); (ii) argue—in a way that would convince a clear-thinking, neutral reader—that *none* of these proofs could possibly work; and (iii) defend your arguments against objections. Now consider what would be required to defend the third thesis. You would have to (i) explain William Paley's teleological argument; (ii) argue—in a way that would convince a clear-thinking, neutral reader—that Paley's argument is flawed in at least one way; and (iii) defend your argument against objections. Defending the third thesis is no piece of cake, but it's certainly more manageable than defending the first thesis. (And note that the more specific project could be considered a contribution toward the more general one.) It's to your advantage, then, to make your thesis as specific as you can. And, again, a helpful way of checking the specificity of your thesis is to figure out the specific question it answers.

In some cases, your thesis may be explicitly conditional, for example:

> If there are no moral facts, a criminal-justice system would still be justifiable.

We say more about conditional claims in Section 10.3.1 but note that this thesis does not say that there are no moral facts. (Nor does it say that there *are* moral facts.) It merely says that *if* there are no moral facts, then something else is true (namely, that a criminal-justice system would be justifiable). This is a worthwhile thesis, and while it is clearly related to the question of whether there are moral facts, its conditional nature means that the author does not have to take a stand on that question. This thesis is thus significantly easier to defend than the following thesis:

> Even though there are no moral facts, a criminal-justice system is still justifiable.

This second thesis is more difficult to defend because it requires establishing *both* the first conditional thesis *and* the claim that there are no moral facts.

Some paper assignments contain ready-made theses to choose from. Suppose, for instance, that you are given the following prompt:

> Write a five-page thesis-defense paper in which you explain whether Locke's or Leibniz's view on innate ideas is correct.

There are two obvious theses you might choose to defend in the assigned paper:

> Leibniz's view on innate ideas is correct.
> Locke's view on innate ideas is correct.

(In the actual paper, you would want to briefly explain Leibniz's or Locke's view when you state your thesis.) More complicated theses are also possible. For example:

> Leibniz's view on innate ideas is more plausible than Locke's, though it has the disadvantage that ....
> Locke's view on innate ideas is more plausible than Leibniz's, with the exception of the claim that ....

Which thesis should you defend? The one that you actually believe. Sometimes students make the mistake of trying to defend a thesis that represents what they think their instructor, or an impressive student in the class, believes about a topic. This is unwise. You will likely not write as convincing a paper in defense of a thesis that you do not believe. (On the other hand, a strong commitment to your thesis may blind you to weaknesses in your argument and lend your writing a distracting tone. See §§2.3.4 & 5.1–5.3 for some advice on these matters.)

But what if you don't know what you believe about the topic at hand? In that case, you should start drafting your paper by explaining a particular view on the topic and arguments for and against that view. As you work on your paper, you will probably find that one view on your topic begins to seem more compelling than others. At that point, you can begin to formulate your thesis. If even this doesn't work, you should seek help from your classmates or instructor.

It is sometimes tempting to defend a thesis according to which two mutually exclusive positions are equally well supported. For example:

> The views of Locke and Leibniz on innate ideas are incompatible, yet equally plausible; there is no good reason to choose one over the other.

You should avoid this kind of thesis if at all possible. Even if this is your honest opinion on the topic at hand, your reader (and instructor) may take it as a sign that you have not thought as carefully and deeply about the topic as you might have. If at all possible, you should decide which position on a topic seems *most* plausible to you, even if it still faces objections to which you cannot figure out how to respond.

Some paper assignments do not include any ready-made theses. For instance, your instructor may ask you to:

> Write a five-page thesis-defense paper on Plato.

"Plato" by itself is too broad a topic for a thesis-defense paper. (What would a thesis on this topic amount to?) "Plato's ethics" is still too broad; entire books are dedicated to this vast topic. "The three-part soul in Plato's *Republic*" is a more workable topic, but you may have to get even more specific than this. You may narrow it down to "the relation between the four cardinal virtues and the three-part soul in Plato's *Republic*" or even focus on only one of those virtues. Again, one way to narrow it down is to ask yourself what specific topics have been the focus of lectures and class discussions. Formulate a specific question that has been debated in class; your answer to that question could be your thesis.

We have discussed formulating your thesis early on because your thesis is such an important part of your thesis-defense paper, and thinking about your thesis is a good way of bringing the specific topic of your paper into focus. But we do not mean to give the impression that you must perfect your thesis before embarking on writing the rest of the paper. On the contrary, you should remain flexible about your thesis. As you work on the body of your paper, you may come to realize that the thesis you began with is not defensible. If so, revise it. Such revision can range from tinkering with the expression of the thesis to taking the opposite stance on your topic. You might think that completely changing your thesis would require completely rewriting your paper, but that gets things the wrong way around. It is in writing your paper—grappling with the arguments for and against various views on your topic—that your own view will develop. Changing your thesis may be like fitting the last piece of a puzzle into place, transforming your paper into a strong, unified case for a thesis. Your thesis should ultimately reflect where your own view on the topic has ended up after thinking it through on the page. Revise that thesis as often as you have to!

Consider one final situation in which you might find yourself: You come to realize that the arguments you have been considering in your draft concern a slightly—or radically—different topic to that of your thesis. Here you must make a choice: Either stick with the material you've drafted and change your topic and thesis, or stick with your original topic and begin drafting again, staying on topic this time. The first option likely entails less work, but the second option may be unavoidable if it turns out you've been writing on a topic that doesn't meet the requirements of the assignment. (We discuss revising your paper in these ways and others in §§3.5 & 3.7.)

3.5 Outlining

Some people find it helpful to begin the process of writing a paper by developing an *initial outline*. This is a plan that enables you to envision the completed paper before you write the first full-length draft. The outline displays what you expect to be the skeleton of the paper, with the main points and subpoints laid out clearly in relation to each other. It can guide your continuing work on the paper, reminding you what arguments and objections you planned to discuss in what order.

In traditional formal outlines, the main sections of the paper—opening paragraph, closing paragraph, and each main point in the body of the paper—are labeled with, say, Roman numerals. Each of these sections may be divided into two or more subsections, labeled with, say, capital letters. Subsections may, in turn, be further divided, and so on. (As with opening and closing paragraphs, such outlines are "formal" because they show the *shape* or *form* of the paper, not because they're the opposite of "informal.") An example follows, but note that in an actual outline, you would include *content*, such as the particular thesis you plan to defend, the particular theories you plan to explain, and so on.

I. Opening paragraph
    A. Motivation of problem
    B. Explanation of problem
    C. Thesis statement
    D. Structural preview
        1. Explanation of theory
        2. Argument for theory
        3. Objection to argument
        4. Reply to objection

II. Explanation of theory [i.e., the same topic as I.D.1]
    A. First part of theory
        1. First aspect of first part of theory
        2. Second aspect of first part of theory
    B. Second part of theory

III. Argument for theory [i.e., the same topic as I.D.2]
    A. First premise
    B. Second premise
    C. Explanation of how A & B imply the theory

IV. Objection to argument [i.e., the same topic as I.D.3–4]
    A. Statement of objection
    B. Reply to objection

1. Response to reply
2. Explanation of why response fails

V. Closing paragraph

A. Structural review

1. Explanation of theory
2. Argument for theory
3. Objection to argument
4. Reply to objection

B. Relevant issues unaddressed in this paper
C. Restatement of thesis

Remember that this is just an example; your outline need not include all of these parts nor be as detailed as this. For instance, it is hard to imagine that all these parts could comfortably fit in, say, a five-page paper. How many main sections you include in your paper and how they are subdivided should be driven by how you think the strongest case can be made for your particular thesis, given the constraints you must work within. And some of these decisions are arbitrary. In the example just given, should the response to the reply (IV.B.1) be given its own Roman-numeraled section? The answer is that *it doesn't matter*. The initial outline is merely an aid to get you started writing. In the finished paper, the structure will be indicated by your signposts (see §§2.2.2 & 5.4), not by the numbers and letters of your outline (with the possible exception of numbered headings in a longer paper).

If you consider more than one objection to a theory or argument, you need to decide whether to state all the objections before you respond to any of them or respond to each before introducing the next. As a general rule, we advise the second approach. If you explain several objections before responding to any of them, then each time you respond to one, your reader will probably have to turn back to remind herself of the objection. That can be irritating. You could, of course, remind the reader of the objection before responding to it, but then you'll be repeating yourself (which can also irk your reader) and using precious words you could instead devote to additional material.

Because the purpose of your initial outline is to get you started writing, as soon as it's finished, it becomes a *working outline*. The difference is that a working outline is always subject to change as your paper develops. Sometimes you find that you cannot argue effectively for one of the claims in your primary argument. You then have to change or remove the claim. That will probably necessitate other changes in your outline. Sometimes you decide that the paper needs to be reorganized because, say, what you originally thought would be a subsection of section III actually fits better in section IV. Or perhaps you realize that what you initially thought was just a reply to an objection in fact deserves to be presented as a central positive argument for your thesis. Occasionally, as mentioned in Section 3.4, you may realize that your view has changed since you wrote your initial outline. You no longer want to defend the thesis you planned to defend originally. This typically does *not* mean that you need to start all over again. Because what you've been writing has led you to a new view on your topic, it should lead your reader to that new view, too. So you can often keep all that material. What you initially considered an objection to your original thesis may now be a positive argument for your new thesis; what was initially an argument for your original thesis may now work as an objection to your new thesis, and so on. This may necessitate large-scale restructuring of your paper, but that may be a relatively easy matter of reordering large chunks of text and revising your signposts. Revising your outline can help you keep track of these changes.

When you are close to completing the paper, anticipating no further major revisions, you should create a *final outline*. This is essentially the working outline revised to show all the changes you've made. A final outline is a very useful check that your paper does all that you think it does. You should compare it carefully with the structural preview and review contained in your opening and closing paragraphs. If there are any discrepancies, you must address them. This may be an easy—but crucial!—matter of, say, adding a line to your structural preview. But it may reveal a serious problem—for instance, that you have not in fact provided an argument for the theory you are defending. This will mean you have further substantial work to do, but it's much better you find that out before submitting the paper than when it's too late to do anything about it.

3.6 Argument Mapping

One way to create your initial outline is by mapping your argument. Begin by writing your tentative thesis near the bottom of a clean sheet of paper. Now think of the best reasons to believe that thesis. Map out these lines of reasoning by drawing a downward arrow from premises to conclusion. Write each separate reason for believing your thesis somewhere above the thesis and connect them with a downward arrow. If one reason for believing your thesis has to be stated in several sentences, draw a plus sign (+) between those sentences, bracket them together, and then draw the downward arrow.

Suppose you are considering the following initial thesis: *Euthanasia for unconscious or mentally impaired patients should be decided by the patient's family*. You begin by writing this at the bottom of a sheet of paper. You then ask yourself why this might be a good proposal. This thought occurs to you: The family knows the patient's character and wishes better than anyone. You reflect for a moment, then add the word "usually": *The patient's family usually knows the patient's character and wishes better than anyone*. You write this above the thesis statement but to the left so you have space to add other reasons. You draw a downward arrow from that sentence to the thesis statement. You reflect again. It is also the family that bears most of the consequences of the decision. After all, they are the ones to deal with the emotional effects of the daily absence of that person from their lives. And the people who are affected most, you reason, should make the decision. You write these reasons to the right of the previous one, and another downward arrow is drawn. The map of this initial reasoning is shown in Figure 3.1.

The plus sign between the two sentences on the right, along with the bracket that groups them, shows that these two work together as *a single reason* for believing the conclusion is true. Neither by itself is a compelling reason to believe the thesis; they combine to make one point. The wording of each shows why the other is relevant. So they have one arrow for the one inference. The arrow on the left represents a different inference—the one about knowing how the patient would feel about the situation and what the patient would want.

You can carry this mapping further. If you want to record some reasons for believing that one of the top three sentences is true, you can write those reasons above and draw an arrow down to that sentence. An extensive map can provide you with most of the

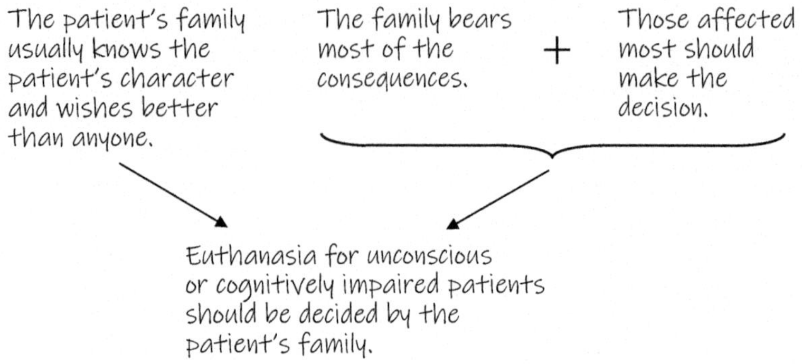

Figure 3.1 A sample argument map.

material that you would place in an outline. You can go straight from the map to the outline and have a large part of the structure of your paper established.

Note that maps can be useful throughout your work on the paper, not just when constructing an initial outline. As you revise, and even do research, mapping can help you visualize the current state of your argument so you can continue to work without losing track of the big picture. (For a detailed explanation of the kind of mapping covered in this section, see Seech, *Open Minds and Everyday Reasoning* 78–95 & 213–32.)

3.7 Revising Drafts

Whether you developed a thesis, then outlined your paper, mapped your arguments, and started writing, or whether you started writing and let your arguments, outline, and thesis emerge from that, at some point you should have enough material to constitute something resembling a complete paper (with or without the opening and closing paragraphs). This is your rough draft. You get from your rough draft to the final version of your paper by *revising* it.

Don't let your first draft be your final version. Nobody writes that well. Some people are surprised when they discover that even great authors revise, rewrite, and edit their work, and that this can be difficult and sometimes frustrating work for them. To do the best writing you are capable of, you have to think, write, rethink, and rewrite. With careful attention to your own work, you will find discrepancies between what you wrote and what you meant. Or you will find that your first thoughts are not your best thoughts. Maybe you write well enough to get an acceptable grade with less revision than it would take to do your best work, but it's only your best work—or something close to it—that you can feel truly proud of when you put your name on the paper.

You need to work through multiple drafts to achieve your best work. But if you read what you have written immediately after writing it, it can be difficult to separate the ideas you wanted to convey from the words you actually wrote. As you reread your own writing, you might be thinking not only of what the words would actually convey to a reader but also of ideas you had in mind when you wrote the passage that did not end up expressed on the page. By starting early, you give yourself time between drafts. Generally, the more time you take between drafts, the fresher your perspective on your paper will be, and thus the more likely you will be to see what you have *actually said* rather than what you were *trying to say*. As a rule of thumb, we suggest allowing at least one good night's sleep between working on your paper and rereading it with an eye to revising it.

The more often you revise your paper, the better it will be. But, happily, revision is often a process of diminishing returns. That is, you will likely make the biggest changes to your paper the first time you revise a complete draft. This is when you may realize that you have not presented your material in the order that makes it easiest for your reader to understand or that you have neglected to include an important part of your case, such as a positive argument for your view or a reply to an objection you consider. Writing new material can be substantial work but, as we have said before (§§3.4 & 3.5), reordering the material in your paper—even radically changing your thesis—can be easier than you might think, more a matter of shifting chunks of text around than of starting over. And if you make substantial revisions to your first draft, it is unlikely that you will have to do so in subsequent rounds of revision, which may consist of tasks such as adding a sign-post, rephrasing a crucial claim, or choosing a better illustrative example. We hope this encourages you to include multiple rounds of revision in your schedule for work on your paper.

3.8 Responding to Criticism

Even if you have made substantial revisions to your rough draft, you will probably be blind to some of its weaknesses. Some language errors or peculiarities, logical fallacies, and plausible lines of objection may elude you but stand out to your reader. The problem, of course, is that the writing and ideas are your own. You already know what you *intended* to say, and that is what comes to mind when you read your draft. In almost every case, the critical comments of others can help you improve a piece of writing. (Recall that, in this context, "critical" means thoughtfully evaluative, not necessarily negative.)

In some philosophy courses, things are arranged so that your instructor or another student will provide this critical feedback. If this is not the case for your paper, you should ask someone to read your draft and make a note of any place he gets lost or has a question that isn't answered in your paper, along with specific recommendations for changes. If your reader is willing to put in a little more time to help you, ask him to provide you with a one-sentence summary of your thesis or one-paragraph summary of your primary argument, in addition to any comments and suggestions. Try not to skew your reader's feedback by giving your own summary or evaluation of any part of the draft as it stands. You may be surprised that passages you thought didn't require any revision are highly confusing to a novice reader, and passages you thought were confusing are actually quite clear.

Who should you ask to critique your draft? In some ways, an excellent candidate would be someone fitting the description of your imagined reader—an intelligent undergraduate with no experience in philosophy. Then again, someone with expertise in your topic, such as your instructor or a fellow student with more experience in philosophy, may be able to give you helpful feedback on the accuracy and cogency of the views and arguments you discuss. Ideally, you would get feedback from both kinds of readers; in practice, you may be limited by who is willing and available, as well as constraints on your own time.

Take seriously *all* the feedback that you receive. The usefulness of criticism depends in large part on how you handle it. When someone tells us that what we've written is confusing or that we missed a plausible objection, most of us become defensive. That is, we respond too quickly with explanations of why we wrote what we did or why what the critic is suggesting isn't a good idea. Responses like these are counterproductive. There is no point in asking for feedback if you are not going to consider it seriously. Even when the critic really has missed something you've said, his response may show that you have not expressed or emphasized it as clearly as you intended to.

If you cannot control your emotions, if you become angry at the critic or feel overwhelmed by his critique, you will find it difficult to recognize when good points are being made. In such cases, take a break from working on the paper. Get a good night's sleep and return to the critical feedback when you're in a more receptive frame of mind. (See also §5.1 on emotional expression in your writing.)

While you should *consider* every comment you receive, you don't need to revise your paper in response to each one. For one thing, you may reasonably disagree, on reflection, with some of the comments you receive. For another, there is never space to consider *everything* relevant to the topic at hand; you will almost certainly have to ignore *some* plausible, relevant arguments. (See §4.1.) Nonetheless, sometimes even a comment that you think is misguided will prompt a new idea about how to revise your paper—an idea not directly suggested by the critic. It would be a shame if you missed a helpful insight because you dismissed some feedback without considering it seriously.

You need to leave yourself enough time to consider any feedback you receive and revise your paper accordingly. If possible, however, you should give your draft to someone for feedback only when you have got it into the best shape you can on your own. If you know that you have to clean up the opening paragraph, do it before you give the draft to your reader. That way, your reader won't waste time telling you something you already know, and you might get helpful feedback on what you thought was now a crystal-clear opening paragraph.

(In Appendix A, we provide sample excerpts from draft philosophy papers, marked up by a reader, along with a version of each excerpt revised in light of the reader's comments.)

3.9 Editing

Once you've revised your first draft as much as you can, you have a final draft. You should leave some time between this and the deadline to do a round of what we'll call *editing*, also known as "copyediting" or "proofreading." During this final stage, you focus on the nitty-gritty of the writing: spelling, grammar, and phrasing. As at the earlier stages of revision, it can help to have someone else read your paper and offer editing suggestions. You know what you meant in the first place and may tend to "see" a corrected reading, overlooking errors that would be obvious to another reader. But to avoid entering even the vague borderlands of plagiarism, make sure that you are the only person who actually makes changes to your own paper. (See §3.11 and Chapter 7 for more on the dangers of plagiarism and how to avoid it.)

For editing at the sentence level, it sometimes helps to hear your paper read aloud, whether by yourself or by someone else. If the reader finds his tongue twisted by a sentence, it should probably be rephrased. If you find yourself losing track of where you are in a sentence or what the sentence is saying, you should revise it—perhaps into two shorter, simpler sentences.

The **grammar checkers** available in word-processing programs and online are increasingly sophisticated. But they can still propose changes that introduce errors or infelicities into perfectly fine text. So, at the very least, do not follow the advice of an automated grammar checker without considering whether the result is prose you are happy presenting as your own. We recommend, however, that you avoid automated grammar checkers altogether in favor of developing your own writing skills. The best way to do this is still by learning from others with good writing skills, whether that's authors you're reading; your family, friends, classmates, and instructors; or staff at your school's writing center.

As for editing at the word level, automated **spellcheckers** are less problematic than grammar checkers, but you should not rely exclusively on them for correct spelling in your paper. For one thing, they may not catch the fact that you've typed the wrong word. For example, if you mistakenly wrote "casual" where you meant "causal," the spellchecker may not alert you to this fact. (See §§6.6 & 6.11 for lists of commonly confused and misspelled words.) A spellchecker will also flag any word that is not in its dictionary, even though the word may be spelled correctly. Many of the technical terms used in philosophy (e.g., "sorites" and "noumenal") and the names of philosophers (e.g., "Unamuno" and "Rorty") will be flagged in this way. You should be able to add such words to your spellchecker's dictionary—but when you do, make sure you spell them correctly!

Finally, be watchful for editing residue. Sometimes when you edit a passage, you'll add a phrase without entirely deleting the phrase it replaces, or you'll change part of a sentence without realizing you need to change, say, a pronoun in another part of the sentence or paragraph. The only way to catch these errors is to reread, with fresh eyes, any material you've altered. Another kind of editing residue is more mechanical. If you copy and paste material into your paper, it may end up in a different font, size, or color from the surrounding material. Sometimes the change is so subtle that you don't notice it—or not until you print out the final version. Either way, your reader may be distracted by it. An easy preventative measure is, as your last editing move, to select the entire text of your paper and apply your standard formatting features (font, including font size and color, line and paragraph spacing, etc.).

3.10 Formatting

Different instructors will ask you to submit your work in different formats. As always, you should follow any instructions you are given. The biggest difference in format is whether you are required to provide a hard copy of the paper or to submit it electronically (or both). Even if the paper is to be submitted electronically, you should format it as if it were going to be printed out (unless your instructor says otherwise).

In case you are not given instructions on some matters, we provide here some standard formatting choices, along with some reasons they have become widespread. These may not be the default settings in the software you use to write your paper. If so, learn how to change them. (This information is easily accessible online.) Word processors are tools—make sure you are the one in charge and not the tool.

3.10.1 General Formatting

12-point, Times New Roman font: Though there is some variation, a serif font, such as Times New Roman, at 12-point size is traditional for philosophical manuscripts, including student papers. *Serifs* are the tiny tails at the end of the strokes making up a letter. "Sans-serif" just means "without serifs." (Look closely at the top and bottom of the letters in this (sans-serif) word and this (serif) word.) There are other common serif fonts, such as Garamond. The most important feature of your choice of font is that your reader does not notice it.

Double line spacing: This became standard since it leaves space between lines for readers to record comments. Even though this is not how comments are usually made in electronic documents, the practice is still standard for papers submitted electronically.

One-inch margins on all four sides of each page: This white space makes the text easier to read and is sometimes used for comments.

Ragged right margin (i.e., paragraphs left-justified only): A margin is "ragged" if the end of each line doesn't align vertically; it is "justified" if the ends do align. Most published text is right- and left-justified, but it is standard for unpublished manuscripts (including student papers) to have a ragged right margin. You may think that justifying the right margin makes your paper look professional but, in fact, most word processors do not achieve professional-level justification, often leaving potentially distracting spaces between words.

Page numbers: Readers often want to refer to different parts of your paper in their comments, and page numbers are a standard way to do this. The top-right and bottom-right corners are standard places to put them, as is the middle of the bottom of the page. The page number may be omitted from the first page.

Clear paragraph divisions: There are two standard ways to indicate a new paragraph: (1) indenting the first line or (2) leaving a gap the width of a (double-spaced) line. Choose *one*. Check that your word processor is not adding unnecessary gaps between paragraphs. (Look for settings such as "space after paragraph" and "space before paragraph.")

3.10.2 Cover Page or No Cover Page?

At the beginning of your paper, you should provide the following information. Some instructors want it on a separate cover page; others prefer it at the top of the first page of the paper; some leave the choice to you. Figures 3.2 and 3.3 illustrate the two options.

Title: Your title should clearly indicate the topic—and, if possible, the thesis—of your paper. Strangely enough, it is standard for paper (and book) titles *not* to be complete grammatical sentences. For instance, if your thesis is that *racial anti-realism is false*, your title might be "The Flaw in Racial Anti-Realism." This is better than "Racial Anti-Realism" or "Assessing Racial Anti-Realism" since these latter titles don't give your reader a sense of where you stand on the topic. Perhaps even better, because it gives your reader a taste of your primary argument, would be "Racial Anti-Realism's Failure to Respect Ordinary Racial Thinking." (For what to capitalize in your title, see §7.4.2.)

You should avoid a humorous title—especially on sensitive topics—unless the joke is deeply connected to your thesis *and* you are pretty sure it will make your instructor laugh out loud.

Your name

The course number and name: Copy this from the syllabus or another authoritative source. If the course number includes a "section" number, be sure to include it.

Assignment number and name (if applicable): If you are responding to one of a numbered list of paper prompts, include that information (e.g., *Question 3a*). It doesn't hurt to include the name of the assignment, either (e.g., *Metaphysics Paper* or *Third Thesis-Defense Paper*).

Character Roles in the Platonic Dialogues

Mariana Rios

PHIL 3105-2: Ancient Greek Philosophy
Second thesis-defense paper
Question 2(a)
Word count: 2,894

1

It is striking that Plato's texts—considered by many to be the founding documents of Western philosophy—are written in the form of dramatic dialogues. While there has been some dispute about which characters, and indeed particular speeches, should be identified with Plato's own views, there has been less discussion of how we should understand the relationships between views that are clearly not Plato's and the characters who express these views. In this paper, I

Figure 3.2 A sample cover page and the beginning of the first page of the paper.

1

Mariana Rios
PHIL 3105-2: Ancient Greek Philosophy
Second thesis-defense paper
Question 2(a)
Word count: 2,894

Character Roles in the Platonic Dialogues

It is striking that Plato's texts—considered by many to be the founding documents of Western philosophy—are written in the form of dramatic dialogues. While there has been some dispute about which characters, and indeed particular speeches, should be identified with Plato's own views, there has been less discussion of how we should understand the relationships between views that are clearly not Plato's and the characters who express these views. In this paper, I

Figure 3.3 What the first page of the same paper would look like without a cover page.

Word count: A word count is not as standardly required as the previous information, but in the age of electronic documents, this is increasingly how instructors measure the length of student papers. At the final stages of editing, record your word count using the word-count feature of your word processor. Different instructors have different rules about whether the word count includes footnotes, your list of works cited, your name, and so on. If that might make a difference (e.g., to whether you receive a penalty for being over or under the required length), check with your instructor.

3.10.3 For Hard-Copy Submissions Only

A staple holding the pages together: If your instructor wants a hard copy of your paper, she will want it to hang together—literally! Paper clips fall out, especially in piles of papers getting moved around. Folding the corner of your paper's pages over does nothing (except perhaps exasperate your instructor). Plastic covers and binders are rarely used at the college level; avoid them unless instructed otherwise.

3.10.4 For Electronic Submissions Only

File type: If your instructor does not specify a file type, you should use a widely accessible type, such as .docx (Word), .pdf (PDF), .odt (Open Office), or .rtf (rich text format).

Identifying file name: The name of the electronic file *containing* your paper is (or can be) different from the *title* of your paper. We recommend that you name your file with your last name and the name of the assignment (e.g., *Ogba, Thesis-Defense Paper 2*) since this is a common way for instructors to keep track of electronically submitted assignments. You can add the subject or title of your paper to the file name (e.g., *Ogba, Thesis-Defense Paper 2, Metaphysics* or *Ogba Thesis-Defense Paper 2, The Problem of Freedom*), but beware that some websites, programs, and operating systems (perhaps those used by your instructor) have difficulty with long file names.

3.11 Acknowledging the Work of Others

If you have read any contemporary philosophy, you may have noticed "acknowledgments" at the front of the book, or in a footnote or endnote, where the author thanks people who have helped her develop her thoughts on her topic. And if you've read any scholarly prose at all, you've doubtless noticed footnotes, endnotes, or parenthetical citations indicating sources the author has used to help her make her points. These kinds of acknowledgments are a sign of the importance that scholars accord to the collaborative nature of their work. The principle that *credit should be given where credit is due* reflects a deep value within the scholarly community. Violations of this principle are taken very seriously by academic communities, including colleges and universities. As a result, the price of **plagiarism** can be high.

The word "plagiarism" comes from a Latin word meaning *thief*. You plagiarize when you present the ideas or words of others in such a way that a reader familiar with the norms of scholarship would infer that those ideas or words originated with you. For professional philosophers, the price of plagiarism may be censure by professional organizations and an irreversible loss of reputation. Students who plagiarize may face a failing grade on the assignment or in the course, academic probation, a record of the violation on their transcript, suspension, or even expulsion.

Sometimes plagiarism is intentional, as when a student purchases a paper from an online "paper mill." The desperate student who is buying the paper "just this once" often reassesses the situation and regrets the decision too late. Avoiding this kind of plagiarism is simple in one sense: Write your own paper. But, of course, what leads students to this kind of plagiarism is often desperation that they are unable to complete—or even begin—writing the paper themselves. If you feel this way, it is a sign that there is a larger problem in your engagement with the course. If you feel totally at sea with respect to the course or the paper assignment, you should talk to your instructor *as soon as possible* to figure out how you can catch up and salvage a passing grade or, if necessary, withdraw from the course. These conversations can be awkward, but they are much less fraught than dealing with an accusation of plagiarism after the fact.

Sometimes plagiarism is unintentional, as when you use a phrase from your notes in your paper without realizing that you took it verbatim (i.e., word for word) from a published text and thus fail to acknowledge it correctly. (We discuss, in Chapter 7, how to acknowledge material you take from others.) The best way to avoid such plagiarism is to *always* clearly mark in your notes or draft *whenever* you have taken material from a published source—whether verbatim or otherwise. (We discuss how to do this in §8.1.1.)

Contemporary word-processing technology has created new gray areas around the edges of plagiarism. In the old days, when you gave your draft to a friend for comments, he might have suggested an alternative way of wording a point by writing it in the margin. If you decided to accept that alternative, you would have to write it out yourself in a new draft of the paper. It would still be good practice to acknowledge your friend's help in a footnote, but since you didn't take this wording from a published source, you would not be required to cite it formally. (See §7.1.) These days, your friend might instead "track changes" in an electronic document, making it easy for you to accept his alternative phrasing at the click of a button—perhaps without even having read it. To some (possibly old-school, but still reasonable) instructors, this looks a lot like your friend wrote part of your paper—and that is plagiarism. As a result, we advise you to err on the safe side by never simply "accepting" a tracked change; *always write out any changes to your paper yourself*. You may be surprised by how often you will want to tweak what your reader has suggested. Either way, you can still acknowledge your reader's help in a footnote.[1]

Professional philosophers, such as your instructor, recognize writing styles and philosophical ideas that alert them to the fact that material in a student paper did not originate with its purported author. Some also use online services to identify plagiarized passages. Professional philosophers are not only intimately familiar with the conventions for acknowledging others' work; they are also deeply committed to the values underlying these conventions. So make sure you have not plagiarized. Check each of the ideas or phrases you borrowed from other sources to see if you have credited the source according to the conventions we discuss in Chapter 7. Remember: Giving credit where credit is due is what distinguishes a scholar from a plagiarist.

1 For instance: Thanks to Julie Post for suggesting the addition of this sample footnote.

4 Making a Strong Case

In the previous two chapters, we've discussed the elements and structure of a thesis-defense paper, and how to go about drafting, revising, editing, and formatting one. In this chapter, we focus on some ways to make the strongest case for your thesis—and some pitfalls to avoid.

4.1 How Much, and What, to Cover

A truly comprehensive case for your view would include all the arguments for it, all the arguments against alternative views on the topic, and explanation and refutation of all the objections to your view and the arguments for it. There is no way you will be able to do that for any worthwhile philosophical topic in the space available to you in a college paper. (Probably no one could do that even in a lengthy book.) Fortunately, such a comprehensive case would probably not be the most convincing case for your view. Many of the arguments considered would likely be of little interest; you would run the risk of losing your reader in the details, distracting her from the main reasons she should believe your thesis.

So how many arguments, alternatives, and objections should you consider—and which ones? There is no easy formula to answer this question, but we can offer two helpful rules of thumb: First, it is better to consider *fewer* arguments (alternatives, objections, etc.) in *more depth* than to consider *more* arguments (alternatives, objections, etc.) in *less depth*. That may seem counterintuitive. Wouldn't *more* positive arguments and the refutation of *more* objections make for a stronger case? It might at first seem so, but other factors will inevitably affect the success of this strategy. For one thing, there's the problem just mentioned of losing your reader in the details. For another, you may face a word limit, in which case every additional argument or objection you explain will take space away from your consideration of something else. At the ridiculous end of this spectrum, you would end up with a bulleted list of arguments, objections, and responses. Such a list might be helpful for some purposes. (It might be a good way to start writing your paper!) But it won't make for a convincing thesis-defense paper in itself because your reader will have questions about each item on the list. Isn't this argument questionable? Does that response to the objection really refute it? It's in the *critical discussion* of these arguments, alternatives, and objections that you will convince your reader of your thesis. Finally, not all arguments are equally strong. The fact that there are, say, two arguments in favor of your view and only one against it doesn't clinch your case. Perhaps the arguments in its favor are weak, and the one against it very strong. So you should err on the side of considering *fewer* arguments, alternatives, and objections in *more depth*.

DOI: 10.4324/9781003512318-4

Now you face the second part of our question: How do you choose which arguments, alternatives, and objections to include? Our second rule of thumb answers this question: You should include the *best* or *strongest* arguments, alternatives, and objections. It's probably obvious that you should include the strongest arguments *for* your view, but doesn't the same reasoning suggest that you should include the *weakest* alternatives and objections? After all, they will allow you to include strong refutations. On the contrary, however, as we mentioned in Section 2.3, you make a stronger case for your view by showing that your thesis is preferable to even the *best* alternatives and can withstand even the *strongest* objections.

Related to this second rule of thumb is **the principle of charity**, according to which you should present the arguments of others in their strongest form. (Compare §2.3.) The name comes from the idea that you are sometimes "charitable" to your opponents by *strengthening* their arguments. Why would you do this? For the reason just given: You strengthen your case by replying to the strongest alternatives and counterarguments. If you are concerned that you *cannot* reply to the strongest versions of these alternatives or objections, you need to revisit your thesis or primary argument.

One pitfall to avoid is a paper that merely summarizes the readings you've been assigned on your topic. As we hope is clear from much that we've said so far, a thesis-defense paper should be about a philosophical *topic* on which you defend a *thesis*. You should use the work of others where it helps you to make that case (see §§3.11 & 4.3, and Chapter 7), but if you find yourself summarizing assigned texts one by one, it's likely a sign that you have not yet come to grips with your own view on the topic at hand. (Some philosophy assignments *require* you to summarize texts—we consider some in Chapters 8 and 9—but these are not thesis-defense papers.)

4.2 Staying on Track

It is often difficult to stay focused on your thesis and primary argument as you draft your paper. It is easy to follow a thread of reasoning from one paragraph to the next, unsure where you will end up. Sometimes this kind of drafting leads to unexpected insights that help you make an even stronger case. But sometimes the thread leads to a **tangent** (related to your topic but unrelated to the case you are making) or even a dead end. This is no problem if you have enough time—and the strength of will—to cut such material out as you revise your paper. In a thesis-defense paper, there is a simple rule for what to include: *If it ultimately serves your primary argument, and thus your thesis, then include it in your paper.* If it's related to your topic but doesn't serve your primary argument and thus your thesis, then leave it out—even if it's interesting or displays your knowledge or intelligence.

4.3 The Roles of Citation and Quotation

We discussed, in Section 2.3.1, the difference between *explaining* a theory or claim and *arguing for* that theory or claim: To explain a theory or claim is to give a value-neutral description of it, while to argue for one is to offer reasons in its favor. It is also important to distinguish argument from citation and quotation.

You **cite** people or texts when you acknowledge them as the source of the ideas or words you are using. This is usually done in a formal way, with quotation marks when you use someone else's very words (see §6.8.7) and—whether or not you use that person's words—a bibliographic citation (see Chapter 7). In some academic disciplines, citation can play the role of "argument by proxy." For instance, in a psychology paper, you might cite a number of studies that collectively establish the truth of some claim. Such argument by proxy is uncommon in philosophy. Certainly, you should not make a claim and then expect your reader to believe it on the basis that it has been defended in print by a professional philosopher—or even many philosophers. (Compare §4.7 on the *appeal to authority*.) If you do not argue for a claim you make, you should state explicitly that you are *assuming* its truth. You might also cite a source where that claim is argued for in a way you endorse, but the claim will still count as an unargued-for assumption in your paper. (See also §5.3.2.)

Similarly, **quotation**—that is, including the words of others in your own paper—is not a form of argument. Many students leave high school thinking that a quotation is a kind of evidence and that one makes a cumulative case in a thesis-defense paper by stringing together a number of quotations. This may be because most high-school students learn how to write essays in English-literature classes. If you're defending a thesis about a novel or poem, then quotations from that novel or poem *can* properly count as evidence in favor of your thesis. If the thesis of your philosophy paper is similarly about a text (e.g., how we should best interpret Descartes's arguments for dualism), then this use of quotation as evidence can be appropriate. But in a philosophy paper where you defend a thesis on a philosophical *topic*, rather than a particular *text*, you should (as a rule of thumb) only quote a source when you need to say something in your paper about *the way the claim is worded* in the material you quote.

As we have already said, you must always cite the source of the words you quote. Since you are always taking the quoted material out of context, however, you must also always *explain* to your reader what the quoted author is saying in the quotation. This makes quotation rather "expensive" in terms of the space you have to make your case. When you use a quotation, you essentially have to state the same idea twice: once in the quotation and once more in your explanation. But if you can explain the idea clearly in your own words, then you should consider whether the quotation is contributing anything to the defense of your thesis. If it is not, you should remove it. If you *cannot* explain the idea expressed in the quotation, you have two options: Either you should discuss in your paper the difficulty of interpreting the quoted material, or you should keep working—perhaps with the help of your classmates or instructor—to figure out what it means.

In sum: While you must always cite any ideas or words you borrow from others, do not confuse citation or quotation with argument. Moreover, make sure you understand how any quotations in your paper contribute to the defense of your thesis. See Chapter 7 for how to cite your sources.

4.4 Universal Claims, Generalizations, and Counterexamples

Think carefully when you use terms such as "all," "every," or "without exception" in a claim. These terms make your claim *universal*—that is, about absolutely everything of the kind you are discussing, with no exceptions (*every* action, *all* events, *everyone*, and so on). As a result, a single counterexample disproves a universal claim. For example, if you claim that *every human action is ultimately motivated by self-interest*, a single example of an action that is *not* ultimately motivated by self-interest is sufficient to show that your claim is false. It is thus important to avoid overstatement. (See also §5.3.) If you can only defend the claim that something is true in *almost all* or *most* cases, say so explicitly and resist the temptation to make a stronger, universal claim. If the several books on logic by Bertrand Russell that you have examined are all very technical, don't claim that "All of

Bertrand Russell's writings are very technical." He also wrote popular articles on ethics and war. They are not technical, so your claim would be false.

In the following two examples, the first word of the sentence makes clear what kind of claim is being made:

> All of Plato's dialogues were written after the Peloponnesian Wars.
> Most theories of truth from before the turn of the twentieth century were foundationalist.

But suppose you read the following sentence in a philosophy textbook:

> Existentialists accept Sartre's view that "existence precedes essence."

Do you think the author means to say that every single existentialist follows Sartre in this matter, or just that this is generally true, but with some exceptions? Sometimes the context will make clear which reading is intended. Still, it is better if your reader does not have to pause to interpret your claim. So you should err on the side of making explicit what kind of claim you are making. When drafting a broad statement, make sure it is clear whether you intend to make a universal claim or a mere generalization.

4.5 Consistency

In philosophy, a lot turns on quite subtle differences, and those differences can only be conveyed—indeed, *will* be conveyed, whether you intend it or not—by subtle differences in language. You must thus strive to say exactly what you mean throughout your paper and to be consistent in what you say.

As should be clear by now, your thesis is a crucial part of your paper: It is the main conclusion you aim to defend. It is thus imperative that you state your thesis consistently throughout your paper. For example, suppose someone states the following thesis in an opening paragraph:

> The existence of God cannot be established through empirical evidence.

Now suppose that in the closing paragraph, the author restates the thesis in one of the following ways:

> God cannot be known.
> There is no reason to believe in God.

These claims are quite different from the original thesis; they are not simply different wordings of it. The adjective "empirical" refers to evidence justified through sensory experience. It may be, then, that the original thesis is true, while the two "restatements" are false. (This would be the case if there is no *empirical* evidence for God's existence, but it could be established, as various philosophers have argued, *a priori*, i.e., independent of any sensory experience.) This author has put the reader in the frustrating position of having to decide which thesis the author is really aiming to defend. (The reader might reasonably wonder if the original "thesis" is intended as partial evidence for the ultimate thesis.) Arguments on this topic are hard enough to understand and evaluate without being unsure what their ultimate conclusion is. So make sure, as you finish revising your paper, that you know *exactly* what your thesis is and that you always state it accurately.

The same point about consistency applies to the names of the theories you discuss, the role of an argument within your paper, the strength of a claim or argument, and so on. Here are some examples: (1) If you call a theory "constructivism" when you introduce it, do not later refer to it as "constructionism." An attentive reader will assume that you have used a different term because you're referring to a different theory, but she will search for this difference in your paper in vain. This kind of inconsistency often arises because different authors you've read refer to the same theory (argument, objection, etc.) with different names, and you've thus come to see them as synonyms. But remember that your reader is unfamiliar with the material you've read on the topic. Pick one name for the theory—the simplest and clearest—and stick with it. (2) Suppose you've considered an objection to an argument you endorse and then replied to the objection. Later on, you might refer to this reply as your "objection" to your opponent's "argument" (the original objection). This is likely to confuse your reader, who will be thinking of what your opponent said as an "objection" and what you said in return as a "reply." So be consistent in how you refer to the various claims and arguments in your paper. (3) In Section 4.4, we emphasized the difference between universal claims and mere generalizations. Having decided exactly what kind of claim you are making, be careful not to muddy the waters by carelessly "restating" the claim so that you are in fact saying something different. Your reader will take you at your word. (See also §5.6.)

4.6 Examples and Analogies

A well-chosen **example** can be a powerful way to draw readers in to your paper (cf. §2.2.3) and to help them understand complex issues, ideas, and arguments. Certain kinds of examples can play a role in an argument (e.g., the counterexamples to universal claims discussed in §4.4). But the kind of example we're discussing here plays no *logical* role in the argument of your paper; these examples are *rhetorical* devices, helpfully illustrating some aspect of your argument without being part of that argument.

Any example you use should be comprehensible to a wide range of readers, so don't, for example, use a character from an obscure comic book that only you and your friends will recognize.

Examples should not be distracting. For instance, an example that uses a good, kind Democrat pitted against an evil, ruthless Republican is likely to irritate any Republican reading your paper—and probably a number of Democrats too. A highly charged example can show that the stakes are high, thus piquing your reader's interest. For instance, examples of people murdering other people are a staple of the literature on free will since they highlight the apparent connection between freedom and morality. But such examples can also distract, since some readers will be upset by the violence. If an example of, say, someone choosing what to have for lunch would work just as well, you should consider that alternative.

If you can, use the same example to illustrate various points throughout your paper. For instance, if you begin your essay on the problem of freedom with Wei choosing between pizza and a sandwich for lunch, then when you come to discuss the influence of past events on people's decisions, you can illustrate the new point with Wei's having had pizza every day of the previous week or with her experience of once getting food-poisoning from eating cold pizza. This saves you space since you don't have to explain a new example from scratch, and it saves your reader the cognitive resources she would have spent imagining a new example, thus helping her to concentrate on your argument.

Analogies are often used in similar ways to examples. In an analogy, you attempt to clarify one thing by comparing it with another that is similar in some way. Often, the things compared are very different; they may be similar in only one respect. Similes and metaphors are simple kinds of analogies, but in argumentative writing, the term "analogy" is often reserved for more complicated comparisons from which an insight or conclusion is to be drawn.

Analogies have been employed in philosophical writing for ages. Plato's *Republic*, for instance, is full of them. In Book V, Socrates is asked whether women, as well as men, should hold the highest offices in an ideal political community. His response is the question: Would a bald person or a long-haired person be a better shoemaker? Obviously, hair length is irrelevant to a cobbler's skill. Socrates suggests *by analogy* that gender is irrelevant to skills of political leadership.

An analogy can help your reader grasp something abstract, unusual, or complex—a concept, theory, or argument—by providing a more concrete, familiar, or simple image that resembles it in key respects. However, you must be cautious when using analogies and considering those of others. The logical power of an analogy is often overestimated. What is a helpful rhetorical device can be treated by an incautious author or reader as an argument. Socrates's cobbling analogy throws into sharp relief the irrelevance of gender to political ability, but it doesn't *argue* for that irrelevance. Someone might respond to Socrates by saying that a person with strong hands would make a better cobbler than someone with weak hands. The question now seems to be whether gender relates to political skill more like hair length or hand strength relates to cobbling skill. But it's unlikely we'll make much progress on the topic by further investigation of shoemaking. At this point, we need some arguments about gender and political skill themselves.

In short, examples and analogies are helpful tools for getting your reader to grasp philosophical concepts, claims, and arguments. But take care that you do not slip into thinking or implying that your illustrative example or analogy is doing substantive argumentative work. (Some writers do discuss something called "argument by analogy" or "analogical reasoning." See, for example, Boardman, Cavender, and Kahane, *Logic and Contemporary Rhetoric* 113–15.)

4.7 Some Common Fallacies

A **fallacy** is a form of reasoning that is unreliable yet psychologically compelling. Fallacies are thus easy to miss in your own thinking and writing, and in the work of others. As with any faulty form of reasoning, fallacies appear both intentionally (in attempts to mislead) and unintentionally (as honest mistakes). For many reasons, then, it's helpful to be aware of the most common fallacies. In this final section, we discuss what are often called *informal fallacies*. (Many good introductory logic and critical-thinking books cover more fallacies than we have space for here. See, for example, Boardman, Cavender, and Kahane's *Logic and Contemporary Rhetoric*. We cover two common *formal* fallacies in §10.3.2.)

You **beg the question**, as philosophers use that phrase, when you argue in a circle, stating or implying your conclusion in one of your premises. A classic example is someone arguing that God exists on the basis that God's existence is implied throughout the Bible and that everything the Bible says or implies is true. The circularity is supposedly in the final premise: *Everything the Bible says or implies is true*. If the existence of God is the issue at hand, this premise stands in need of defense. One way of defending it is by claiming that the Bible is the word of God. But the Bible can be the word of God only if God exists. So it seems that this argument begs the question—it assumes (implicitly) that God exists in order to argue that God exists. (See also §10.2.3.)

Notice, however, that we've made an assumption about how the person offering this argument would defend the questionable premise. If he has some other (noncircular) way of defending that premise, then he has not begged the question. One moral is that you should be as explicit as possible about your reasons for endorsing a controversial claim.

A note on terminology: Unfortunately, the phrase "beg the question" is used more and more commonly to mean "raise the question." For example, someone might say that the rise in tuition fees "begs the question" of how students will cover the cost. Clearly, this person is not making an accusation of circular reasoning. You should remember, then, that "beg the question" is a technical term in philosophy. Just as you wouldn't use "weight" when you mean "mass" on a physics test, even though you might do so outside the physics classroom, you should only use the phrase "beg the question" to mean "argue in a circle" in your philosophical writing.

You set up a **straw man** whenever you attack a misrepresentation of someone's position or argument that is weaker than the original.[1] For example, suppose someone advocates the regulation of handguns. If she is criticized on the grounds that a complete ban on firearms would be unconstitutional, then the critic has "attacked a straw man": The regulation of handguns could occur without a complete ban on firearms, so criticism of the second view may leave the first view untouched. Straw men are easier to attack than the actual position or argument at issue and thus can make a weak case (that of the person attacking the straw man) appear stronger than it is. You might see setting up a straw man as the opposite of *the principle of charity* (see §4.1), according to which you should present the arguments of others in as strong a form as possible.

You create a **false dilemma** (or false dichotomy) when you present two alternatives as if they were the only possibilities when in fact a third alternative exists—or perhaps many more. Note that not all dilemmas are "false." For instance, either you are taller than everyone else in the room or you aren't. The author of a false dilemma typically argues as follows: Either A or B is true. A is unacceptable (for some reason). So B must be true. For example, a proponent of capital punishment might argue that *we must universally adopt capital punishment unless we want crime running rampant in every street*. It seems implausible that, without capital punishment, law and order will not be enforced anywhere. This author thus owes us at least an argument for that claim, i.e., an argument that the dilemma is not false.

The fallacy of the **slippery slope** is committed when the writer argues—without good reason—that one claim (at the top of the metaphorical slope) implies, through a kind of domino effect, a series of similar claims, ending in a final claim (at the bottom of the slope). The fallacy is that the first claim implies the final claim. The final claim may be endorsed, or it may be presented as so objectionable (for some reason) that we must reject the initial claim. For example, someone might oppose teaching about the beliefs of

1 Unfortunately, no gender-neutral alternative to the phrase "straw man" has become standard in formal English. The use of "strawman" as a transitive verb (e.g., "Perales strawmans Stevenson") is quite recent and is currently considered too informal for scholarly prose.

major religions in a public-school curriculum by asserting that this will lead to some religions being presented in a more favorable light than others; that will lead to the explicit endorsement of some religions and the denigration of others; that will spread beyond the public schools to other social institutions; and ultimately, the separation between church and state will be destroyed. It's surely *possible* that all these things will come to pass, but this person has not shown that the first will lead inevitably to the last.

To avoid the slippery-slope fallacy, you must *either* establish that the slope really is slippery—that is, that each step in the series of implications really is inevitable—*or* refrain from claiming such inevitability.

Another fallacy is closely related to the slippery-slope fallacy. Consider that some things are red (this apple, for instance), and some things are yellow (this banana). Can you specify exactly where on the color spectrum red ends and yellow begins? No. Does that show that nothing is actually red or that there's no difference between red and yellow? Of course not. You commit the **continuum** fallacy when you argue that a category (e.g., red things) does not exist simply because there is a continuum between things supposedly in that category (e.g., this apple) and things not in it (e.g., this banana).

For a more complex philosophical example, suppose you were defending the idea that killing one innocent person to save the life of a million others is morally acceptable. You don't think that it would be acceptable to kill an innocent person to save only a *single* other life, but a million lives is a different story. Now suppose someone challenges you to specify the smallest number of lives saved that would justify killing one innocent person. You balk. How could you pick a particular number of saved lives that *would* justify sacrificing an innocent person such that just one fewer saved life would *not* justify the sacrifice? You are tempted to withdraw your original claim. (That is, you are succumbing to your opponent's argument that nothing falls into the category *morally justified sacrifice of an innocent life to save others*.) But your challenger is committing the continuum fallacy. Perhaps your original claim is wrong, but your challenger hasn't shown that yet.

You commit the **genetic** fallacy when you reason on the basis of the *origin* or *source* of an idea or argument rather than its content. This fallacy is particularly seductive when you're arguing against an idea that is defended by a person or group you are disposed against. If, for instance, you dismiss an argument against abortion simply because it is endorsed by the Catholic Church, then you have committed the genetic fallacy. (It would be equally fallacious, of course, to claim that an argument is *compelling* simply because it is endorsed by a particular organization.) The argument in question is either rationally compelling or not; its source doesn't affect its strength. The **ad hominem** fallacy, named with a Latin phrase that means "at the person," is an instance of the genetic fallacy that focuses on a particular individual. For example: "You can't trust Marisa's view about health care—she's a libertarian!"

The **appeal to authority** is a version of the genetic fallacy in which you claim that something is true because it is endorsed by someone with a particular social status. Perhaps the "authority" to which you appeal is an elected official, is a religious leader, or has a Ph.D. The point is not that we should not trust such people; indeed, we may have good reason for thinking that what they say is true. Perhaps it's extremely unlikely that the governor would warn people that a hurricane threatens her state if there were not good evidence that a hurricane really is on the way. Perhaps you've asked a professor in the physics department about current theories of quantum mechanics because they're relevant to your paper on the metaphysics of time and he's an expert on the topic. But there are two reasons for caution. First, a person's sphere of authority may be irrelevant to the claim in question. A Ph.D. in chemistry, for instance, is no evidence of expertise in ethics. Second, even when a person's sphere of authority *is* relevant to the claim in question, you should not believe the claim is true—or expect others to—*merely* because an authority endorses it. Notice that in the cases of the governor and physics professor, we have good reason to think that the authorities in question believe what they do because of further evidence they could appeal to. If you are, in essence, appealing to that evidence by proxy, you are not committing a fallacy. But it wouldn't hurt to make that appeal explicit. (Compare §4.3.)

The fallacy of **common belief** could be considered an instance of the appeal to authority. In this case, the "authority" is popular opinion. The implicit reasoning is that if the claim were false, then it would not be believed by so many people. Unfortunately, false beliefs about the nature of the world, the human psyche, and certain groups of people have often been widespread. They were not thereby true. It would surely be unjustified to assume that we have arrived at a point in history where there are no such widespread false beliefs. When a claim is prefaced with such phrases as "Everybody knows ...," "Who would deny ...," or "It's a well-known fact that ..." be on your guard for this fallacy.

The fallacy that **two wrongs make a right** is committed when an action is justified by the fact that it has been performed before. The fact that an action *has* (or has not) been performed has no bearing on whether it *ought* to be performed—or is even acceptable. Nevertheless, in politics and on various social topics, adults continue to commit this childhood fallacy. It would be committed if, for example, someone attempted a moral justification of the government's violation of some individuals' civil rights simply by observing that other nations have committed similar acts.

Closely related to the idea that two wrongs make a right is the ***tu quoque*** fallacy, named with a Latin phrase that means "you too." In this case, an author defends his reasoning by pointing out that some aspect of it that has been criticized is also used by the critic. For instance, suppose that while defending determinism, you must reply to an indeterminist's criticism that you have not provided empirical evidence for your view. If you decide to turn the tables and point out that *he* has not provided empirical evidence that *indeterminism* is true, you have committed the *tu quoque* fallacy. Even if you're right that he needs to provide such empirical evidence, that doesn't address the fact that your case is lacking in the same way.

The **appeal to ignorance** is a fallacy in which the lack of evidence for a claim is taken to demonstrate that the claim is false. The slogan that *absence of evidence is not evidence of absence* is a warning against a version of this fallacy. Suppose you wonder if anyone has dropped by your place while you were out to lunch with your roommate. If your roommate claims that clearly no one has since there's no note on the door, no messages on either of your phones, and so on, he is appealing to your collective ignorance to establish the absence of any visitor while you were at lunch. Yet someone might, of course, have dropped by without leaving a note or any other evidence of a visit. It is not always obvious when this fallacy is being committed, however: Sometimes absence of evidence *is* evidence of absence. If you are convinced that your evil cousin stole your grandmother's ring from your bedroom, but a high-tech sweep of your room turns up not a single trace of your cousin's DNA, the absence of such evidence is surely *some* reason to revise your belief.

5 Language

Stylistic Matters

In your professional life, you may often be expected to explain something in writing to an intelligent reader who has an excellent grasp of the English language yet is unfamiliar with the material you are explaining. The writing skills we cover in this chapter and the next are thus useful for much more than just doing well on your philosophy paper.

You wouldn't write an email to your professor like a poem, and you wouldn't write a short story like an instruction manual. Different kinds of writing serve different purposes. You also wouldn't write a children's book using the same language you would use if you were addressing professional anthropologists or attorneys—even if you were trying to communicate the same ideas to these different audiences. You should thus use language in your philosophy paper in ways that best help you achieve your purpose. That means keeping in mind not only *what* you are trying to say but also *to whom* you are saying it—your audience.

A single idea can, in some sense, be expressed in different words. An obvious example of this is translation: The sentence *Mia is a philosopher* says the same thing as the sentence *Mia es filósofa*. Even sticking to one language, we can understand the sense in which the following two sentences say the same thing: *The paper contains many excellent arguments. Many excellent arguments are contained in the paper.*

In another sense, however, the sentences in each of these pairs might convey something slightly different. In the first pair of examples, how the word "filósofa" is used in Spanish—its historical and colloquial uses, the fact that it is grammatically gendered—may mean that the Spanish sentence conveys something slightly different about Mia than the English sentence does. Indeed, the Spanish sentence may convey something different in Spain than it does in Mexico, in Oaxaca than it does in Mexico City, or between one pair of Oaxacan friends and another. Because you are writing for a general audience rather than a specific person, and you can assume that your audience realizes this, you don't have to worry about people's idiosyncratic associations (e.g., that they have a cat named Mia). By the same token, though, you need to understand the generally accepted meanings of words and ways of phrasing things.

In the second pair of examples, because the first sentence (*The paper contains many excellent arguments*) is the default way of structuring this sentence, the alternative (*Many excellent arguments are contained in the paper*) slightly emphasizes the "many excellent arguments" by putting it first in the sentence and making it the grammatical subject.

The moral of these examples—one that underlies much of the advice in this chapter and the next—is that with a few exceptions (e.g., correct spelling and grammar), *the*

DOI: 10.4324/9781003512318-5

language and content of written work are not separable. Your word choice and phrasing determine the meaning conveyed by your prose. Most importantly for philosophical prose, subtle changes in wording can significantly affect what claims you are making. This can then alter the truth of the claims and the evidence needed to support them. So cultivating a curiosity about and sensitivity to language will help you communicate with others more effectively. Moreover, because of the relationship between language and thought, it will help you think more clearly.[1]

In this chapter, we discuss some aspects of *style*—different ways of using language to express roughly the same idea—that commonly affect the success of student philosophy papers. (In the next chapter, we discuss aspects of language that are more a matter of using language correctly or incorrectly.) Much of our advice in this chapter serves three essential features of good argumentative prose: *clarity*, *accuracy*, and *concision.*

Clarity is a matter of using language in such a way that your audience easily grasps what you are communicating. Your prose should be like a clean pane of glass, offering a transparent window into your thoughts. Reading perfectly clear prose can seem like you are directly encountering the author's ideas, but such clarity is an achievement, and acquiring the necessary skills requires both attention to detail and lots of practice.

Accuracy is a matter of communicating someone's ideas *correctly*. Notice that the explanation of a theory could be very clear while getting the theory wrong. That's wasted clarity. Accuracy is important when conveying not only other people's ideas but also your own. It is very easy to communicate something different from what you intended, so you must be vigilant that the language you are using accurately reflects what you are trying to say.

Concision is a matter of using the fewest words to communicate what you are trying to say. Being concise can help you to say more in the same number of words or pages and is thus an important skill to develop. Concision is obviously important when you are working within a page or word limit, but you should aim for concision in all your argumentative writing. If you ramble on, or repeat the same idea in several different ways, your reader may become bored or confused, or lose the thread. On the other hand, boiling things down too much may result in inaccuracy—you might not use enough words to communicate precisely what you need to.

Let us offer a couple of cautionary notes before we dive into our specific advice in this chapter and the next: First, don't let what we say in this chapter slow you down when drafting your philosophy paper. Your draft is a draft, not your final version; it doesn't matter if it's poorly written. If it helps you get on with your paper to exaggerate your claims, use rhetorical questions, and omit all punctuation (things we advise against in what follows), go for it! Just make sure you leave enough time to fix all those things as you revise your paper. Most of the advice we give in this chapter and the next can be applied when you revise your paper without substantially rethinking its structure or content.

Second, you are doubtless already familiar with some of the advice we give in this chapter. You can obviously skim or skip the advice you don't need. But make a list of the

1 These paragraphs skate over many fascinating issues in philosophy of language. For an introduction, see Wolf, "Philosophy of Language."

advice that's new to you or that you know you don't always apply. Then keep that list by your side as you revise your paper.

5.1 Emotion and Emotional Expression

You should be aware of the effects that your emotions might have on your own thinking—and thus writing—as well as the effects that emotional expression in your writing might have on your audience. Generally speaking, Western thought has arguably overemphasized the tension between emotion and reason. Perhaps your anger at some injustice, rather than clouding your ability to think about it, will spur you to find new arguments for your moral views. Nonetheless, most of us have had the experience of being unable to think clearly about a topic because of how we feel about it. We can only do our best, when writing a philosophy paper, to try to ensure that this isn't happening to us.

It is easier, perhaps, to be aware of emotional *expression* in our writing. There is nothing in itself wrong with passionate philosophical writing, but you should be aware that an unbiased reader may become suspicious when you are so enthusiastic about your own ideas or so scornful of ideas you disagree with that you may *appear* to have oversimplified the topic or become closed-minded. This problem is like a conflict of interest. If a judge has something to gain from a particular court case (because, say, she is friends with the person on trial), we might expect her to recuse herself (i.e., step down) from the case to avoid the *appearance* of injustice—even if everyone involved agrees that she is capable of making an impartial decision. Similarly, even if you are confident that your reasoning is watertight or your opponent's reasoning shoddy, you will more effectively make your case by simply stating your reasoning and trusting your reader to see its cogency. Overly emotional writing can distract your reader from your case and thus reduce your paper's clarity.

5.2 Empty Rhetoric

Rhetoric is the use of language to persuade. *Empty* rhetoric is persuasive language in the absence of good reasoning. Are you convinced by the politician who obviously exaggerates the strengths of his favored view and the weaknesses of the one he disagrees with? No. Instead, you get the impression that persuasion is more important to him than accuracy and fairness. You might suspect that claims he presents as facts are misleading or even made up. Obviously, you don't want to make that kind of impression on your audience. If there's a flaw in an argument you are critiquing, don't gleefully take it as an opportunity to belittle the opposing view: *This reasoning is so patently absurd that it barely deserves to be called an argument.* Simply point out the flaw: *The second premise is false.*

An open-minded writer does not treat other views unfairly—let alone insult people—so you should avoid derogatory language. In a paper advocating a "pro-choice" position on abortion, don't refer to "anyone so foolish and insensitive to think that a woman has no right whatsoever over her own body." In a paper advocating a "pro-life" position, don't refer to "the degenerates who feel that their personal convenience is more important than a human life."

Your reader will be looking for good reasoning. Like overly emotional writing, empty rhetoric will only distract her from your case and raise questions in her mind about your character.

5.3 Overstatement

5.3.1 Claims

In informal conversation, overstatement is commonplace. Someone might say, for instance, that his favorite soccer player *didn't do a thing right on the field today*, when that claim is literally false because, despite an exceptional number of errors and misjudgments, she sometimes—even frequently—dribbled and passed the ball effectively. This is often no problem in everyday conversation. In the case just given, the speaker wanted to render a striking evaluation of the player's performance that would be understood by his actual audience. If you pointed out that what he said was technically false, you might reasonably be accused of pedantry. Conversational exaggeration of this sort is frequent and often harmless.

This habitual overstatement, however, creeps into both informal and formal discussions of politics and other weighty matters. A liberal may say that conservatives "give no thought to the poor in this country." A conservative may say that liberals "are completely irresponsible in dealing with the nation's finances." These broad generalizations, because of the words "no" and "completely," invite us to ignore—by ignoring themselves—the variety of people who belong to the huge, vague categories of "liberal" and "conservative." You can find examples of such indefensible overstatement in just about any piece of electoral-campaign rhetoric or opinion journalism on hot political and social topics. The habit of overstatement also infects our professional and social lives, from job applications to gossip, where it can do serious damage.

Because most of us have acquired the habit of overstatement to some extent, it is not surprising that it shows up in our writing. But in a philosophy paper, precision of expression and rational defense of one's claims are of the utmost importance. Overstatement is, by definition, inaccurate. It thus affects your arguments, whether it appears in the expression of your thesis, a premise, conclusion, inference, objection, ... indeed, *anywhere* in your paper.

So, whether you are wording the thesis itself or constructing a line of argument to support it, choose your words carefully. Don't write "Abortion is the same as murder" if you mean that *all abortions are murders*. Whatever your views on abortion, it is a distinct concept from that of murder since, after all, no one thinks that all murders are abortions. Don't write "Existentialists think that constructing theories is a waste of time" if you mean that *most existentialists believe that theorizing, as opposed to reflection that leads to action, has too long been the focus of philosophy*. A clear statement of this second claim requires more words than the first. The first claim sacrifices accuracy for brevity: It uses fewer words than the second but at the cost of failing to convey the precise idea the writer is trying to express. (See also §4.4.)

5.3.2 Plausibility, Assumptions, and Reasoning

Your conclusions should be supported by well-thought-out reasoning that would be compelling to open-minded readers who are neutral toward, or even skeptical about, the view you offer. "Compelling" here doesn't imply that every reader will be powerless to resist your reasoning. It means that no reasonable reader could simply dismiss it as obviously misguided; anyone making a comprehensive case against your view would have to address your reasoning.

To make a compelling case, you must be aware of how **plausible** your claims and reasoning are. "Plausible" means, roughly, *believable.* If someone told us that 70% of ice cream sold in the United States last year contained some form of chocolate, we would find it plausible. That doesn't mean *we would believe* the claim, but it seems like it *could* be true—it's believ*able.* If someone told us that 99% of ice cream sold in the United States last year was mint chocolate chip, we would find it implausible. We can't believe that that is true, given even our slight knowledge of the U.S. ice-cream market. That doesn't mean it's *not* true, but someone would have to provide us with some evidence. Clearly, plausibility is a matter of degree. The claim that 98% of ice cream sold in the United States last year was mint chocolate chip is pretty implausible, but it's not *as* implausible as the claim that 99% was.

Since you are trying to convince your reader of your view through your reasoning, it is easy to fall into the trap of *overstating* the plausibility of your claims. Suppose that a crucial premise in your argument is that *killing an innocent person is always morally wrong*. You might worry about baldly stating this claim. Is it really true? What about accidental and unforeseeable killings? What about the killing of soldiers during a war? It can be tempting to hurry past these worries by writing something like one of the following sentences:[2]

> Obviously, killing an innocent person is always morally wrong.
> Of course, killing an innocent person is always morally wrong.
> Only a fool would deny that killing an innocent person is always morally wrong.

Do not succumb to this temptation. Careful readers will not be taken in by such bluster; the same questions that have occurred to you (and possibly other questions) may well occur to them—and they are unlikely to appreciate being called fools. You thus have two options: Argue for this claim or state explicitly that it is an assumption you are making in order to proceed with your case.

You will have to make *some* **assumptions** in your paper; if you provided an argument for every claim, you would get stuck in an infinite regress. (Each premise would have to be the conclusion of a subsidiary argument. But then each premise of that subsidiary argument would have to be the conclusion of a further subsidiary argument, and so on.) If your assumptions are highly plausible (e.g., *there are differences between dogs and cats*), so much the better. But it is more difficult to draw worthwhile conclusions uncontroversially from obviously true claims. If the premises are obviously true and the reasoning uncontroversial, most people will likely have arrived at the conclusion before reading your paper. You may, then, have to make some controversial assumptions in your paper. That's fine, as long as you explicitly label them as assumptions. You could say:

> I assume throughout this paper that killing an innocent person is always morally wrong.

If the assumption is highly controversial or plays a significant role in your argument, you might acknowledge that in your closing paragraph:

> My case does rest on the controversial assumption that killing an innocent person is always morally wrong.

2 In our examples, we underline words to highlight them. The words would not be underlined in an actual paper.

A common rhetorical move is to suggest that you *could* defend your assumption if only you had the space:

> Though there is no space to argue for the claim here, I assume, throughout this paper, that killing an innocent person is always morally wrong.

To make this move in good conscience, however, you should be able to say *something* in defense of your assumption if asked about it. (Otherwise, this is an empty rhetorical move.)

Finally, if you're aware of a published argument you endorse for the assumption, you can cite it:

> Though there is no space to argue for the claim here, I endorse Peter Kim's argument that killing an innocent person is always morally wrong (46–9). I thus take that claim for granted throughout this paper.

Similar advice applies to the strength of your reasoning. Sometimes your reasoning will firmly establish the conclusions that you draw in your paper. At other times, you will have to settle for less. Be sure you don't claim that you have established a conclusion more firmly than you actually have. We say more about signaling such strength in the following section; we discuss different kinds of reasoning in Chapter 10.

5.4 Indicators and Signposts

In Section 2.2.2, we introduced and explained the importance of *signposts*—sentences at the beginning or end of a paragraph that help orient your reader within the overall structure of your paper. What we call **indicators** are smaller signposts that indicate the kind of claim you are making, such as a premise, conclusion, or objection.

The most common *premise indicators* are "since" and "because." But there are many other possibilities, such as "for the following reasons" or "is implied by." In the interest of concision, you should favor shorter premise indicators. Why say "due to the fact that" when you could simply say "because"?[3]

The most common *conclusion indicators* are "so," "thus," and "therefore." As with premise indicators, there are many alternatives, such as "consequently" and "hence," and you should prefer these shorter indicators over phrases such as "it follows that" or "this leads to." Note that "leads to" often indicates nonlogical connections, such as causation (e.g., *anger leads to hate*) or mere succession, for instance, when a banquet speaker says, "That leads me to my final point" (which bears no logical connection to what came before). Your reader may thus be unsure what you mean by this phrase. You should be explicit and as precise as possible about the relationship between the premises and conclusion of any argument you make. Use "therefore," "makes probable," or whatever is both specific and accurate. (We discuss the relative strength of different kinds of arguments in §§10.2 & 10.5.)

3 For other problems with this phrase, see Garner, *Garner's Modern English Usage*, s.v. "due to" and "due to the fact that."

Indicating an *objection* typically takes a few more words than indicating a premise or conclusion. (Indeed, objection indicators may be better classified as signposts.) For example, you might write:

> A critic may object to this line of reasoning on the following grounds.

Then you would explain the concern and respond to it. If the objection has actually been offered in print, you can indicate its source:

> Ivica Moreno has objected to this kind of argument by saying ....

You must include a citation in such cases. (See Chapter 7 for details.) Sometimes, you can think of an objection that a particular thinker might make, even though she has not (to your knowledge) actually made it. You can indicate this as follows:

> Anscombe would almost certainly object to this argument.

Because you are referring to the views of a particular person, this kind of claim should also include a citation of the material that leads you to think this person would make this objection. In other cases, you may attribute the objection not to a particular thinker but to someone with a particular kind of view. For instance:

> A libertarian would likely object that ....

Though you do not refer to a particular libertarian here, if something you have read has suggested this line of objection, you should cite it.

5.5 Vagueness

Vagueness is insufficient specificity. It gives your reader an experience like that of looking at something through frosted glass. You can see that something is there and its rough size, shape, and color, but you cannot tell exactly what it is. Just as glass can be more or less frosted, language can be more or less vague. Vagueness is also a matter of context. A pane of glass that would count as crystal clear if used for a window might be hopelessly flawed as material for a telescope lens. Similarly, whether a word, phrase, or sentence in your paper counts as vague, i.e., *insufficiently* specific, will depend on its function within your paper as a whole.

People sometimes choose frosted glass for windows in their bathrooms or front doors: They want light to come in, but they don't want everyone to be able to see (clearly) into their house. Similarly, sometimes vagueness in writing is desirable or unavoidable. One can almost always ask for more specificity about a claim. Suppose someone read the first sentence of this paragraph and then accused us (the authors) of vagueness: Who are these people who choose frosted glass for their windows? What proportion of people choose frosted over clear glass for their bathroom windows? Are we considering *internal* windows or just those in the exterior walls? These are silly questions in this context. We're just giving an analogy to help explain vagueness. More specificity would distract from our purpose. But in another context—for instance, a meeting of the management of a glass manufacturer—these questions might be reasonable, even vital.

Vagueness becomes a problem in your philosophy paper, then, when you use language that is *less specific than it needs to be* to achieve your purpose. If, for instance, you criticize an argument by saying *only* that "it doesn't establish its conclusion," your reader may reasonably complain that this is vague. You need to be more specific. Is the problem that one of the argument's premises is false? If so, which one? Or is the problem that even though the premises are true, they do not establish the conclusion?

For another example, consider this sentence from a paper on the philosophy of race:

> Haslanger believes that race goes beyond biological features and is more a matter of social or cultural factors.

Even if Haslanger's views are not the focus of this paper, this sentence is unhelpfully vague. When the author says that (according to Haslanger) race "goes beyond" biological features, does he mean that it *includes* but is *not exclusively* a matter of biological features? Or does he mean that biological features play no role in race (on this view)? It also looks like the author is distinguishing social from cultural factors. But what is this distinction? Aren't cultural factors a kind of social factor? And does the author mean that race can be *either* social *or* cultural (according to Haslanger), or is the idea that Haslanger is herself unclear on what kinds of factors are relevant? Of course, if Haslanger's views play a central role in the paper, these questions are all the more pressing and the vagueness all the more problematic.

5.6 Definition and Equivocation

When an important word or phrase in your paper can be used to mean different things, you should define it to clarify how *you* are using it. For example, in a paper in which you discuss various traditional Western arguments for the existence of God, you should define "God." Some of those arguments establish (at most) the existence of a powerful creative entity rather than, say, a being with the attributes of omniscience and omnipotence. So the definition of "God" will affect whether these arguments succeed. Moreover, in the absence of a definition, "God" might mean quite different things to different readers.

Similarly, by "communism," do you mean the political systems that were formerly in place in Eastern Europe, the Soviet Union, and China? Or do you mean a theoretical utopia of shared resources that has never actually been realized on a large scale? By "self-interest," do you mean egotistical preoccupation with oneself or the prudent advancement of one's own benefit? Terms as commonplace as "human nature," "idea," "free will," "rights," "essence," "responsibility," "art," "consequences," "substance," and "belief" are regularly used differently in philosophy from how they are used in everyday discourse. They are also used differently by different philosophers. So you must explain what you mean by such terms if they play a role in your argument.

The same goes for any technical terms you use. If your audience is someone with no experience in philosophy, you cannot use a term such as "*a priori*" without explaining what it means. Even if you are writing for a philosophically sophisticated reader, such terms are used differently by different philosophers, so you may well need to define them to avoid vagueness or ambiguity, especially if they play a crucial role in your argument.

We do *not* recommend that you define such terms by quoting a dictionary. As we've said, these terms require definition because their philosophical use often differs from their ordinary use. You should be guided by how the term is used in the course materials related to your paper. If in doubt, consult your instructor. (See also §6.3.)

After you have defined an expression, be consistent in your own use of it. (Compare §4.5.) Be wary of **equivocation,** which occurs when you use a term twice with different meanings each time but without signaling this shift in meaning. Equivocation is dangerous because it can create the impression that a conclusion follows from some premises when it really doesn't. In a paper on free will, "free" may be used in one paragraph to mean *without physical restraint*, in another paragraph to mean *able to do anything one wishes*, and in the conclusion or thesis statement to mean *able to choose differently in identical circumstances*. Since these are quite different concepts, establishing (for instance) that we are free in *one* of these senses does not, without further argument, establish that we are free in another of them. The solution to this problem is *not* to redefine the term "freedom" each time you want to use a different one of these concepts. That would make your reader's head spin. It will be much clearer for your reader if you use a *different term* for each concept. Ideally, you should use ordinary words that bear some relation to the concepts you're using them for. For instance, you could call these different senses of freedom "physical freedom," "absolute freedom," and "psychological freedom." In principle, you could call these different concepts "freedom_1," "freedom_2," and "freedom_3" or "freedom," "phreedom," and "shreedom," but these are going to be hard for your reader to keep straight. The creation of jargon is a bane of philosophy (and many other disciplines), but perhaps this example helps you understand the temptation.

5.7 Concision

One passage is more concise than another when it conveys the same content using fewer words. Concision is much easier to define than to achieve. The best we can do here is point to a few ways that writers tend to use more words than they need to. As you revise more and more of your own prose, you will develop a sense of where and how you can trim it.

5.7.1 Eliminate Filler

You may find that your draft contains whole sentences or even paragraphs that don't contribute anything to the defense of your thesis. Consider the following example:

> Many philosophers have discussed this question, offering various answers.

This is relevant only to the extent that you consider many philosophers' answers to this question. But presumably, you explain the question and the best answers to it elsewhere in the paper. So this sentence does not say anything that helps your audience understand your case for your thesis. The entire sentence can be deleted.

One place to be eagle-eyed for filler is your opening sentences—especially if these were the first sentences you wrote as you began to draft your paper. It's very common to write empty phrases to get yourself going. This is how openings such as "Since the dawn of time ..." have come to irritate teachers everywhere. Ask yourself: Does this sentence help my audience understand my case for my thesis? If not, delete it.

5.7.2 Define Technical Terms Once, Then Use Them

One reason for the appeal of technical terms in any discipline is that they let you use one word or phrase to communicate something that would otherwise require many words. As we said in Section 5.6, you must define any technical term the first time you use it. However, after that, you can trust your reader to remember what the term means. So use it, and save yourself some space. For example:

Verbose:	Some would argue that there can be freedom in a world entirely governed by causal laws of nature. The problem with the view that freedom is compatible with the world's being entirely governed by causal laws of nature, however, is that	(41 words)
Concise:	Compatibilism is the view that there can be freedom in a world entirely governed by causal laws of nature. The problem with compatibilism, however, is that	(26 words)

5.7.3 Eliminate Repetition

Strategic repetition (e.g., in your closing paragraph) can helpfully remind your reader of what you have said earlier. But repetition at close quarters is almost always a waste of words. For example:

Verbose:	We are now in a position to understand Dretske's epistemological externalism. Dretske's theory is as follows: "Externalism in epistemology requires that all mistakes in fact be avoided ..." (Dretske 106).	(27 words)
Concise:	We are now in a position to understand Dretske's epistemological theory: "Externalism ... requires that all mistakes in fact be avoided ..." (Dretske 106).	(20 words)

5.7.4 Be Wary of the Verb "To Be"

There is nothing wrong with the verb "to be" and its various forms ("am," "are," "being," etc.), but it does occur in many verbose constructions. So it can be helpful to keep an eye out for this verb when looking for opportunities to prune your prose. Here are some examples:

Verbose:	<u>I will be arguing</u> that the best solution is anti-realism.	(10 words)
Concise:	<u>I argue</u> that the best solution is anti-realism.	(8 words)
Verbose:	This counterexample <u>is indicative of</u> a problem with the argument.	(10 words)
Concise:	This counterexample <u>indicates</u> a problem with the argument.	(8 words)

Concise:	This counterexample shows a problem with the argument.	(8 words—one of which is simpler than in the preceding sentence)
Verbose:	There is the possibility that a person could live her life without ever doing something morally wrong.	(17 words, including unnecessary repetition)
Concise:	A person could live her life without ever doing something morally wrong.	(12 words)

(For more examples, see Garner, *Garner's Modern English Usage*, s.v. "Be-Verbs: B. Circumlocution with *Be*-Verbs.")

5.8 Three Cautions

In this final section, we mention three stylistic problems that often mar philosophical writing. Keep an eye out for these as you revise your paper.

5.8.1 Big Words and Long Sentences

Sometimes a long, complex, or unusual word is just what you need in order to communicate an idea concisely. This is the point of technical terms, but many ordinary words (i.e., those not specific to an academic discipline) are also helpful in this way. (See our next heading for an example.) Less often, a long or complicated sentence may be helpful for conveying a particular idea. However, if someone could express the same idea with a shorter, simpler word or sentence, why wouldn't he? As we mentioned in Section 3.2, the answer to that question is sometimes that the writer is not confident that he understands the topic and thus (consciously or unconsciously) resorts to obscure vocabulary and grammar. Another answer is that the writer thinks, on the basis of the texts he's read or classes he's attended, that this is just how philosophy is done. We can assure you, however, that this is not how *good* philosophy is done. If your instructor has assigned you a text with lots of obscure terms, it will be because she believes that the text is worth grappling with *despite*—not because of—its difficult prose. So, if you can replace a long or difficult word in your draft with a shorter or simpler one, you should do it. If you can replace a long or complicated sentence with a shorter or simpler one—possibly two shorter and simpler ones—you should do it.

5.8.2 Anthropomorphism

Anthropomorphism occurs when you write about something that is not a person as if it were. This can be a powerful rhetorical technique when used well, but unintended anthropomorphism can result in awkward sentences that distract your reader. In philosophy papers, unintended anthropomorphism occurs when your writing implies that, for instance, a theory argues something. Claims, theories, arguments, and so on are *things*—not people—so they don't believe, claim, or argue anything. *People* believe, claim, and argue things. It's often easy to revise a problematic sentence so that the inanimate thing (e.g., a theory) isn't impossibly performing some action or so that an animate thing (e.g., a theorist) is performing the action. For instance:

Awkward: Compatibilism believes [claims, argues] that determinism is true.
Fine: Compatibilists believe [claim, argue] that determinism is true.
Fine: According to compatibilism, determinism is true.

It is not always clear whether a construction is anthropomorphic, and even thoughtful readers differ in their tolerance for anthropomorphism. So, as with other stylistic choices, you will sometimes have to use your judgment to decide whether a particular anthropomorphism is better than any revision that eliminates it.

5.8.3 Rhetorical Questions

A **rhetorical question** is a sentence in the *form* of a question that doesn't really *function* as a question since the person posing the question does not intend his audience to answer it. A rhetorical question is often used to make an assertion. The idea is that the answer to the question is so obvious that every reader will supply it. One example is the question, "Is the pope Catholic?" The speaker assumes that everyone knows the answer is "yes," so the apparent question is really a way of saying "yes." Such clichés are too informal for scholarly prose, but it can be tempting to use a rhetorical question when you feel that some claim is obviously true or that you've made a strong case for it. For instance, in a paper on epistemology, you might draft the following sentence:

> How could someone know something without being aware that one knows it?

If this is followed by an explanation of how someone *could* know something without being aware of it, there is no problem with the sentence. Because you're answering it, the question is not rhetorical. But if the idea is that the answer to the question is obvious (in this case, presumably: *one couldn't*), then it is an unhelpful rhetorical question. The problem is that some philosophers believe that a person *can* know something without knowing she knows it. If you want to claim that such philosophers are wrong about this, state it explicitly. Because it's a controversial claim, you will, of course, have to either argue for it or state explicitly that you are assuming its truth in order to make some further point.

In short, you should avoid using a rhetorical question to assert a controversial claim since some readers will answer the question differently from how you intend them to.

6 Language

Usage Matters

Consider the following sentence, which one of us encountered in a travel guide while drafting this chapter:

> Though the native Kulin Nation Aborigines bitterly resisted the burgeoning settlement evolved into the hub of a thriving pastoral community.

If two-thirds of the way through the sentence, you had to go back and reread it, you're not alone. It's natural, when first reading the sentence, to think that *the burgeoning settlement* is what the Kulin people resisted. But, reading on, you realize that can't be the case because if it were, the rest of the sentence wouldn't make grammatical sense. What the writer is trying to say is that the settlement evolved despite the Kulin people's resistance. The original sentence is an example of what Bryan Garner calls a "miscue": Because the noun phrase "the burgeoning settlement" directly follows the verb phrase "bitterly resisted," the sentence leads you to expect one grammatical structure, when in fact it has another (*GMEU*, "Miscues").[1] (We review basic grammatical vocabulary such as "noun phrase" and "direct object" in §6.4.)

Notice that the problem with this sentence is not that it's ambiguous—it's clear on rereading the sentence what its meaning must be. The problem is simply that the way the sentence is structured slows readers down by distracting them from the content—*what* is being communicated—drawing their attention to the *way in which* it is being communicated. Most of the advice we give in this chapter is aimed at avoiding this kind of distraction. Some of our advice may seem mysterious to you—our examples of incorrect usage may strike you as perfectly acceptable. Like it or not, however, the imagined reader for whom you are writing your philosophy paper, despite knowing nothing about philosophy, is thoroughly familiar with the conventions of formal writing and will be distracted by any departures you make from those conventions.

Solutions to such problems can often be surprisingly simple. For instance, a single comma would prevent the miscue in our opening example:

> Though the native Kulin Nation Aborigines bitterly resisted, the burgeoning settlement evolved into the hub of a thriving pastoral community.

1 Throughout this chapter, we use the abbreviation *GMEU* for *Garner's Modern English Usage*, by Bryan Garner, typically followed by the name of the relevant entry. For more on this book, see Section 6.3.

DOI: 10.4324/9781003512318-6

But you shouldn't always choose the solution to a usage problem that requires the fewest changes. Rewriting a sentence from scratch often leads to a clearer expression of the idea. Consider the following possibility, for instance:

> Despite the bitter resistance of the native Kulin Nation Aborigines, the burgeoning settlement evolved into the hub of a thriving pastoral community.

6.1 Usage Rules

In the previous chapter, we discussed *style*—differences between equally correct ways of expressing something. In this chapter, we discuss *usage*—differences between correct and incorrect ways to use language. The very idea that there are correct and incorrect ways to use language is controversial. We will consider that controversy in the following section. For now, however, let's say something about the sense of "correct" in play here. We presume you have sometimes had the experience, while writing, of pausing to wonder whether a word you've used really means what you are trying to express or whether a sentence you've written is grammatically correct. However you choose to respond to such experiences, they demonstrate your awareness that some aspects of language are beyond your immediate control: Words mean certain things independently of what you want or intend them to mean. A sentence that seems perfectly fine to you may violate a rule of grammar of which you're unaware or which you don't know how to apply in this case.

These rules, about what words mean and how they are properly combined into sentences, are not laws of nature or moral principles; they are *conventions*. That is, they are almost all *contingent* (i.e., the rules could have been different) and *arbitrary* (i.e., there's no reason a rule should require what it does rather than something else). These two features of usage rules can be seen in both the great variety of languages across the globe and also the ways in which a single language changes across time. (They also help explain why the rules are so hard to learn.) Consider, for example, that any competent English speaker would surely raise an eyebrow at the following sentence: *Aiko had Sam the bottle given*. But the same grammatical structure is standard in German: *Aiko hatte Sam die Flasche gegeben*. Presumably, neither the English nor the German way of constructing sentences is inherently better; they're just different.

For an example of change within a single language, consider that several hundred years ago the English word "naughty" meant something much stronger than it does today—something more like *evil*. Back then, it might have been appropriate to call a serial killer *naughty*, but today that would be decidedly odd. There's nothing essential to the collection of letters "naughty" that makes it better for expressing a weaker rather than a stronger concept, though. So why not use "naughty" in the older, stronger sense? For that matter, why use the standard English way of constructing your sentences rather than combining English words with German grammar? We hope the answer to these questions is obvious: Your writing will be more easily understood if you use standard English. The fact that a rule is conventional—i.e., contingent and arbitrary—does not mean that it has no force. Consider traffic laws (e.g., which side of the road you must drive on) or the rules of your favorite sport.

Where do the rules of language use come from, and how do they change? The basic answer is that the rules and their changes come from how people use the language.

Linguists could tell detailed stories about these changes, but we presume that the differences between English and German grammar, for instance, are largely the result of random forces in the early development of the two languages. As for the changing meaning of "naughty," presumably as more people used the word hyperbolically (i.e., in a kind of overstatement) to describe things that were less than evil (such as misbehaving children), the word came to have the milder sense as its primary, literal meaning. In short, language is a little like the law in a democratic state. It comprises rules that you are governed by, and while you have some say in what those rules are (by your vote in the legal case and your language use in the linguistic case), your *individual* influence over the rules is slight. Linguistic change is a matter of *collective* trends or decisions.

Your motivation to think carefully about usage is thus two-sided. On the one hand, you need to be aware of how your audience will understand what you write. On the other hand, how you use language will contribute (albeit slightly) to the language that future readers and writers will inherit. Being careless about usage is thus analogous to being careless about politics (e.g., voting in ignorance of the candidates' platforms) or, to change the analogy, to littering. One less vote or one more piece of litter rarely makes a significant difference to the political or environmental landscape. Yet it doesn't follow from this that you shouldn't care about whether you vote or litter. Not only do individual actions in these cases have significant collective effects, but we might also hope to foster a culture in which people care about politics and the environment. Like politics and the environment, language affects us all, and we are responsible for what we do with it.

How, then, should you do your duty when it comes to language use? At the bare minimum, you should always write with both a dictionary and a usage guide by your side so that you can continue to learn about how the language is currently used. (We say more about these resources in §6.3.) But you should also remember that the language is constantly changing. You may be aware of a meaning that a word has acquired since the dictionary or usage guide you are consulting was written—though you should also bear in mind the possibility that you are mistaken! Moreover, the rules of language can be broken for communicative effect. We nonetheless recommend conservatism as your basic approach to usage. If you are tempted to break a rule given in this chapter (or in another authoritative source), ask yourself whether you could say the same thing as effectively (perhaps in a quite different way) without breaking the rule. If the answer is "yes," we recommend taking this alternative course.

6.2 The Politics of Usage

We've mentioned differences between languages and within one language over time. But what about differences between language use in a single language at a single time? Not all native English speakers in the United States, for example, grow up speaking the same kind of English. On the contrary, there's a great variety of English-language communities in the United States. So how did the particular version of English that is our focus in this chapter become standard for formal writing in the United States?

The answer to this question is doubtless extremely complicated, and we are not qualified to give it in any detail. But it is undeniable that a large part of the answer will involve histories of injustice. Consider just a couple of obvious examples: The standard language of formal writing in the contemporary United States is not an indigenous Native American language because those languages, along with the rest of the culture of the indigenous peoples of North America—not to mention the people themselves—were brutally oppressed over centuries of colonization. The standard language of formal writing in the contemporary United States is also not an African language because the earliest African people to arrive in the United States were taken there by force and deliberately separated from other members of their cultures, including their own families. One result was that they usually had to learn English to communicate with one another. The version of English that has become standard for formal writing in the United States is the English that those with political and socioeconomic power were familiar with; it is the English (very roughly speaking) of upper-middle-class white people.

One might respond to this fact by lamenting the history of the situation we find ourselves in but acknowledging that, after all, if we want to be able to communicate with the widest possible audience, a single shared language is extremely useful, and formal U.S. English is the one we find ourselves with. But there are at least four plausible arguments that things are not so simple.

First, formal U.S. English is *not* the only formal variety of English. Most notably, "standard British English" is widely used for scholarly prose in English-speaking countries other than the United States, and speakers of U.S. English have little difficulty understanding such prose.

Second, consider the argument that the supposedly gender-neutral use of male pronouns (e.g., "he") to refer to anyone whose gender is unknown reinforces the idea that masculinity is normal and other genders are departures from the norm. If the argument is plausible then, similarly, maintaining the English of a certain social position (say, upper-middle-class whiteness) as the standard language of formal communication presumably reinforces the idea that that social position is normal and other social positions are departures from the norm. This is (or should be) false and may well contribute to injustice. (We discuss gendered language in more detail in §6.5.)

Third, if formal U.S. English is the language of upper-middle-class white people, it seems likely that such people will find it easier to use that language than people in other social positions (e.g., working-class black people) and thus have an advantage over them where language use is evaluated—for instance, in college philosophy papers or job applications. This seems likely to unjustly reinforce social hierarchies.

Fourth, because of the close connection between language and thought, it is plausible that some thoughts are more easily expressed in one language than another. So, in restricting the language available to us, formal U.S. English might make the communication of some ideas more difficult.

Despite our sympathy with these arguments, we are going to encourage you to learn the rules of formal U.S. English and follow them in your philosophy papers. Three main considerations lead us to think that this is morally acceptable despite the plausibility of the arguments just considered.

First, practically speaking, you may have no choice but to write in formal U.S. English. Your instructor may require it, and even if this is ultimately unjust, you may not be in a position to convince your instructor of this nor to sacrifice your success in the course for this reason. As one theorist puts it, borrowing a line from the poet Adrienne Rich, sometimes "this is the oppressor's language yet I need it to talk to you" (qtd. in hooks 167).

Second, if it is true that formal English is, in some sense, the language of social and political power, it will be useful for those with less social and political power to learn it, even if one of their aims is to revolutionize the relationships between language and power. This argument is often countered by considerations usefully summarized by the slogan:

The master's tools will never dismantle the master's house (the title of an influential essay by Audrey Lorde). We cannot consider these arguments in detail here, but even if it is true that the master's tools *alone* will never dismantle the master's house, we are cautiously optimistic that the master's tools may be used to *contribute* to the dismantling, especially if they are used by the oppressed. (Indeed, we think that Lorde suggests this view in her essay.)

Third, for all we've said about the differences between language communities, there is a lot of overlap between different Englishes, and the differences between them are located primarily in *spoken* rather than *written* language. We believe that much of the advice we give here about how to use language (e.g., the difference between "i.e." and "e.g.") does not violate the conventions of other forms of English.

It's also worth remembering that which form of English you use in your paper is not an all-or-nothing affair. Using language from another form of English or introducing a term from another language—in a paper otherwise written in formal U.S. English—can be a very effective way of communicating your point. One example from scholarly prose is the introduction of the term "signifyin'" to name a kind of allusiveness characteristic of some Black art. And the nonstandard verb "ain't" has been strikingly used by thinkers as different as Sojourner Truth ("Ain't I a woman?") and Hilary Putnam ("'meanings' just ain't in the head!").[2]

The conventions of language use that we discuss in this chapter belong to what is usually called "standard American English." However, as we've already noted, this variety of English is standard at most for formal prose, so we use the term "formal" instead of "standard." Moreover, the use of "American" to refer to what's associated with just one of the many nations comprised by the Americas (namely, the United States) is potentially confusing and politically objectionable to some. We thus use "U.S." rather than "American" when we need to distinguish this variety of formal English from others.

We hope that much of this book will be useful to readers in places where other varieties of English are the standard language of formal prose. As already noted, "standard British English" is the language of formal prose in many predominantly English-speaking countries. Unfortunately, we do not have enough space to cover both U.S. and British usage. Where they differ, we give only the U.S. convention. A good usage guide (see below) should cover U.S. and British variants.

6.3 Resources

You should write, as you read, with a **dictionary** at hand so that you can look up any word whose meaning you are unsure of. The gold standard is the *Oxford English Dictionary* (www.oed.com), commonly referred to by scholars as "the OED." It contains not only definitions but also etymologies (word histories), examples of each word's use across the history of the English language, and much more. It is unfortunately not freely available, but you can probably access it through the website of your school or public library—it's worth the effort. Good dictionaries available free online include

2 In fact, Sojourner Truth herself seems not to have uttered the words "Ain't [or Ar'n't] I a woman?" in her famous 1851 speech, but the phrase has certainly been historically influential. For more information, including the full text of different versions of the speech, see Podell, *The Sojourner Truth Project*. The Putnam quotation is from "The Meaning of 'Meaning,'" p. 227.

Merriam-Webster (www.merriam-webster.com) and *Collins* (www.collinsdictionary.com). Wiktionary (en.wiktionary.org) is crowd-sourced, so we advise some caution, but it contains a lot of helpful information. Despite its authoritative domain name, Dictionary.com is, in our view, inferior to the other readily available dictionaries; we advise you to avoid it.

Two warnings: First, dictionaries tend toward comprehensiveness—that is, they aim to include all the ways in which a word is, or even has been, used. Occasionally, this means that an entry will include a definition that is incorrect according to formal U.S. English. (Good dictionaries should indicate this, but some do not.) Moreover, it will not always be obvious whether a particular meaning listed in a dictionary is the one your reader will assume you are using. A dictionary is an essential tool for a writer, but it is no substitute for reading widely and paying attention to how language is used by good writers.

Second, ordinary dictionaries are not good resources for definitions of technical philosophical terms. You should be guided primarily by the course materials related to your paper, but if you want to consult a reference work, turn to a philosophical source, such as the *Shorter Routledge Encyclopedia of Philosophy*, the *Cambridge Dictionary of Philosophy*, or the *Oxford Companion to Philosophy.* Your library may have online access to one of these.

A **thesaurus** groups words with similar meanings so that you can look up near-synonyms (words with close to the same meaning). It is thus sometimes helpful when a particular word is on the tip of your tongue, but you can't quite find it. You should *not* use a thesaurus to find new words to use in your paper. There are very few complete synonyms in the English language. Some of what is signified or connoted by one word will fail to carry over to a listed near-synonym. So fishing in a thesaurus for new vocabulary will likely result in saying something you do not mean. If you are tempted to use a word you've found in a thesaurus (or anywhere else), be sure to look it up in a good dictionary first. Moreover, we have emphasized the importance of *consistency* in vocabulary. (See §4.5.) Despite what writing instructors in the past or in other disciplines may have told you, in a philosophy paper, you should *not* vary your vocabulary to hold your reader's interest.

A **usage guide** (or usage dictionary) provides advice about aspects of using language that people are often unsure, confused, or mistaken about. In our view, it is the most underrated tool for the student writer. If you care about writing well, you should acquire a good usage guide. We highly recommend *Garner's Modern English Usage*. It is comprehensive and reliable, and its preface includes thoughtful discussion of both the value of usage guides generally and Garner's empirically informed methodology.[3] Guides such as Garner's are arranged like a dictionary. So, for instance, if you want to check you're using the abbreviation "e.g." correctly, you just look it up under "E"; if you remember that you need to be careful about the word "unique," but you can't remember why, look it up under "U." That said, there is a lot of useful information in the book that is not so easy to find. The cross-references within entries are helpful, but here is a list of entries

3 The most recent edition of *Garner's Modern English Usage* is the fifth, published in 2022. The first edition was titled *A Dictionary of Modern American Usage*, and the second and third *Garner's Modern American Usage*, but the changes in title do not signify a substantial change in subject matter or methodology, just a gradual shift toward including more information about non-U.S. Englishes, particularly British English. Secondhand copies of earlier editions are cheaply available online.

that we recommend you read at some point since they cover topics (beyond those we cover below) that frequently cause problems in philosophical prose.

because	Punctuation
Concord	Race-Related Terms
Danglers	Remote Relatives
due to	so
Pointing Words	whether
Preventive Grammar	

In our discussion of many usage points below, we are indebted to Garner's sage advice.

Many colleges have a **writing center** where you can get help with various aspects of writing a paper. It must be said, however, that the quality of advice offered at these centers can vary widely from campus to campus and even advisor to advisor. You should keep your college's writing center in mind as one possible resource, but you should not take every piece of advice you receive uncritically. One thing to keep in mind is whether the person giving you advice has expertise in *philosophical* writing in particular. Another is that your instructor's requirements should trump anything others say. Some campus writing centers have open-access websites with lots of helpful information about writing papers, including usage. Two resources we recommend are the "Tips and Tools" page of the writing center at the University of North Carolina, Chapel Hill (https://writingcenter.unc.edu/tips-and-tools/) and Purdue University's "Online Writing Lab" (https://owl.purdue.edu/owl/).

6.4 Grammar

For much of what follows in this chapter—and for improving your writing more generally—it helps to know at least the basics of grammar. We cannot provide you with the kind of comprehensive review of grammar that you can find in a standard guide.[4] However, we can remind you of a few points that often lead to problems in college philosophy papers.

6.4.1 Grammatical Categories and Functions

One set of grammatical terms groups words into the "parts of speech"—that is, different categories or kinds of words. You should know that a **noun** is a word naming a *thing*, whether physical (e.g., "table") or mental ("joy"), concrete ("brick") or abstract ("justice"). A **verb** names what something *does* or something that *happens*. This includes actions ("run," "think," "argue"), processes ("grow," "evaporate"), and states ("be," "remain"). An **adjective** "modifies" a noun, describing it in some way ("red," "loud," "valid," "absurd"). Despite its name, an **adverb** modifies not just verbs but also adjectives and occasionally other adverbs ("slowly," "barely," "well," "more"). A **preposition**

4 We recommend parts B ("Basic Grammar") and G ("Grammatical Sentences") of Hacker and Sommers, *A Writer's Reference*; and parts I ("Parts of Speech") and II ("Syntax") of Garner, *The Chicago Guide to Grammar, Usage, and Punctuation*.

precedes a noun phrase, indicating some relationship between it and something else ("to," "for," "through," "under").

Most **pronouns** are generic terms that stand for (and thus save you from repeating) a previously used noun (e.g., "she," "which," "that," "whom"). **Personal pronouns** are those that stand for people (e.g., "she") rather than things ("it"). They can be singular ("me") or plural ("us") and are categorized by "person": First-person pronouns refer to the speaker ("I" and "we"), second-person pronouns to the audience ("you"), and third-person pronouns to others ("he," "she," "they").

A different set of terms name the grammatical *functions* of words and phrases within a sentence. The **subject** of a sentence is what "performs the action" of the verb.

The sun rose.[5]

The **predicate** is everything else in a sentence. It provides information about the subject. It must contain a verb.

The sun rose early, warming all the philosophers gathered in the sheep pen.

The **object** of a sentence is what the verb "acts upon." (A sentence does not have to have an object, as the previous two examples demonstrate.) A **direct object** names what the verb acts directly upon.

I raised two objections.

An **indirect object** names what the verb is done "for" or "to." An indirect object is thus often preceded by a preposition; where it is not, supplying a preposition can help you identify the indirect object, even if the result is unacceptable in formal English.

I raised two objections to Johnson's argument.
I gave [to] Jorge a book.

A **dependent** (or **subordinate**) **clause** is a group of words including a subject and predicate, but that falls short of being a complete sentence; that is, it cannot stand alone. Consider the following sentence:

Johnson dismissed my objection, which was admittedly weak.

The underlined words are a clause that modifies "my objection." The subject of the clause is "which" (a pronoun standing for "objection"); the rest of the clause is its predicate. But the clause couldn't be a sentence by itself since "which" can't function as the subject of a complete sentence.

A **phrase** is a group of words that form a unit but not a complete clause, let alone a sentence. Consider the following sentence:

The terms of the agreement were difficult to understand.

5 As in Chapter 5, we underline words to highlight them. The words would not be underlined in an actual paper.

The words "of the agreement" are a phrase that modifies the noun "terms," but it is not a clause because it has no subject or predicate. Because this example begins with a preposition ("of"), it is called a **prepositional phrase**.

6.4.2 Sentences

In formal writing, you should always use **complete sentences**, each containing a subject and main verb.

Wrong: Descartes resolved to doubt everything that was doubtable. Which initially led him to an extreme skepticism.
Right: Descartes resolved to doubt everything that was doubtable, which initially led him to an extreme skepticism.
Right: Descartes resolved to doubt everything that was doubtable. This initially led him to an extreme skepticism.

The dependent clause that was incorrectly set off as a separate sentence in the first example is joined with the main clause in the second example and becomes an independent sentence in the third.

Sometimes two sentences that should be separate are joined into one cumbersome and faulty sentence, as in the following examples.

Wrong: Descartes resolved to doubt everything that was doubtable this initially led him to an extreme skepticism.
Wrong: Descartes resolved to doubt everything that was doubtable, this initially led him to an extreme skepticism.

In the first example, nothing separates the two sentences. (This error is often called a "run-on sentence.") In the second example, a comma separates the two sentences. (This error is often called a "comma splice.") You can correct these errors by joining the two sentences with a "coordinating conjunction" ("and," "but," "nor," etc.). This requires inserting a comma before the conjunction:

Acceptable: Descartes resolved to doubt everything that was doubtable, and this initially led him to an extreme skepticism.

The resulting sentence, while grammatically correct, can still be cumbersome (as in this example). It's often best simply to separate the two sentences with a period:

Better: Descartes resolved to doubt everything that was doubtable. This initially led him to an extreme skepticism.

Alternatively, you can meld the two ideas into a single—if longer and more complicated—sentence:

Also better: Descartes's resolve to doubt everything that was doubtable initially led him to an extreme skepticism.

The subject and main verb of a sentence must **agree in number**; that is, they must both be singular or both plural. This usually poses no problem for college students. For instance, you are unlikely to (intentionally!) write a sentence like the following:

Wrong: John write well.

One tricky case, however, is a sentence with two subjects, one of which is singular while the other is plural, when the subjects are joined by "or" or "nor." Should you use a singular or plural verb form? Generally, the verb should agree with the subject nearer the verb.

Wrong: Either the Greek philosopher Pythagoras or the later Pythagoreans was responsible for the now famous Pythagorean theorem.
Right: Either the Greek philosopher Pythagoras or the later Pythagoreans were responsible for the now famous Pythagorean theorem.
Wrong: Either the later Pythagoreans or the Greek philosopher Pythagoras, their founder, were responsible for the now famous Pythagorean theory.
Right: Either the later Pythagoreans or the Greek philosopher Pythagoras, their founder, was responsible for the now famous Pythagorean theory.

Confusion over number agreement can be caused by nouns or pronouns that modify the subject and occur between the subject and verb.

Wrong: The complexity of Nietzsche's interwoven themes frustrate some readers.
Right: The complexity of Nietzsche's interwoven themes frustrates some readers.

"Complexity" is the subject of the sentence and is singular, so the appropriate verb form is "frustrates." The noun nearer the verb ("themes") is plural, but it is not the subject of the sentence. It is the object of a prepositional phrase, "of Nietzsche's interwoven themes," which modifies the subject.

(For more on this topic, see *GMEU*, "Concord, §A. Subject–Verb Disagreement.")

Words, phrases, or sentences presented in series should be in **parallel form**. That is, multiple items at the same conceptual or functional level should be grammatically the same.

Wrong: Wittgenstein wrote *Tractatus Logico-Philosophicus*, was the author of *Philosophical Investigations*, writing also "A Lecture on Ethics."
Right: Wittgenstein wrote *Tractatus Logico-Philosophicus*, *Philosophical Investigations*, and "A Lecture on Ethics."

In the preceding example, the problem is solved by using one introductory verb and separating the items with commas. Sometimes different verbs must be used with various items in the series, but they should have the same grammatical form:

Wrong: The pre-Socratic philosophers of ancient Greece wondered at the complexity of the world, had looked for a principle of unity in all the diversity, and positing a principle of permanence in a sea of change.

Right: The pre-Socratic philosophers of ancient Greece wondered at the complexity of the world, looked for a principle of unity in all the diversity, and posited a principle of permanence in a sea of change.

Writing a list can easily lead to violations of parallelism. Consider these two versions of the same list:

Wrong: Philosophical activities are diverse. Philosophers may:
- a. write papers for publication in professional journals
- b. they teach college classes
- c. internships and residencies in prisons, schools, and even art museums.

Right: Philosophical activities are diverse. Philosophers may:
- a. write papers for publication in professional journals,
- b. teach college classes, and
- c. have internships and residencies in prisons, schools, and even art museums.

In the corrected version, parallel structure has been achieved by rewriting several of the items so that any one of them could follow the introductory "Philosophers may …." Note also the punctuation added at the end of each item, and the "and" added before the last item. This shows that the list (together with its introduction) is a complete sentence that the writer has formatted as a list for clarity. It could be formatted as a sentence instead:

Right: Philosophical activities are diverse. Philosophers may write papers for publication in professional journals; teach college classes; and have internships and residencies in prisons, schools, and even art museums.

In this case, semicolons rather than commas are used between items because one item in the list (the third) itself contains commas, so using commas to separate the parallel items would be confusing. (See also §6.8.3.) Finally, you might format the list like a sentence but retain labels for each item:

Right: Philosophical activities are diverse. Philosophers may (a) write papers for publication in professional journals; (b) teach college classes; and (c) have internships and residencies in prisons, schools, and even art museums.

Which of the three acceptable versions would you prefer to encounter in something you were reading?

(For more on this topic, see *GMEU*, "Parallelism.")

The **location** of a word or phrase within a sentence can make a big difference in what the sentence says or how easily it is understood. Notice in the following examples what happens when the word "only" is put in a different place in otherwise identical sentences. Each sentence is grammatically correct, yet each says something quite different.

> Sondra Wu claims that Socrates wrote only poetry.
> (That is, she claims that Socrates wrote nothing besides poetry.)

> Sondra Wu claims that only Socrates wrote poetry.
> (That is, she claims that no one else wrote poetry.)

> Sondra Wu claims only that Socrates wrote poetry.
> (That is, she claims nothing else.)

> Only Sondra Wu claims that Socrates wrote poetry.
> (That is, no one else claims this.)

Entire phrases can be misplaced. Consider this sentence:

> J. L. Austin examines the concept of responsibility in his essay "A Plea for Excuses," which is very important in moral philosophy.

What is "very important in moral philosophy," according to the writer of this sentence? On one natural reading, it is *Austin's essay* since the relative clause ("which ...") immediately follows the essay's title. But the writer probably meant the relative clause to be about *the concept of responsibility*. The writer could have avoided confusion by writing:

> J. L. Austin examines the concept of responsibility, which is very important in moral philosophy, in his essay "A Plea for Excuses."

Or alternatively:

> In his essay "A Plea for Excuses," J. L. Austin examines the concept of responsibility, which is very important in moral philosophy.

Generally speaking, if a word or phrase *modifies* or *is about* another word or phrase, the two should be placed as close together as possible.

(For more on this topic, see *GMEU*, "Miscues, §B. Misplaced Modifiers" and "Remote Relatives.")

6.4.3 Pronouns

Most pronouns must have an explicit **referent**, that is, a noun for which the pronoun stands.[6] (The exceptions are **indefinite pronouns**, such as *anyone*, *no one*, and *somebody*.) In the following example, "he" is the pronoun, and "Liu" the referent.

> Liu makes a compelling case, but he faces a serious objection.

6 Another word for a pronoun's referent is "antecedent," but we prefer to reserve the latter term for the logical concept explained in Section 10.3.1.

If a pronoun's referent does not appear in the same sentence, or in the immediately preceding sentence, you should repeat the referent itself rather than using a pronoun. Otherwise, your reader may have to search back through what she has already read to find the referent, which will, at the very least, distract her.

Sometimes a writer has a referent in mind but fails to make it explicit. For instance, someone who has been writing about rationalism may use the word "they" to refer to rationalists, although the word "rationalists" has not been used. This is yet another example where what is clear to the writer may not be clear to the reader. The passage must thus be rewritten.

A pronoun must **agree in number** with its referent, just as a verb must agree with its subject. If the referent is singular, the pronoun must be singular; if the referent is plural, the pronoun must be plural.

Wrong: Libertarianism is attractive, but they face serious objections.
Right: Libertarianism is attractive, but it faces serious objections.
Wrong: Libertarians argue powerfully, but it faces serious objections.
Right: Libertarians argue powerfully, but they face serious objections.
Right: Libertarians argue powerfully, but their theory faces serious objections.

It might be argued that the above sentences we've labeled "wrong" are examples of missing referents rather than disagreement in number. More important than their correct classification, however, is that they must be rewritten. (For more on this topic, see *GMEU*, "Concord, §B. Noun–Pronoun Disagreement.")

A pronoun's **case** is the form it takes to display its role in the sentence as a subject, object, or possessor. Subjects take the *nominative* case (e.g., "I," "we," "he," "she," "they," "who"). Objects of a verb or preposition take the *objective* case ("me," "us," "him," "her," "them," "whom"). The *possessive* case shows some kind of ownership ("my," "our," "his," "her," "their," "whose").

Wrong: Kierkegaard and me would agree that the ethical level of being is more advanced than the aesthetic.
Right: Kierkegaard and I would agree that the ethical level of being is more advanced than the aesthetic.

Kierkegaard and the writer are the **compound** (i.e., joint) subject of the verb "would agree" and thus of the sentence. So the pronoun should be in the nominative case (i.e., "I"). A helpful test is to consider a version of the sentence with only the pronoun as the subject. Would you say, "Me would agree that ...," or "I would agree that ..."?

Wrong: John Wisdom and her are the only philosophers to approach language in that way.
Right: John Wisdom and she are the only philosophers to approach language in that way.

John Wisdom and the woman (presumably named in the previous sentence) are the compound subject of this sentence. So the pronoun should be in the nominative case (i.e., "she"). Would you say, "Her is the only philosopher ...," or "She is the only philosopher ..."?

Wrong: The tutor sharply criticized Devon and I.
Right: The tutor sharply criticized Devon and me.

Devon and the writer are the compound object of the verb "criticized." So the pronoun should be in the objective case (i.e., "me"). Would you say, "The tutor criticized I," or "The tutor criticized me"?

Wrong: Strawson is a better writer than him.
Right: Strawson is a better writer than he.

This last example is tricky because you have to realize that the verb governing the pronoun has been omitted. Putting the verb back in, we can see that the sentence says, "Strawson is a better writer than he is." It would clearly be wrong to say, "Strawson is a better writer than him is."

You should be **consistent** in using the same pronoun for the same referent.

Wrong: When one watches a film, we imagine that the fictional events are really happening.
Right: When we watch a film, we imagine that the fictional events are really happening.
Wrong: When one watches a film, they imagine that the fictional events are really happening.
Right: When people watch a film, they imagine that the fictional events are really happening.
Right: When one watches a film, one imagines that the fictional events are really happening.

(For more on pronouns, see §6.5, §6.7 on "I, you," and *GMEU*, "Pronouns.")

6.5 Gendered Language

Some previously accepted uses of language should be avoided because of the pernicious ideas about gender they suggest and arguably reinforce. To refer to the human race as "man," for instance, suggests that men (in the narrower sense) are the primary or typical examples of humanity. When there is a gender-neutral alternative to such a term, you should use it. Replace the generic "man" or "mankind" with "humanity" or "humankind." Gendered terms for roles or occupations, such as "chairman" or "mailman," are increasingly uncommon. You should encourage this shift in the language by avoiding such terms in favor of their gender-neutral equivalents (e.g., "chair," "mail carrier").

One of the most difficult problems for writers aiming for both gender neutrality and undistracting prose arises from the historical lack of a gender-neutral third-person singular personal pronoun in formal English. For instance, it was traditionally considered grammatically incorrect to write a sentence such as the following:

A utilitarian must anticipate the actions of people they have never met.

The criticism was that the subject of the sentence ("a utilitarian") is grammatically singular, and so it cannot properly be referred to with a plural pronoun ("they"). The traditional solution was to use a masculine pronoun to refer to someone whose gender is unknown or indeterminate:

> <u>A utilitarian</u> must anticipate the actions of people <u>he</u> has never met.

The result, however, was the dominance of the masculine pronoun across formal English, which was problematic for the same reasons as the supposedly gender-neutral "man." (A related issue arises in connection with some topics in the philosophy of religion. When using a pronoun to refer to a divine being, consider the implications of your choice.)

Perhaps the biggest change in formal English since the previous edition of this book was published is the increased acceptance of "they" as a third-person singular pronoun (and, correlatively, "are" as a third-person, singular verb form). Proponents of this change point to a long history of the use of "they" to refer to an unknown individual. (For instance, you might walk past a car on which a large tree branch has fallen and say, referring to the car's owner: *They're not going to be happy about that!*) But even if the singular "they" has been unacceptable in formal English until very recently (or even still is), recall from the beginning of this chapter that languages (like governments) change not just because of random forces but also thanks to the deliberate actions—the choices—of people. If you believe that gendered pronouns are ethically or politically problematic, you should consider encouraging the use of the singular "they" in formal English by employing it in your own formal writing.

If, for some reason, you prefer to (or must) avoid the singular "they," you have other nonsexist options in formal English. One is alternating between masculine and feminine pronouns. If you are writing an essay comparing utilitarianism and deontology, you might consider using masculine pronouns to refer to a utilitarian and feminine pronouns to refer to a deontologist (or vice versa). If you employ this strategy, make sure you keep your "characters" distinct. For instance, don't simply alternate between masculine and feminine pronouns sentence by sentence. One drawback of this strategy is that it can be distracting or misleading. Your reader may wonder if you are implying that utilitarianism is somehow masculine and deontology feminine. Your reader might even be subconsciously affected by this gendered pattern.

Another option is to use "he or she." (We recommend this over the alternative "s/he" as more elegant.)

> <u>A utilitarian</u> must anticipate the actions of people <u>he or she</u> has never met.

The biggest drawback of this solution is that, over the course of a paper, it constantly highlights gender and thus distracts your reader.

Note that while the previous two solutions aim at gender *equality*, they are not gender-*neutral* in the sense of avoiding gender altogether. Indeed, for the reason just mentioned, they arguably reinforce the idea that there are only two genders and that which gender one belongs to is of great importance. Many gender theorists argue that this is itself problematic. Two further solutions to the problem of gendered pronouns achieve gender neutrality while conforming to the traditional rules of formal English. One is to pluralize the noun in question:

Utilitarians must anticipate the actions of people they have never met.

Another is to use the third-person, singular pronoun "one":

According to utilitarianism, one must anticipate the actions of people one has never met.

As you will discover when you write with these issues in mind, it is not always easy to employ one of these strategies in a given sentence, let alone throughout a paper. Moreover, it is impossible in *traditional* formal English to do away with gendered pronouns altogether since it is traditional to use gendered pronouns to refer to actual individuals whose work you are discussing. For example:

In much of her work, Haslanger treats gender and race in parallel.

Some philosophers of gender are keen to depart from this tradition by, for example, using "they" as an all-purpose third-person pronoun:

In much of their work, Haslanger treats gender and race in parallel.

As we write this book, this usage has not yet become part of formal English. But it is impossible to predict whether—and, if so, when—this usage will become standard in formal English.

When thinking about these issues, you might ponder an experience one of your authors had when preparing an essay for publication. He was discussing the work of a philosopher with a gender-neutral name. To conform with the rules of formal English (required by the journal in which he was publishing the essay), he had to find out the philosopher's gender. He thus spent a considerable amount of time doing what frankly felt like snooping on the internet to find clues to the philosopher's gender. The philosopher's gender, of course, had nothing to do with the arguments under discussion. Is this a sign that formal English has a gender problem?

(For more on the philosophical issues raised by gendered language, see §1 of Saul, Diaz-Leon, and Hesni, "Feminist Philosophy of Language.")

6.6 Commonly Confused Terms

In this section, we discuss terms that mean quite different things yet are often mistakenly used in place of one another in philosophical writing because of their similar spelling or sound.

causal *and* casual

"Causal" means *to do with causes*, and the *s* is pronounced as a *z*: KAW-zell. "Casual" means *informal*, and the *s* is soft (like the *s* in "pleasure"): KAH-zhu-ill.

conscience, conscious, *and* consciousness

Your *conscience* (a noun) is something like an internal moral guide. You are *conscious* (an adjective) if you are aware or having experiences. (In Freudian psychology, it also functions as a technical-term noun.) *Consciousness* (a noun) is usually the feature of being conscious or sometimes a thing that is conscious.

Right: Her conscience was bothering her since she had lied.
Right: She was conscious that she had lied.
Right: After the accident, she briefly lost consciousness.

disinterested *and* uninterested

The opposite of being interested in something is being uninterested in it. *Disinterestedness* is a much less common phenomenon. You are *disinterested* with respect to something if you have no practical stake in it. The sense of "interest" involved is the same as in the phrase "conflict of interest."

Wrong: I am disinterested in your excuses for his behavior.
Right: I am uninterested in your excuses for his behavior.
Wrong: A judge should be an uninterested observer of the case before her.
Right: A judge should be a disinterested observer of the case before her.

effect *and* affect

"Effect" is usually a noun, meaning something like *result* or *consequence*, but it is sometimes a verb, meaning *bring about*. "Affect" is usually a verb, meaning *influence* or *have an effect on*. But it is occasionally a noun, meaning something like *feeling* or *emotional character*; the adjectival form of this noun ("affective") is more common in philosophy than the noun itself. All the following examples are correct.

Common:	The drug had a strange effect on me.
Uncommon:	The revolt effected a change in government.
Common:	The drug affected me strangely.
Uncommon:	He was in a peculiar affective state.
Very uncommon:	The drug induced a peculiar affect in me, a kind of joyful sadness.

e.g. *and* i.e.

These abbreviations serve quite different purposes.

The abbreviation "e.g." introduces one or more *examples*. You might remember this by thinking of it as short for "egzample," but it is actually an abbreviation of the Latin phrase *exempli gratia*, meaning "for the sake of example."

The abbreviation "i.e." introduces an expression equivalent to the one it follows. That is, it's used to explain something you've just written in other words. It is an abbreviation of the Latin phrase *id est*, meaning "that is."

Though you should know what these expressions mean so that you can understand texts that contain them, you can easily avoid using them incorrectly in your own writing by simply not using them at all. Generally speaking, in formal prose, it is better to use the phrases "for example" or "for instance" instead of "e.g.," and "that is" or "in other words" instead of "i.e." If used at all, the abbreviations should be reserved for parenthetical material. Each instance should always include the periods and be followed by a comma (e.g., like this).

(See also the discussion of these abbreviations in §6.10.2.)

except *and* accept

Except is most commonly used as a preposition (though it can be used as a verb, meaning *make an exception of*). *Accept* is always a verb, meaning (roughly) *to allow*.

Right: All existentialists except Lagardo wrote novels.
(That is, Lagardo was the only one who didn't.)
Right: All existentialists accept Lagardo wrote novels.
(That is, they all agree that Lagardo wrote novels. Note that inserting a "that" after "accept" would prevent a miscue here. See §6.7 on "that, which, how.")

exists *and* true

Beginning philosophers are often confused or careless about the distinction between *existence* and *truth*. A *thing* exists or doesn't exist; a claim (or sentence, proposition, premise, etc.) is true or false.

Wrong: Despite the argument from evil, an omniscient, omnipotent, wholly benevolent being could be true.
Right: Despite the argument from evil, an omniscient, omnipotent, wholly benevolent being could exist.

Confusion may arise when a noun refers to a claim or theory. For instance, it's easy to forget that you've defined "determinism" as a certain *claim* (e.g., that every complete set of events can have only one complete set of effects) and start using the term as if it refers to a possible feature of the world. But your reader will not have forgotten.

Wrong: As I have demonstrated, however, determinism does not exist.
Right: As I have demonstrated, however, determinism is not true.

former *and* latter

"Former" and "latter" are used to refer to one or the other of two things that have been directly referred to in the immediately preceding sentence. "Former" refers to the first (the two *f*s can help you remember this); "latter" refers to the second (its similarity to "later" might help). If the two things are referred to any earlier than the immediately preceding sentence, you should not use "former" or "latter." If more than two things are in the relevant group, you can't use "former" or "latter" to refer to any of them. (The same goes for other binary phrases, such as "on the other hand" or "the other side of this coin.") Given the work these terms impose on your reader, you should use them sparingly, if at all.

Wrong: Hegel, Schlegel, and Schelling are rarely confused; the former is by far the most well-known.
Right: Hegel, Schlegel, and Schelling are rarely confused; the first is by far the most well-known.
Right: Hegel, Schlegel, and Schelling are rarely confused; Hegel is by far the most well-known.
Right: Hegel and Schlegel are rarely confused; the former is much better known.
Right: Hegel and Schlegel are rarely confused; Hegel is much better known.

problem of *and* problem with

A problem *with* something is necessarily negative, such as a problem with your lungs. When philosophers refer to the problem *of* something, it is negative in the sense that the problem needs solving, but the problem is not *with* the thing that raises the problem.

Wrong: The problem with freedom is how we can be free in a world governed by laws of nature.
Right: The problem of freedom is how we can be free in a world governed by laws of nature.
Wrong: The problem of freedom is that it's hard to make decisions.
Right: The problem with freedom is that it's hard to make decisions.

rebut *and* refute

When you *rebut* someone's argument, you *attempt* to show that it fails; you object to it. When you *refute* someone's argument, you *succeed* in showing that it fails. You thus probably do not want to claim that someone else has refuted your argument. In fact, you should generally be careful about attributing refutation to others and refrain from claiming that you've refuted someone else's argument unless you are sure that you have succeeded.

refer *and* reference

You should usually use "refer" as a verb and "reference" as a noun. For example:

Wrong: Gaunilo references Anselm's ontological argument.
Right: Gaunilo refers to Anselm's ontological argument.
Right: It would be impossible to follow up all the references in Nguyen's article.

There is a growing tendency to use "reference" as a verb meaning "refer to" or "cite." You should avoid this tendency on the grounds that shorter, simpler words are better and that we should discourage the proliferation of exact synonyms.

use ***(noun) and*** **usage**

Usage is the use of language. If you are talking about the use of anything else, you should *not* use the word "usage." If you *are* talking about the use of language *and* you use the word "usage," you should not include the word "language" (or "word," "punctuation," etc.) since it would be redundant.

Wrong: The usage of teleological arguments in ethics is uncommon.
Right: The use of teleological arguments in ethics is uncommon.
Wrong: This is another example of poor language usage.
Right: This is another example of poor usage.
Right: This is another example of the poor use of language.

use ***(verb) and*** **utilize**

To *use* something is to employ it to some end. To *utilize* something is to *make it useful or usable*. For instance:

> At home I always used a can-opener. On the desert island, I had to utilize a sharp rock.

There is a growing tendency to write "utilize" where "use" would do. (Indeed, it could be argued that "use" would do in the second sentence of the example above.) You should avoid this tendency on the grounds that shorter, simpler words are better and that we should discourage the proliferation of exact synonyms. At least nine times out of ten, it would be better to replace "utilize" with "use."

6.7 Miscellaneous Usage Points

In this section, we consider an assortment of usage issues that often cause problems in philosophical writing. We discuss them in alphabetical order by our (sometimes idiosyncratic) headings.

Absolute Adjectives

Most adjectives describe features that admit of degrees. One thing can be *colder* than another, for instance, or *very cold*. But some adjectives are "absolute" in the sense that they do *not* admit of degrees. For instance, to describe something as *complete* is to say that it has all its parts. Nothing can be *very* complete or *less complete* than something else. While absolute features do not admit of degrees, things can be *nearer to* or *further from* absolute states. For instance, a sentence lacking a period may be *almost* complete, and one person may be *closer to* moral perfection than another.

Some common absolute adjectives (e.g., "unique") cause problems in philosophical writing. But many technical and quasi-technical philosophical terms are also absolute, such as "possible," "impossible," "necessary," and "sufficient."

Wrong: <u>The most unique feature</u> of Korsgaard's view is her distinction between instrumental and extrinsic value.
Right: <u>A unique feature</u> of Korsgaard's view is her distinction between instrumental and extrinsic value.
Right: <u>An unusual feature</u> of Korsgaard's view is her distinction between instrumental and extrinsic value.

(The two last examples are both right as far as usage goes. Which one is right in terms of *content* depends on whether this distinction really is *unique* to Korsgaard's view or merely unusual.)

Wrong: It's very possible that a person may perform one bad action yet live a good life.
Right: It's possible that a person may perform one bad action yet live a good life.
Right: A person can perform one bad action yet live a good life.
Right: Performing one bad action has no implications for whether a person has a good life.

Again, which acceptable sentence is the right one for your paper depends on what you are trying to say. Misuse of an absolute adjective is sometimes a sign that you are trying to say something that would be better put in nonabsolute terms.

(For more on this topic, see *GMEU*, "Adjectives, §B. Noncomparable Adjectives.")

and/or

In casual settings, it's usually clear what "and/or" means: You can take one or the other of two options or both. Even here, though, "or" is usually a better choice since it typically includes the possibility of taking both options. For instance, if someone says, "You have to complete a paper and/or give a presentation to pass the course," he presumably means that you have to do *at least one* of those things (otherwise, he would have used "and"). But then he could have kept the sentence simpler by saying, "You have to complete a paper or give a presentation ...."

Anyway, the phrase is too informal for academic writing. In philosophical writing in particular, whether you are making a conjunctive ("and") or disjunctive ("or") claim makes a big difference, so you should think about precisely what claim you are making and use "and" or "or" as appropriate. In the rare case when you need to make explicit that there are two options and you can take one or the other *or both* (or one or the other *but not both*), you should say so explicitly.

Wrong: A student can earn a philosophy major and/or minor.
Right: A student can earn a philosophy major or minor (or both).
Right: A student can earn a philosophy major or minor—but not both.
Wrong: According to Ogba's theory, membership in a racial group requires having certain biological features and/or social experiences.
Right: According to Ogba's theory, membership in a racial group requires having certain biological features and social experiences.
Right: According to Ogba's theory, membership in a racial group requires having certain biological features or social experiences.
Right: According to Ogba's theory, membership in a racial group requires having certain biological features or social experiences (or both).

Note that the last two examples say the same thing; the very last one just makes the possibility of meeting both conditions explicit. Of course, which one of these last three examples is right in terms of *content* depends on what Ogba's theory actually is.

Finally, note that "and/or" can sometimes cause genuine confusion. For instance, on arriving in Canada in 2021, one of your authors encountered the following rule:

> If you are a traveller entering Canada via Quebec, you are required to take a COVID-19 test on Day 1 and/or Day 8 following arrival.

He had taken a test on day 1. Now, is he required to take a test on day 8? It depends on whether the "and/or" here means *and* or *or*. Whoever wrote this rule should have considered whether the requirement was disjunctive or conjunctive and used the appropriate word.

The Aspectual as

The word "as" is used in many different ways. What we call the *aspectual* "as" introduces a phrase that picks out one aspect (among many) of the thing it modifies. For instance, Miyo might say that *as your friend*, she forgives you for your actions, but *as a member of the Honor Council*, she must treat you like any other plagiarist. This construction is perfectly fine if you mean to draw your reader's attention to one specific aspect of the thing described (perhaps in contrast to another).

Right: As human beings, we are mortal; but as souls, we are immortal.

If you do not mean to focus on a specific aspect of what the phrase modifies, you should eliminate the aspectual "as":

Wrong: <u>As humans, we</u> typically consider ourselves morally responsible.
Right: <u>We</u> typically consider ourselves morally responsible.
Wrong: <u>As people, we</u> are subject to society's laws.
Right: <u>People</u> are subject to society's laws.

based on

Things are *based on* other things; they are not "based off" or (worse) "based off of" other things.

Wrong: Her theory is <u>based off</u> an aesthetic conception of music.
Worse: Her theory is <u>based off of</u> an aesthetic conception of music.
Right: Her theory is <u>based on</u> an aesthetic conception of music.

comprise

"Comprise" means something like *include* or *embrace*. So the whole *comprises* the parts, but not vice versa. However, it is commonly misused to mean something like *makes up* or *constitutes*, leading to confusion about the relationship between the items.

Wrong: The legislative, judicial, and executive branches <u>comprise</u> the government.
Right: The government <u>comprises</u> the legislative, judicial, and executive branches.
Right: The legislative, judicial, and executive branches <u>make up</u> the government.

One phrase to look out for is "comprised of," which doesn't make sense if you know what "comprise" means. Just as you would never say that *the whole is included of the parts*, or *the whole is embraced of the parts*, you should never say that *the whole is comprised of the parts*.

Wrong: The academic year is comprised of two regular semesters and a summer session.
Right: The academic year comprises two regular semesters and a summer session.
Right: The academic year is made up of two regular semesters and a summer session.

(See also *GMEU*, "comprise.")

counterargument, counterexample

A *counterargument* is an argument against (i.e., counter to) something. A *counterexample* is an example that shows a universal claim to be false. (See §4.4.) To divide either word into two words is a mistake and may miscue your reader into thinking that you are making a point about counters.

Wrong: This counter argument is invalid.
Right: This counterargument is invalid.

dilemma

A *dilemma* is a choice between two mutually exclusive—usually unappealing—options. For instance, whether to save your drowning grandfather or the six strangers tied to the train tracks may be a moral dilemma. (Both options are unappealing because they entail the death of innocent people.) The word is commonly misused to mean *problem* more broadly. The following sentence is acceptable *only* if the writer goes on to explain that there are two mutually exclusive, unappealing ways to answer the objection. Otherwise (as we assume for the sake of this example), it misuses the word "dilemma."

Wrong: How to answer this objection is a serious dilemma.
Right: How to answer this objection is a serious problem.
Right: It is difficult to answer this objection.

The two options presented by dilemma are traditionally called its "horns."

Right: If we reject indeterminism, we find ourselves on the other horn of the dilemma: Our actions are not free.

(See also *GMEU*, "dilemma.")

disagree

Do not use the phrase "disagree that"; it usually leads to ambiguity and confusion. Consider the following sentence:

Wrong: Williams disagrees that there are limits to our moral obligations.

Is the writer saying that (1) Williams disagrees *with the claim* that there are such limits, thus implying that there are no such limits, or that (2) Williams disagrees with something else, claiming rather that there *are* such limits? Such sentences should be rewritten. (Which of the following is correct depends on Williams's actual views.)

Right: Williams does not agree that there are limits to our moral obligations.
Right: Williams disagrees, claiming that there are limits to our moral obligations.

I, you

In philosophical prose, it is usually perfectly acceptable to use the first-person pronoun ("I") to indicate what you believe and what you are doing in your paper. In some other disciplines, this is considered bad usage, and you are taught to paraphrase yourself away by using the passive voice, attributing your actions to the paper itself, or using locutions such as "the present writer." But in philosophy, writers are up-front about their contributions.

Awkward: This paper argues that there is no such thing as freedom, at least as that word is commonly understood.
Awkward: In this paper, it is argued that there is no such thing as freedom, at least as that word is commonly understood.
Awkward: The present author argues that there is no such thing as freedom, at least as that word is commonly understood.
Right: I argue that there is no such thing as freedom, at least as that word is commonly understood.

You can also use the second-person pronoun, "you," but be aware that your reader will take this personally. Since you don't know what your reader thinks about the topics you discuss, it is advisable to use noncommittal language in attributing views to her.

Wrong: You can see that this argument is deeply flawed.
Right: You might already have seen that this argument is deeply flawed.

issue

An *issue* is (traditionally) a topic, but the word is increasingly used to mean something like *problem* (especially in the phrase "have issues with," which is too informal for academic prose). Since the traditional meaning is a useful one, and the new usage may sometimes cause confusion, we encourage you to preserve the traditional meaning.

Wrong: I see three issues with this argument.
Right: I see three problems with this argument.
Right: This argument raises three issues.

The last example is right, that is, assuming that the three things are issues or topics—not problems.

(See also *GMEU*, "issue.")

like

In everyday speech and prose, the word "like" is used in several different ways. It sometimes introduces an example:

> Wizards, like Harry, always carry a wand.
> (That is, Harry is one example.)

It sometimes introduces a contrastive comparison:

> Witches, like Harry, always carry a wand.
> (That is, witches are like Harry (a nonwitch) in this respect.)

And it sometimes introduces a *restrictive clause*—that is, a clause that restricts the range of reference of what the clause is attached to:

> Wizards like Harry always carry a wand.
> (That is, we're only talking about *wizards like Harry*; perhaps wizards *unlike* Harry *don't* carry wands.)

It's often clear from the context how "like" is being used. Sometimes the context won't be enough, however, and in philosophical writing it is better to be safe than sorry. So we recommend that you follow these guidelines:

1. Don't use "like" to introduce an example. There are plenty of other ways to do this:

   Wizards (for example, Harry) always carry a wand.
   Wizards, such as Harry, always carry a wand.
   Wizards always carry a wand; Harry is one example.

2. When using "like" to introduce a comparison, make sure that it's contrastive, i.e., that the thing being compared does not belong to the class of things with which it's being compared. (If you think that you're introducing a comparison but it is not contrastive, you are probably giving an example. You should thus follow guideline #1.) The "like" clause must be set off from the rest of the sentence with commas. For example:

   Haslanger, like cultural constructivists, denies that race is biological.

   This sentence implies that Haslanger is not a cultural constructivist but says that she agrees with cultural constructivists that race is not biological.

3. When using "like" to introduce a restrictive clause, *do not* set the clause off from the rest of the sentence with commas. You can think of the restrictive clause as an extension of the thing it restricts, so you want them to be as closely connected as possible. For example:

Right: Philosophers like Quine deny that there is a sharp distinction between the *a priori* and *a posteriori.*

It can help to imagine that the restrictive clause is connected to what it restricts: *Philosophers-like-Quine deny that there is a sharp distinction between the* a priori *and* a posteriori. (But you shouldn't include the hyphens in your writing.)

(Compare our advice about restrictive and nonrestrictive clauses under "that, which, how," below. For other pitfalls, see *GMEU*, "like.")

Names

If you use a philosopher's name in your paper, make sure you get it right. If you don't, your reader may infer that this carelessness extends to your consideration of the philosopher's ideas. The first time you refer to a particular philosopher, you should use the person's full name. In all other references, use just the last name. You should never use titles, such as "Dr." or "Professor," nor refer to the institution at which the person is employed (e.g., "the University of Pennsylvania"). This is appropriate in some kinds of writing, but in argumentative prose, it can give the impression that you're appealing to the authority of the person's qualifications, institutional affiliation, or social position rather than the strength of his arguments. (See our discussion of fallacious appeals to authority in §4.7.)

Wrong: This argument is defended by Dr. Haslanger, Professor of Philosophy at MIT. But Sally Haslanger does not consider the following objection.
Right: This argument is defended by Sally Haslanger. But Haslanger does not consider the following objection.

(On formatting names in citations, see §7.4.1.)

Notes

Footnotes (which appear at the bottom of a page) and endnotes (which appear at the end of the paper, before the list of works cited) serve a variety of functions. In some scholarly styles, citations appear in notes. Notes may also be used to acknowledge help. We discuss these uses in Chapter 7.

Commentary notes include material that is relevant to the paper but less important for making the case for your thesis than anything in the main text. (A note is similar to parenthetical material: The author wants to include it but also to indicate that it is less important than the surrounding material.) Our advice to beginning philosophical writers is to avoid using such notes if at all possible. One of the hardest tasks you face as a writer is deciding what to include in your paper and what to leave out. (See §4.1.) Notes can seem to offer a panacea: You can *sort of* include that material in your paper, but not really. To your reader, however, they may seem more like a weird limbo. (Is this material important for the author's argument or not?) You would do better to decide whether the material in question is important enough to include in your paper (given all the other constraints, such as your word limit). If it is, you should put it in the main text of the paper; if not, you should cut it.

Numbers

In general, use words (e.g., "three") instead of numerals (e.g., "3") to express numbers below 11; use numerals to express numbers above ten.

Wrong: I have 3 objections to the claim that there have been precisely four thousand, five hundred and sixty philosophers in the history of humanity.
Right: I have three objections to the claim that there have been precisely 4,560 philosophers in the history of humanity.

(For exceptions, and much more about using numerals and numbers, see *GMEU*, "Numerals.")

Passive Voice

Writing in the **passive voice** is a matter of using verbs in such a way that the grammatical subject of the sentence is the *recipient* of the verb's action rather than the *agent* of that action. It is contrasted with the more usual (and thus more easily understood) **active voice**. You can express the same idea actively or passively:

Active: Anna objected to Kazuo's argument.
Passive: Kazuo's argument was objected to by Anna.

There is nothing inherently wrong with the passive voice, but it has become a bugbear of writing instructors because some students use it far too frequently, mistakenly thinking that it gives their prose a scholarly air. Our advice is to use the passive voice sparingly and deliberately. When revising your paper, try rewriting in active voice any sentence you've drafted in passive voice. If it works just as well, go with the active version. (For more on this topic, see *GMEU*, "Passive Voice.")

Plurals

In formal English, a **plural** (the form of a noun referring to more than one of the things named) is normally formed by adding an *s* or *es*: *one apple, two apples; one near miss, two near misses*. But you are doubtless familiar with many exceptions, e.g., *one child, two children; one tooth, two teeth*. More confusing are words that have been borrowed from other languages and retain the original plural form. Many examples that crop up in philosophical prose (including all the examples below) are taken from Ancient Greek. These simply have to be learned, though you can quickly infer some rules of thumb from these examples.

Singular	*Plural*
analysis	analyses
crisis	crises
criterion	criteria

(*Continued*)

Singular	*Plural*
hypothesis	hypotheses
phenomenon	phenomena
schema	schemata
thesis	theses

"Criteria" and "phenomena" are plural forms commonly misused as singular.

Wrong: This action doesn't meet a single criteria.
Right: This action doesn't meet a single criterion.
Wrong: It is a very common phenomena.
Right: It is a very common phenomenon.

The other words in the list above have plural forms with which many people are unfamiliar.

"Media" is a particularly tricky example. It was originally a plural form of the Latin word "medium," one meaning of which in contemporary English is *a means of communication*. Thus "the media" refers to various (i.e., plural) means of mass communication (television, newspapers, etc.) or artistic materials (paint, marble, etc.). However, the mass-communication sense has come to be used also (but not exclusively) as a singular noun, so that you may write sentences such as: *The media tends to make this problem worse.*

Questions

A **direct question** is simply put to the reader (or reflexively to the writer). For example:

Right: What is the meaning of life?

Direct questions alone cause few problems; most writers know that a direct question is a complete sentence and thus must begin with a capital letter and end with a question mark. The problems begin when the question is somehow embedded in a larger sentence. If you are simply introducing a direct question, it must be set off from the introduction in some way.

Wrong: We must then ask what is the meaning of life?
Right: We must then ask, "What is the meaning of life?"
Right: We must then ask: What is the meaning of life?

The example with quotation marks is the traditional way of punctuating a direct question in formal U.S. English, though we think the example with a colon is acceptable and more elegant. (Some would insist on a lowercase "w" following the colon. In line with our discussion of colons in §6.8.3, we think an uppercase "W" is better since the direct question is a complete sentence.)

An **indirect question** is more deeply integrated into a larger sentence. The question is *referred to* rather than *asked*, so its grammar is different, and it does not take a question mark.

Right: Many philosophers have asked what the meaning of life is.
Wrong: Many philosophers have asked what the meaning of life is?
Wrong: Many philosophers have asked what is the meaning of life.

The second example here gets the grammar right for an indirect question but mistakenly adds a question mark. The third example omits the question mark, but its second half is grammatically a direct question. If this is the word order you want, it needs to be written like one of the examples of direct questions given above.

(See also our advice on rhetorical questions in §5.8.3 and *GMEU*, "Questions, Direct and Indirect.")

said *as a Pointing Word*

Do not use "said" as a "pointing word" to refer to something mentioned earlier. It has an air of pompous legalese and can usually be replaced with a more common pointing word (such as "this" or "that"), the definite article ("the"), or the original referent.

Wrong: One problem with <u>said theory</u> is that it is incoherent.
Right: One problem with <u>this theory</u> is that it is incoherent.
Right: One problem with <u>the theory</u> is that it is incoherent.
Right: One problem with <u>compatibilism</u> is that it is incoherent.

Technical Terms

We discussed the introduction of technical terms in your paper in Section 5.7.2. Some of these terms have been borrowed from ordinary English and put to special use in philosophy. You should take care not to use such words in their ordinary ways in a philosophy paper. Two words that commonly cause problems are "valid" and "sound." Because the logical meanings of these terms are so important in philosophy (see §10.2), you should reserve them for such uses in philosophical writing.

Wrong: These claims about animals are <u>valid</u>, but they do not hold up under scrutiny.
Right: These claims about animals are <u>plausible at first glance</u>, but they do not hold up under scrutiny.
Wrong: Spinoza's reasoning is <u>sound</u>, but because he begins with a false premise, it does not establish his conclusion.
Right: Spinoza's reasoning is <u>valid</u>, but because he begins with a false premise, it does not establish his conclusion.

The last example is right only if the reader really means to attribute the logical property of validity to Spinoza's reasoning. (See also our discussion of "beg the question" in §4.7.)

Tenses

When discussing philosophical arguments and theories, it is standard to use the present tense.

Wrong: The first premise of Descartes's ontological argument was false.
Right: The first premise of Descartes's ontological argument is false.

The idea behind this is that the nature and quality of an argument are unrelated to how old it is. Descartes's arguments for the existence of God, for instance, are just as good or bad now as they were when he wrote them down several centuries ago. If you're making a *historical* claim, however, the past tense is appropriate.

Wrong: The *Discourse on Method* is published in 1637.
Right: The *Discourse on Method* was published in 1637.

that, which, how

Restrictive and Nonrestrictive Clauses

In formal U.S. English, the words "that" and "which" function differently when they introduce a dependent clause. The distinction is worth knowing, not only so that you can use it to communicate your own ideas more clearly but also because it will help you to understand others' writing more easily.

The two words mark the difference between a *restrictive* and a *nonrestrictive* clause (also known as *defining* and *descriptive* clauses or *essential* and *nonessential* clauses). Restrictive clauses are introduced by "that"; nonrestrictive clauses by "which." A *restrictive* clause restricts the range of reference of what the clause is attached to; it further specifies that thing. Consider the following sentence.

Right: The problem that the libertarian can't avoid is explaining the nature of the agent.

The phrase "that the libertarian can't avoid" restricts the reference of "the problem"; it specifies which particular problem we're talking about. So it's introduced by "that." Notice that you couldn't remove the clause without changing the meaning of the sentence (by changing the meaning of its subject: "the problem"). It can thus help to think of the restrictive clause as connected to what it restricts: *The problem-that-the-libertarian-can't-avoid is explaining the nature of the agent.* (Compare our remarks about restrictive clauses in our earlier discussion of "like.")

Perhaps this is one reason the word "that" is often omitted in sentences like these—it brings the restrictive clause even closer to what it restricts. For instance:

The problem the libertarian can't avoid is explaining the nature of the agent.

Though there is nothing grammatically wrong with this last example, and it is unlikely to miscue the reader, we advise you to err on the side of introducing a restrictive clause with "that" since it can only make the structure of your sentence clearer. (See also our discussion of the omitted "that" below.)

A *nonrestrictive* clause does *not* restrict the reference of what it is attached to. Rather, it adds some extra information. Unlike restrictive clauses, nonrestrictive clauses can be removed from a sentence without changing the meaning of what remains. For this reason, nonrestrictive clauses are set off by commas. For example:

Right: The problem, which the libertarian can't avoid, is explaining the nature of the agent.

Which particular problem the author is referring to has presumably been specified earlier. With the clause "which the libertarian can't avoid," the author is merely adding some extra information about this problem (namely, that it's unavoidable).

In short, to master using "that" and "which" to introduce dependent clauses correctly, make sure you understand (1) the difference between a restrictive and nonrestrictive clause, (2) that "that" introduces the former and "which" introduces the latter, and (3) that the nonrestrictive clause is set off with a pair of commas while the restrictive clause is not.

Omitted that

Another "that"-related problem to look out for is miscues caused by an *omitted* "that." We often omit a "that" that would otherwise introduce the content of what philosophers call a "propositional attitude," such as *believing*, *saying*, or *hoping*. Usually, this is unproblematic. But sometimes it results in a miscue. Consider the following example:

> On this point, Khan believes compatibilists are mistaken.

By the time you get to the end of the sentence, it's clear what it means, but it risks miscuing the reader since before you get to the "are," you may (unconsciously) parse the sentence as follows:

> On this point, Khan believes compatibilists.

Of course, this second sentence says virtually the opposite of what the first says, so it's potentially confusing in addition to the basic miscue problem (namely, that your reader may have to go back and reread the sentence). The solution is to include the "that":

> On this point, Khan believes that compatibilists are mistaken.

Now, you could just be on your guard for potential miscues of this sort, but we recommend that you get into the habit of including the introductory "that" in sentences like these. It helps your reader to see the claim that you say is being believed, hoped, denied, or whatever. The only situations in which you have a *reason* to omit such "that"s are (1) when you're desperate to cut a few words to get under a word limit and (2) when the sentence has so many "that"s that it's distracting.

(For more on "that" and "which," see *GMEU*, "that.")

that *and* how

In casual contexts, "how" is sometimes substituted for "that" in introducing a claim. This is considered incorrect in formal English. For example:

Wrong: The problem is how souls are not physical objects.
Right: The problem is that souls are not physical objects.

Titles of Works

Titles of longer or larger works (books, scholarly journals, films, musicals, etc.) should be italicized. (Never underline words—italicize them instead. Underlining is how italics were indicated to publishers when authors had only handwriting or typewriters at their disposal.) Titles of shorter or smaller works (chapters, journal articles, short stories, songs, etc.) should be placed in quotation marks. If you are unsure about a particular case, consult an authoritative source, such as the *MLA Handbook*, the *Chicago Manual of Style*, or your instructor.

Wrong: The essay *Are Folk Races Like Dingoes, Dimes, or Dodos?* was specially commissioned for inclusion in "The Norton Introduction to Philosophy."
Right: The essay "Are Folk Races Like Dingoes, Dimes, or Dodos?" was specially commissioned for inclusion in *The Norton Introduction to Philosophy*.

why

Because philosophers often talk about reasons, they are particularly sensitive to language about reasons, including the word "why," which is commonly used to introduce a direct or indirect question about reasons. For example:

Right: Why would happiness be considered the sole source of value in the universe?
Right: You might wonder why happiness would be considered the sole source of value in the universe.

As a result, the common phrase "the reason why" can sound repetitive to philosophical ears. We thus advise that you avoid it. (Though we label the first example below *wrong*, many would consider that too strong.)

Wrong: The certainty that I'm free is the reason why I'm a libertarian.
Right: The certainty that I'm free is the reason I'm a libertarian.
Right: The certainty that I'm free is why I'm a libertarian.

(See *GMEU*, "reason is because" and "reason why.")

6.8 Punctuation

The conventions governing the use of punctuation are part of formal U.S. English. Your imagined reader will understand how these peculiar marks standardly function in formal prose, so you should too. Again, we can only cover the punctuation marks most commonly misused in philosophy papers. For a more thorough review, see *GMEU*, "Punctuation."

6.8.1 The Apostrophe

The **apostrophe** (') has two main functions: to show possession or contraction. To show possession in the singular, you usually place an apostrophe at the end of the word and add an *s* (e.g., "Maria's idea"). To show possession in the plural, you usually place an apostrophe after the final *s* that indicates that the word is plural. "The empiricist's assumption" refers to the assumption of one empiricist (who perhaps represents others). "The empiricists' assumption" refers to the assumption of more than one empiricist (possibly all empiricists).

The cases to watch out for are singular nouns (including names) that end in *s* and plural nouns that don't. The latter are straightforward. For instance, we write "the children's rights" because "children" is a plural noun that (unusually) doesn't end with an *s*. The basic rule for singular nouns that end in *s* is also straightforward: Add an apostrophe and another *s*, following the usual rule.[7]

Wrong: The consciousness' self-awareness is puzzling.
Right: The consciousness's self-awareness is puzzling.
Wrong: James' ideas were revolutionary.
Right: James's ideas were revolutionary.

Unfortunately, there are exceptions to this rule. The most common in philosophy papers is that Ancient Greek names ending in *s* take only an apostrophe:

Wrong: Socrates's ideas were revolutionary.
Right: Socrates' ideas were revolutionary.

Finally, note that possessive pronouns do not take apostrophes:

Wrong: The fault was our's.
Right: The fault was ours.
Wrong: The problem is it's circularity.
Right: The problem is its circularity.
Wrong: But who's fault was it?
Right: But whose fault was it?

(For much more on apostrophes and indicating possession, see *GMEU*, "Possessives.")

When an apostrophe is used to signal the contraction of two words into one, it is placed where a letter (or more than one letter) has been omitted. We write "doesn't" rather than "doe'snt" because the omitted letter is the *o* from the word "not." (See also *GMEU*, "Contractions.") If you understand this rule and the previous one (about possessive pronouns), you should be able to avoid confusing "its" and "it's": Only write "it's" if you can replace it with "it is." Otherwise, write "its" (which means "of it").

7 Some authorities would dispute our judgment of some of the following examples, but such authorities are in the minority, and their alternative conventions are needlessly complex. For discussion, see *GMEU*, "Possessives."

Contractions were traditionally considered unacceptable in formal English, but the most common contractions (e.g., "don't," "can't," and "it's") are increasingly common in such prose. If your instructor holds the traditional view, we advise you to follow it. You can easily remove contractions during the editing process by searching for apostrophes.

6.8.2 The Comma

The **comma** (,) is perhaps the least rule-governed punctuation mark, and thus the most difficult to use well (and to give advice about!). It generally functions to mark off a unit of grammar or sense but in a subtler way than other punctuation, such as colons, semicolons, or dashes.

Items in a list are separated by commas. The final comma precedes the "and" before the last item:

Right: The world contains substances, properties, and events.

If a single item in a list includes a comma, use semicolons to separate the items. (We give examples in our discussion of the semicolon below.)

The two parts of a conditional claim are separated by a comma:

Right: If your action is free, then you are morally responsible for it.

(For more on conditional claims, see §10.3.1.)

Nonrestrictive clauses are marked off with commas. (See §6.7 on "like" and "that, which, how.") But so are many other clauses that interrupt or are added to the basic structure of the sentence. For example:

Right: Having established this premise, Barnes proceeds to her final conclusion.
Right: Runga's argument, no less than Abel's, makes a strong case for vegetarianism.
Right: Gender, in the sense of public adherence to or departure from gender norms, is highly malleable.

In the previous two examples, it would be possible to use parentheses or dashes to set off the material enclosed in commas. Commas are a neutral way of setting off such material. **Parentheses** (()) *de-emphasize* the material they enclose, while **dashes** *highlight* the material. Compare the following two examples with the previous one.

Right: Gender (in the sense of public adherence to or departure from gender norms) is highly malleable.
Right: Gender—in the sense of public adherence to or departure from gender norms—is highly malleable.

(We say more about dashes in §6.8.4.)

You should *not* use a comma to connect two complete sentences. (See §6.4.2.) Nor should you use a comma to separate the subject from its verb, the verb from its object, or an adjective from its noun when these things occur next to one another.

Wrong: Both intentions and consequences, are relevant to moral evaluation.
Right: Both intentions and consequences are relevant to moral evaluation.
Wrong: Longford identifies, several problems with this argument.
Right: Longford identifies several problems with this argument.
Wrong: Achebe provides powerful, arguments for this claim.
Right: Achebe provides powerful arguments for this claim.

6.8.3 The Colon and Semicolon

These two punctuation marks are often confused, but despite their similar names and appearances, they have quite distinct functions. A **semicolon** (;) is primarily used to show a close relationship between the two main clauses that it separates, each of which could stand alone as a complete sentence. It can thus be replaced with a period with only a slight loss in what's communicated to the reader. ("Semiperiod" might be a better name for it when used in this way.)

Right: Empiricists believe that all knowledge ultimately derives from the senses. Rationalists deny this.
Right: Empiricists believe that all knowledge ultimately derives from the senses; rationalists deny this.
Right: Empiricists believe that all knowledge ultimately derives from the senses; they think nothing is known *a priori.*

One common misuse of the semicolon occurs when the words on one side of it could not constitute a complete sentence. The solution is sometimes to replace the semicolon with a comma, sometimes to replace it with a period. But these solutions often entail some further rewriting:

Wrong: Rationalists believe that we cannot go wrong if we initiate a line of reasoning with clear and distinct ideas; though it is not always clear what qualifies an idea as clear and distinct.
Right: Rationalists believe that we cannot go wrong if we initiate a line of reasoning with clear and distinct ideas, though it is not always clear what qualifies an idea as clear and distinct.
Right: Rationalists believe that we cannot go wrong if we initiate a line of reasoning with clear and distinct ideas. It is not always clear, however, what qualifies an idea as clear and distinct.

Another use of the semicolon is to separate items in a list when some of the items themselves contain commas. (In such cases, "megacomma" might be a better name for it.)

Wrong: The world contains particles, atoms, and molecules, minerals, plants, and animals, and beliefs, desires, and hopes.

Right: The world contains particles, atoms, and molecules; minerals, plants, and animals; and beliefs, desires, and hopes.

A **colon** (:) is a punctuational pointer: It follows an introductory phrase and directs the reader's attention to what follows. Unlike the main use of a semicolon, what precedes or follows the colon need not constitute a complete sentence.

Wrong: Nietzsche introduces two important concepts; the Apollonian and the Dionysian.
Right: Nietzsche introduces two important concepts: the Apollonian and the Dionysian.

Some argue that what follows a colon should always begin with a lowercase letter since a colon occurs *within* a sentence, not at its end. However, we believe that if what follows the colon can function as a complete sentence, it is helpful to indicate this to your reader by beginning it with a capital letter.

Acceptable: I cannot, however, agree with the following claim: all nonhuman animals have the same rights.
Better? I cannot, however, agree with the following claim: All nonhuman animals have the same rights.

6.8.4 Dashes

As mentioned in our discussion of the comma, a dash can be used to set off a phrase from the rest of the sentence. Unlike neutral commas or de-emphasizing parentheses, dashes *highlight* the material they introduce or enclose.

Right: The argument—one that must be considered by anyone addressing this topic—makes a strong case for the rationality of religious belief.
Right: Jones's objection is strong—but not quite strong enough to defeat the argument.

The dashes in these sentences are **em dashes** (—), so-called because they are traditionally the width of a capital *M*. There should be no space between an em dash and the letters on either side of it.

The **en dash** (–), traditionally the width of a capital *N*, is much less common in formal U.S. English. (It is used in place of an em dash in formal *British* English, in which case there is a space between the en dash and the letters on either side.) But it can perform a useful function as a kind of *tensile hyphen*, yoking together two terms between which there is some tension. There is no space between the letters on either side of the en dash used in this way. For example:

Wrong: The mind/body problem continues to puzzle philosophers.
Acceptable: The mind-body problem continues to puzzle philosophers.
Better: The mind–body problem continues to puzzle philosophers.

Wrong: The Mexican/American War lasted just over two years.
Acceptable: The Mexican-American War lasted just over two years.
Better: The Mexican–American War lasted just over two years.

It is surely unlikely that anyone would be miscued into thinking that "Mexican-American War" refers to a war among Mexican-Americans, but if you have mastered the en dash, you needn't worry about even this unlikely possibility.

One reason some writers make little use of dashes is that they don't know how to get them into an electronic document. This is also a source of the misuse of hyphens in place of dashes. (See the following subsection.) But all word processors enable you to insert dashes quite easily. If you're not sure how to do it, a web search will quickly inform you.

6.8.5 The Hyphen

A **hyphen** (-) is not a dash, so it should not be used in any of the ways discussed in the previous subsection. Its most important use is in **phrasal adjectives**—that is, adjectives made up of more than one word. The hyphen yokes the words of a phrasal adjective together, preventing miscues and making the structure of the noun phrase clear to your reader.

Wrong: One problem with open source software is determining what the open source is.
Right: One problem with open-source software is determining what the open source is.

In the first half of the sentence, "source" is part of the phrasal adjective ("open-source") modifying the noun "software," so the phrasal adjective requires a hyphen. In the second half of the sentence, "source" is a noun modified by the single adjective "open," so no hyphen is required.

There are a couple of exceptions to this rule. First, if the *first* word of a phrasal adjective is an adverb ending in *-ly*, it doesn't take a hyphen.

Right: Ribeiro fashions expertly crafted sentences.

Second, if the items in a phrase are already joined in some other way (e.g., because they are capitalized or in quotation marks), the hyphen should be omitted. For example:

Right: She is among the foremost Latin American philosophers.

According to the conventions of formal U.S. English, the following sentence is unambiguous:

Of the three, I preferred the middle school orchestra.

The sentence is about a school orchestra in the middle of two others. However, a reader might obviously be miscued into thinking that the sentence is about the orchestra of a middle school. The best course in this case is probably to revise the sentence. For instance:

Of the three, I preferred the second school orchestra.

If such revision is not desirable for some reason, you should consider using a hyphen to indicate a "phrasal noun." For example:

The result was an <u>authentic work-performance</u>.

6.8.6 Quotation Marks, Square Brackets, and Ellipsis Dots

Despite their name, **quotation marks** (" ") are used for much more than just indicating that the words they enclose are being quoted (i.e., borrowed verbatim) from another writer. In philosophical writing, some other common uses include introducing a term, mentioning a term, and distancing oneself from a term. All these uses—like the indication of a quotation—are similar in that they draw attention to the particular words enclosed in quotation marks rather than simply using those words. (A further use, discussed in §6.7, is to indicate the titles of shorter works.) You should *not* use quotation marks for emphasis; that's what italics are for.

When you **introduce** a term, especially a neologism (i.e., a new, made-up word), placing it in quotation marks alerts your reader:

Right: Napoleon calls this fantastical beast a "liger."

Philosophers distinguish between **using** a term and **mentioning** a term. We *use* words all the time; when we *mention* one (in this technical sense) we draw attention to the word itself rather than using it for its ordinary meaning:

Right: Trees contain water and fibrous material.
Wrong: Trees contains five letters.
Right: "Trees" contains five letters.

(Note that the verb is singular in the last example since *the word* "trees"—as opposed to what it refers to—is one thing, not many.)

Wrong: Race motivates discrimination and celebration, but what does race really mean?
Right: Race motivates discrimination and celebration, but what does "race" really mean?

(Note that the author of the last example first *uses* the word "race" and then *mentions* it.)

So-called **scare quotes** indicate that you want to distance yourself from the literal meaning of the term. You're using scare quotes correctly if you can remove the quotation marks and add "so-called" before the term:

Right: Barber's "philosophy" is really just a collection of clichés.
Right: Barber's so-called philosophy is really just a collection of clichés.

Use scare quotes sparingly. If you're distancing yourself from the literal meaning of a term, consider whether there is a different term that you could use literally.

When you **quote** a passage, you must use quotation marks immediately before and after the borrowed words. (You must also supply a citation. We discuss how to do that in Chapter 7.) The quotation marks must surround every word you have taken from the source. Sometimes you may want to leave out some words within a quoted passage because they're irrelevant to your concerns, they may confuse your reader, or you are under length constraints. Similarly, you may sometimes want to add or change some words inside a quotation to clarify something for your reader or to integrate the quoted material into the structure of your sentence. This is perfectly fine, as long as (1) you don't thereby misrepresent the meaning or grammatical coherence of the quoted material and (2) you use **ellipsis dots** (**…**) to indicate any *omissions* and **square brackets** ([ ]) to indicate any *additions or alterations*. (An *ellipsis* is an omission, hence the name of this punctuation mark. If you type three periods in a row, most word processors will replace them with a single character comprising three ellipsis dots. If your word processor doesn't do this, you should put a space between each pair of periods.)

For example, you might want to quote part of the first sentence in the second paragraph of John Stuart Mill's *On Liberty*:

> The struggle between Liberty and Authority is the most conspicuous feature in the portions of history with which we are earliest familiar, particularly in that of Greece, Rome, and England.[8]

If this quotation appears after you've introduced the topic of a conflict between liberty and authority, you may choose to delete the words "between Liberty and Authority" to avoid repetition. This is acceptable, but the omission must be signaled to the reader:

> According to Mill, this "struggle … is the most conspicuous feature in the portions of history with which we are earliest familiar, particularly in that of Greece, Rome, and England" (Mill 5).

Alternatively, you might want to simplify Mill's thought in the second half of the sentence by replacing and omitting some words:

> According to Mill, "the struggle between Liberty and Authority is the most conspicuous feature in the [earliest known] history … of Greece, Rome, and England" (Mill 5).

Note that it's acceptable to change the first letter of the quotation from uppercase to lowercase to integrate it into your own sentence without indicating this change with square brackets. Most would also accept modernizing (i.e., eliminating) Mill's capitalization of the common nouns "liberty" and "authority." But some authors use square

8 We haven't supplied quotation marks or a citation here since they might be counterproductive in this context!

brackets to indicate even such minor changes. If in doubt, err on the side of indicating any change you make to quoted material.

It's easy to get tripped up by other punctuation marks that occur in the same place as closing quotation marks. The basic rules are simple, however: (1) Punctuate the *entire sentence* (not just the material in quotation marks) as if the quotation marks weren't there. (2) If a *comma* or *period* occurs right next to the *closing* quotation marks, put it *inside* the quotation marks. (3) If *any other punctuation* occurs right next to the closing quotation marks, put it *outside* the quotation marks. For example:

Wrong: Napoleon calls this fantastical beast a "liger".
Right: Napoleon calls this fantastical beast a "liger."
Right: Napoleon calls this fantastical beast a "liger," among other names.
Right: Napoleon calls this fantastical beast a "liger"; what the liger calls Napoleon is unrecorded.
Right: One character, however, was not a "liger": Napoleon.
Right: Why does Napoleon call this fantastical beast a "liger"?

A parenthetical citation is part of the sentence, clause, or phrase to which it is attached but not part of the quotation, so it goes between the closing quotation marks and any immediately following punctuation:

Wrong: Davies claims that this "is not an experience of space and movement. (79)"
Wrong: Davies claims that this "is not an experience of space and movement." (79)
Right: Davies claims that this "is not an experience of space and movement" (79).
Wrong: Davies claims that this "is not an experience of space and movement," (79) which is controversial.
Right: Davies claims that this "is not an experience of space and movement" (79), which is controversial.
Right: Davies claims that this "is not an experience of space and movement," which is controversial (79).

A footnote or endnote mark, by contrast, goes after the last punctuation mark of whatever it's attached to—typically at the end of the sentence.

Wrong: Davies claims that this "is not an experience of space and movement.[3]"
Wrong: Davies claims that this "is not an experience of space and movement".[3]
Wrong: Davies claims that this "is not an experience of space and movement"[3].
Right: Davies claims that this "is not an experience of space and movement."[3]
Wrong: Davies claims that this "is not an experience of space and movement,[3]" which is controversial.
Right: Davies claims that this "is not an experience of space and movement,"[3] which is controversial.
Right: Davies claims that this "is not an experience of space and movement," which is controversial.[3]

Some students have been taught that they should always put a comma right before any opening quotation marks and inside any closing quotation marks not right at the end of the sentence. This is an approximation of the rules for writing dialogue (e.g., in a short story). Since such writing is rare in philosophical prose, you should ignore this advice and follow the rules given above (though consider our discussion of direct questions in §6.7 under "Questions").

(For more on these punctuation marks, see *GMEU*, "Quotations" and "Punctuation.")

6.8.7 The Slash

The **slash** (/) should be avoided in philosophical writing. We have yet to see a sentence containing a slash in a philosophy paper that could not be improved by removing the slash (together with some rewriting). The slash is often used colloquially to mean "or" or "and"; this is too informal for philosophical prose and likely ambiguous. Don't do it in your philosophy paper. (The use of "and/or," discussed in §6.7, is a particularly egregious case of this.)

Wrong: Lee argues that race is culturally/politically constructed.
Right: Lee argues that race is both culturally and politically constructed.
Right: Lee argues that race can be constructed culturally or politically.

(Of course, which of these is right in terms of *content* depends on Lee's view.)

Sometimes a slash is used to separate (or join?) two similar words. This is usually an indication that the author cannot decide which word to use.

Wrong: This confusing/incoherent argument is difficult to assess.

An argument may be confusing or incoherent (or both), but these are quite different things. If you find yourself using a slash in this way, think about which word is best and delete the other—and the slash. If you need both, use both; but rewrite, deleting the slash.

Right: This confusing argument is difficult to assess.
Right: This incoherent argument is difficult to assess.
Right: This confusing argument is difficult to assess, but I will show that it is ultimately incoherent.

Sometimes a slash should be replaced with an en dash. See Section 6.8.4.

6.9 Capitalization

The basic rules of capitalization are simple: Capitalize the first letter of every sentence, and capitalize proper nouns wherever they occur. **Proper nouns** are the names of specific people, places, things, or events; **common nouns** refer to items of a general kind. We have underlined the proper noun and italicized the corresponding common noun in the following examples.

Elizabeth Anscombe was an influential twentieth-century *philosopher*.
The only *city* with more philosophers was Athens.
The Statue of Liberty is one such famous *monument*.
The best-known baseball *tournament* is misleadingly named the World Series.

Unfortunately, it is not always easy to tell a proper from a common noun. You should resist the tendency to capitalize technical terms, grand concepts, and the names of arguments and theories (even though the last—as names—might be considered proper nouns).[9]

Wrong: The question is whether we have Freedom.
Right: The question is whether we have freedom.
Wrong: One objection to Externalism is that it precludes our knowing what we know.
Right: One objection to externalism is that it precludes our knowing what we know.

One generally accepted class of exceptions to this rule is technical terms that are formed out of proper nouns.

Wrong: It is true that platonism faces serious objections.
Right: It is true that Platonism faces serious objections.

Do not capitalize simply for emphasis; use italics (but do so sparingly). *Never* use all caps (i.e., spelling a word with all capital letters). One exception may be in headings, but even there, they can give the impression that you are shouting at your reader.

Wrong: Plato did NOT claim that ideal human love lacks a sexual aspect.
Wrong: Plato did Not claim that ideal human love lacks a sexual aspect.
Right: Plato did *not* claim that ideal human love lacks a sexual aspect.

Try structuring the sentence so that the emphasis is clear without italics.

Acceptable: The medium of *film* is the only one that allows such immersion.
Arguably better: Film is the only medium that allows such immersion.
Another possibility: There is only one medium that allows such immersion: film.

6.10 Scholarly Terms

Many scholarly terms have been passed down from the time, centuries ago, when Latin was the universal language of Western scholars, with the result that what would once have been as familiar and casual as the present-day "FYI" can now seem an obscure and confusing code. It's useful to know these terms, not just so that you understand them when you encounter them in your reading but also because many of them are useful space-saving devices. However, as with all technical terms, you should resist any

9 You may recall a violation of this rule by John Stuart Mill in an example in Section 6.8.6, but it wasn't a rule in his day.

tendency you may have to use this language merely to show off. It is difficult to imagine a situation, for instance, in which it would be better to use the scholarly term "ergo" than the ordinary word "so." If you can say the same thing in ordinary English, you should do so. (There is more on most of these terms in *GMEU*.)

In what follows, we list the most common such terms (in bold), each followed by a direct translation (in square brackets), its grammatical category when used in formal English (often different from its original grammatical role), a short definition, and an example of its correct use. Many of these terms are italicized because they are not considered English words. Those that have been fully assimilated into formal English (for instance, "e.g.") are no longer italicized. Many terms are in an intermediate state and thus might be italicized or not. Just make sure you treat each term consistently. (For more on this issue, see *GMEU*, "Italics, §B. Foreign Phrases.")

6.10.1 Words and Phrases

a fortiori [from a stronger position], adverb: it follows all the more that.

> Such a being would not be conscious; *a fortiori*, such a being would not be self-conscious.

contra [against], preposition: against.

> I will argue, *contra* Hoch, that such mechanisms do not exist.

ergo [therefore], adverb: therefore.

> The argument from design fails to establish divine omnipotence; *ergo*, it is insufficient as a basis for belief in the Christian God.

modus ponens [mode of positing], noun and adjective: a form of argument in which the consequent of a conditional claim is inferred from the conditional and the affirmation of its antecedent. (See §10.3.2.)

> The form of the argument is *modus ponens*.
> It is a straightforward *modus ponens* argument.

modus tollens [mode of removing], noun and adjective: a form of argument in which the antecedent of a conditional claim is denied by inference from the conditional and the denial of its consequent. (See §10.3.2.)

> She establishes her conclusion by *modus tollens*.
> A *modus tollens* argument suggests itself.

non sequitur [it doesn't follow], noun: an argument in which the premises are irrelevant to the conclusion, or the conclusion of such an argument.

> Unfortunately, this argument is a *non sequitur*. The color of Johnson's shoes has nothing to do with his moral character.

Leoni's claim is a *non sequitur*; the color of Johnson's shoes has nothing to do with his moral character.

pace [with peace], preposition: despite the views of [someone].

There is no doubt, *pace* Descartes, that animals are sentient beings.

(et) passim [(and) everywhere], adverb: (and) throughout [a text]. Used only in citations.

Gulley (*passim*) and Irwin (36–38 *et passim*) have argued this before me.

prima facie [on first face], adverb and adjective: at first glance, on the face of it.

Perhaps there are exceptions, but killing an innocent person is *prima facie* wrong.
The *prima facie* justification for the view is its simplicity.

qua [insofar as], preposition: as, considered as, in the role of.

She discusses human beings *qua* decision-makers.

reductio (ad absurdum) [reduction (to absurdity)], noun: An argument against a view that proceeds by showing that the view implies a contradiction and thus must be false.

He presented the reductio that such a policy would lead to some people being both citizens and noncitizens.

sic [thus], adverb: as originally printed. The term indicates that the error or peculiarity in quoted material occurs in the original source. Unless the error or peculiarity plays a role in why you quoted the passage, it's better simply to correct it (using appropriate punctuation).

Unnecessary:	He writes that "this is a characteristically mail [*sic*] approach to ethical problem solving" (73).
Good:	He writes that "this is a characteristically [male] approach to ethical problem solving" (73).
Good:	Confusingly, he seems to endorse the opposite of what his argument shows: "races are not [*sic*] culturally constructed" (237).

simpliciter [simply], adverb: simply, without additions or qualifications.

We must distinguish language *simpliciter* from its artistic uses.

sine qua non [without which not], noun: a necessary thing.

The capacity for language is a *sine qua non* for higher intelligence.

sui generis [kind of one's own], adjective: one of a kind, unique.

> Are the attributes of the gods *sui generis*, or do they also occur in some form in human beings?

6.10.2 Abbreviations

Immediately following each abbreviation is the full phrase it is abbreviated from. Note that the period following an abbreviation is part of it (indicating that it is an abbreviation). Such periods should never be omitted. However, if the abbreviation occurs at the end of a sentence, the period does double duty—it should not be repeated.

Wrong: He provides theories, arguments, objections, <u>etc..</u>
Right: He provides theories, arguments, objections, <u>etc.</u>

ca., circa [around], preposition: around. Used to indicate vagueness or uncertainty, especially with respect to dates.

> The manuscript was lost in the 13th century (ca. 1275).

cf., confer [compare], verb: compare. Used only in citations and cross-references.

> Williams is not alone in this (cf. Pater 53).

e.g., exempli gratia [for the sake of example], adverb: for example. (Note that this is always followed by a comma in formal U.S. English.) You should avoid using *both* "e.g.," *and* "etc." with one list of examples since each renders the other redundant: On the one hand, if these are just examples (so you use "e.g."), there are presumably many others (so you don't need "etc."). On the other hand, if there are other items that could be listed (so you use "etc."), those listed are presumably just examples (so you don't need "e.g.").

> The titles of Austin's essays (e.g., "Three Ways of Spilling Ink" and "How to Talk—Some Simple Ways") may strike us as peculiar.

et al., et alii [and others], noun: and other authors (or editors). Used only in citations.

> The introduction to the section on free will is especially helpful (Rosen et al. 571–4).

etc., et cetera [and the other things], noun: and so on. See "e.g." (above) for why you should avoid using *both* "e.g." *and* "etc." with one list of examples.

> Many biological fruits are not called "fruit" in ordinary English (pea pods, peppers, pumpkins, etc.).

et seq., et sequens [and the following (material)], noun: and the following material. Used only in citations. You should use it only if it would be more helpful to your reader than providing a precise page range.

For Wittgenstein's own explanation of "language games," see *The Blue Book* (17 *et seq.*) in addition to the references given above.

ff., folio [page], noun: and the following pages. Used only in citations. Sometimes it is preceded by a space; sometimes not. You should use it only if it would be more helpful to your reader than providing a precise page range.

For Wittgenstein's own explanation of "language games," see *The Blue Book* (17ff.) in addition to the references given above.

ibid., ibidem [in the same place], noun: the same source [as the previous one]. (Typically used only in footnote and endnote citations.)

[3] *Ibid.*, p. 45.

i.e., id est [that is], adverb: in other words. Note that this is always followed by a comma in formal U.S. English.

She is a person in the relevant sense (i.e., a being with moral responsibility).

iff; if, and only if, conjunction. This phrase indicates a *biconditional* claim—that is, a claim in which one thing logically implies another and is logically implied by it. In other words, "A if, and only if, B" (or "A iff B") is equivalent to "If A, then B; and if B, then A." (See §10.3.1 for an introduction to conditional, i.e., *if–then*, claims.)

X is an aunt iff X is female and has a sibling or sibling-in-law with a child.

op. cit., opere citato [in the work (previously) quoted], noun: the work (previously) cited. Typically used only in footnote and endnote citations.

[3] *Op. cit.*, p. 45.

qtd. in, quoted in. Used in citations to indicate that the material cited appears as a quotation from another source within the source cited. (See §7.7.3.)

Appiah claims that "there are no races" (qtd. in Spencer 572).

s.v., sub verbo [under the word], adverb: under the headword. Used to refer to a particular entry in a reference work.

For some amusing examples, see *Garner's Modern English Usage*, s.v. "Mondegreens."

viz., videlicet [it is permissible to see], adverb: namely, that is. This term is better avoided in favor of the more common "i.e." or "namely."

Kant analyzed aesthetics in what is known as his "third critique," *viz.*, the *Critique of Judgment.*

6.11 Commonly Misspelled Words

We end this chapter with a list of words that are commonly misspelled in philosophy papers and thus distract readers. Proofreaders and spellcheckers are helpful but not fool-proof. As with every aspect of your paper, the ultimate responsibility for correct spelling is yours. (For the meanings of these terms, consult one of the philosophical reference works listed in §6.3.)

aesthetic ("esthetic" is an outdated spelling)
analytic
anarchy
argument (the *u* is not followed by an *e)*
atheist
coherence (an *e*—not an *a*—follows the *r*)
conceive (follows the rule: *i* before *e*, except after *c*)
deceive (follows the rule: *i* before *e*, except after *c*)
deism
deontological
dialectical
dialogue
dualism
empirical
empiricism
epiphenomenalism
existence (an *e*—not an *a*—follows the *t)*
existentialism
fallacy
medieval
necessary
ontological
perceive (follows the rule: *i* before *e*, except after *c*)
phenomenology
philosophical
premise ("premiss" is an outdated spelling)
scholasticism
skepticism (the *k* is replaced by a *c* in many other varieties of English)
solipsism
tautology
teleological
theism
theory
utilitarian

7 Acknowledging the Work of Others

A default assumption your reader will make is that everything in your paper originates with you—from the overall structure, through the arguments you discuss, to the particular way each sentence is written. So if anything in your paper does *not* originate with you, you must acknowledge its source. As we said in Section 3.11, giving credit where credit is due is what distinguishes a scholar from a plagiarist. Clearly indicating the sources that have influenced your paper is useful for other reasons too. Sometimes a reader will want to follow up your citation of a source to learn more about the idea that you've briefly mentioned, to compare how you've characterized it with how its original author did, or to check that you've quoted someone accurately.

There are widely accepted, clearly defined (if exasperatingly detailed!) conventions for acknowledging published sources, and most of this chapter is devoted to introducing those conventions. We begin, however, with two other kinds of sources you are likely to draw on in writing your paper, yet which there are no clearly defined conventions for acknowledging.

7.1 Acknowledging the Help of Friends, Family, and Classmates

You have probably benefited from either discussing the topic of your paper with classmates or listening to others discuss it in class. And if you follow our advice earlier in this book, you will receive feedback on drafts of your paper from friends and family who are not in the course for which you are writing your paper. Acknowledging such help became more and more common in scholarly publications over the course of the twentieth century, and in the twenty-first century, more and more instructors are encouraging such acknowledgments in student papers—perhaps as part of a growing concern to show that philosophy has always been a collaborative endeavor, despite the way its history has sometimes been presented.

The most common way to acknowledge such help is in footnotes or endnotes. Help with the paper in general is usually acknowledged in a note at the very beginning or very end of the paper. For example:

> [1] Thanks to my classmates in *PHIL 3444: Latinx Philosophy* for useful discussion of the topic of this paper and to my mother for help with my spelling and grammar.

DOI: 10.4324/9781003512318-7

Help with a particular part of the paper can be acknowledged where you made use of it. For instance:

> [5] Thanks to Gabriela Peters for helpful discussion of how best to respond to this objection.
> [9] Thanks to Harry Leung for helping me to formulate this argument more clearly.

7.2 Acknowledging the Help of Your Instructor

You have doubtless also benefited from your instructor's lectures and other materials, such as slide presentations, handouts, or videos. It might seem surprising, given the high importance most instructors place on acknowledging your paper's sources, that you are usually *not* required to acknowledge these influential sources. This is because many instructors consider their teaching in a very different light from their scholarship. Where scholarly publications are additions to a somewhat impersonal public record, teaching is a more personal relationship (albeit within a highly institutionalized context). Thus, many instructors consider their lectures and other teaching materials as a kind of gift to students, which become the student's own if properly assimilated.

Having said that, it is better to err on the side of acknowledging a source—including material provided by your instructor. You can do this in a note, following the examples in the previous section. If in doubt, you should ask your instructor how to proceed.

7.3 Citing Published Sources

For the remainder of this chapter, when we talk of a *source*, we mean something you have made use of in writing your paper that has been *published*, whether in a formal venue, such as a book, journal, or online encyclopedia, or an informal venue, such as a blog or YouTube. We will call the acknowledgment of such sources *citation.*

You must cite *all* the sources that have had an influence on the final form of your paper. Merely mentioning the author or title of a source is not enough. Scholars have developed detailed systems of conventions for citing sources, and you should learn the basics of one of them. Different scholarly disciplines use different systems, and there is no single system used in all philosophical scholarship, but we will introduce you to the basics (slightly simplified in places) of one system widely used in philosophy: **MLA style,** named for the Modern Language Association, which established the system. (The other most commonly used system is **Chicago style**, named for the *Chicago Manual of Style*, in which it is set out.)

7.3.1 Quotation and Paraphrase

Obviously, a source has influenced your paper when you have copied some words from it into your paper. This is **quotation**. Any language you quote must be enclosed in quotation marks and cited. In Section 6.8.6, we discuss how to punctuate quotations, including how to handle any additions and omissions you make to the quoted material, and how to punctuate the end of the quotation and the citation.

If a quotation is longer than about three lines or 50 words, it is indicated not by quotation marks but as a **block quotation:**

> This is not a true quotation, but we have formatted it as a block quotation to give you an example. It is a separate paragraph but with every line indented at the left. (If you don't know how to do this, a web search will quickly inform you.) In a student paper, however, the block quotation should be double-spaced, as with the rest of the paper. We cover parenthetical, in-text citations in Section 7.7. For now, just notice that the in-text citation for a block quotation comes *after* the final period of the quotation and is separated from it by a space. (Murgatroyd 57)

However, for the same reason that we recommend avoiding quotation where possible (see §4.3), we recommend avoiding block quotations: It is better to put the ideas you discuss in your paper in your own words, even if the ideas are not originally your own.

Putting the ideas of others in your own words is often called **paraphrase**. However, we recommend that you do not think of what you are doing as paraphrase since to many students that term dangerously suggests taking the words of others, changing them slightly, and then presenting them without quotation marks. Beware: Even if you cite the source of such an idea, this is plagiarism! The problem is that although you have acknowledged that you borrowed the *idea*, you have not acknowledged that you borrowed the *expression* of the idea. (That would require using quotation marks.) If a sentence in your paper closely resembles a sentence in a source you have consulted, you must present it as a quotation, with any alterations indicated. (See §6.8.6.) The best way to avoid unintended plagiarism of this sort is always to have your sources out of your sight when you are writing individual sentences of your paper. You must also be scrupulous to record when you have taken material verbatim in your notes; otherwise, you may think you are rewriting your own words from your notes when in fact they come from the source you took the notes on. (We discuss this topic further in §8.1.)

7.3.2 Lists of Works Cited and Bibliographies

A **list of works cited** (or **works cited** for short) is precisely what it sounds like: a list of *all and only* the works (i.e., sources) that you have cited in the body of your paper. One of the items on your final-formatting checklist should be to confirm that every source you cite in your paper appears in your list of works cited and that every source in the list is cited somewhere in your paper.

Your list of works cited goes at the end of your paper, announced with a heading: Works Cited. It traditionally begins on a new page, but we see no harm in starting it immediately below the body of your paper, especially if it will fit entirely on that page. The items are listed in alphabetical order by the first piece of information in each. This is usually the author's last name (the *first* author's last name if the item is co-authored). If a source has no stated author, it is listed by its title. Each item has its own paragraph with a **hanging indent.** (That is, the first line is flush with the left margin, but every other line is indented. You can easily discover how to do this online.) You should either leave a line between each item or double-space the entire list of works cited (or both). These formatting details are important since they help your reader make use of your paper. When using your list of works cited, your reader will be looking for a particular entry, following up on one of your in-text citations. She will thus be scanning the list, looking, in the first instance, for the last name of the author you've cited. The hanging indent, in particular, makes finding the relevant item much easier. (For a sample list of works cited, see the end of the sample essay in Appendix B.)

Sometimes the word "bibliography" is used as a synonym for "list of works cited." It has two further distinct meanings, however. First, a list of sources at the end of your paper is a **bibliography** (as opposed to a list of works cited) when it includes not only sources cited in the body of the paper but also other works on the topic. Second, some bibliographies are self-contained works in their own right—lists of useful sources on some topic. You may encounter such bibliographies in your research (see §9.3.1 on "Other Scholarly Sources"), or you may be given the assignment of compiling such a bibliography. In Section 9.1.1, we discuss one kind of stand-alone bibliography that students are sometimes required to write in philosophy courses: an annotated bibliography. In this chapter, we do not consider bibliographies, discussing only lists of works cited.

7.3.3 *Citations*

Your reader should be able to find not only any source you are citing but also *the particular material within* that source that contributes to your paper at the point where the citation occurs. MLA style clearly distinguishes these two tasks by combining (1) a list of works cited at the end of the paper, which contains the full details of each source cited in the paper (enabling the reader to locate each source) with (2) individual **in-text citations** appearing at each place in your paper where it has been influenced by a source. Each in-text citation gives a brief indication of (a) which source is being cited and (b) the particular place within that source where the influencing material appears.

In **note citation** systems, a superscript number appears in the text (i.e., a small number raised above the rest of the type, e.g., [6]), directing the reader to a corresponding note at the bottom of the page (in **footnote** systems) or the end of the paper (in **endnote** systems). We do not cover note citation systems in this book. If your instructor requires you to use such a system but doesn't provide you with resources on how to do so, we recommend the *Chicago Manual of Style*.

How many in-text citations should your paper include? Obviously, there's no magic number that answers this question for all papers, but remember that you should provide a citation for every idea that does not originate with you. For reasons we've discussed earlier in the book, a lot of the ideas in your paper are likely to fit this description. However, you don't introduce a new idea in every sentence of your paper. It is the *paragraph* that is the unit of thought in your paper. (See §2.2.1.) So, as a rule of thumb, you might expect to provide something like one citation per paragraph, on average. But this is a *very* rough approximation. Perhaps it would be less misleading to say that, for almost any paper, one citation per sentence would be too many, and no citations at all would be too few. The only hard and fast rule, again, is that you must provide a citation for every idea in your paper that does not originate with you.

7.3.4 *Looking Ahead and Further Resources*

In the following three sections (7.4–7.6), we explain how to create a **full bibliographic reference** for the most common kinds of sources you are likely to use in your paper—that is, all the information about the source you need to include in your list of works cited, formatted according to MLA style.[1] For each kind of source, we (a) describe its

1 Apart from the fact that we cover only the basics of MLA style, we make some simplifying departures from it. We note these where they occur.

distinguishing features, (b) list the information you'll need from a source of that kind to complete a full bibliographic reference, (c) explain how to find that information, and (d) provide a template and examples demonstrating how to format it. Pay close attention to the details of the formatting—what is capitalized, what punctuation is used, and where exactly the punctuation goes. These details may seem trivial, but departures from the style will distract a reader familiar with the conventions (such as your instructor), who may consider them important. Finally, in Section 7.7, we turn to the creation of in-text citations.

There are many resources available to help you cite sources correctly in your paper. Many college-library and writing-center **websites** have information on how to cite sources according to various scholarly systems, including tools to help you create your citations. Though most are perfectly adequate, we particularly recommend those of the University of North Carolina, Chapel Hill (https://guides.lib.unc.edu/citing-information) and Purdue University's "Online Writing Lab" (https://owl.purdue.edu/owl/research_and_citation).

A **citation-management tool** is a program, app, or website that stores your citation information and helps generate citations for you. Such tools may be more trouble than they are worth if you're just starting out in philosophy; they're of more use to people doing advanced research and keeping track of numerous sources. If you do use a citation-management tool, you should treat it like a spell- or grammar checker—that is, with a healthy skepticism, checking its results against your knowledge of the citation system you're using. It remains your responsibility to ensure that your citations are complete and correctly formatted.

The ultimate source of the conventions of MLA style is the *MLA Handbook*. It is available in print and e-book format and contains a *lot* more information than we can cover in this chapter. (The ultimate source of the conventions of Chicago style is the *Chicago Manual of Style*. It is available in print and e-book format, and there is also the *Chicago Manual of Style Online* (https://www.chicagomanualofstyle.org/home.html) to which your library may have a subscription.)

7.4 Formatting Names, Titles, and Numbers

Before we look at the various kinds of sources you may cite, it is worth covering some basics about how to format names (of authors, editors, etc.), titles (of books, articles, etc.), and numbers (of pages, volumes, etc.) that appear in bibliographic references.

7.4.1 Names

You should record people's names as they appear in the sources you are citing. If an author includes his middle initial, you should include it too. If another spells out her middle name, that's what you should do. If a third uses only initials for his first name(s), you should too. Be sure to reproduce any accents or diacritics in a person's name (e.g., María José Alcaraz Léon). If you're not sure how to include such marks in your text, a web search can usually inform you.

Because items in your list of works cited are listed alphabetically by the author's last name (or, if there is more than one author, the *first* author's last name), the first and last names of that author get flipped. But note that *no other names get flipped*—because no other names are used to list the source in alphabetical order. So, in the example below, the first and last names of the first author (John Bishop) get flipped, but the names of his co-author (Daniel J. McKaughan) and the editors of the encyclopedia (Edward N. Zalta and Uri Nodelman) appear in their normal order.

Bishop, John and Daniel J. McKaughan. "Faith." *The Stanford Encyclopedia of Philosophy*, edited by Edward N. Zalta and Uri Nodelman, Fall 2022 ed., 15 July 2022, https://plato.stanford.edu/archives/fall2022/entries/faith/.

If there are three or more people in one role (author, editor, etc.), you can list only the first, followed by the abbreviation "et al." (short for *et alii*, Latin for "and others"). But be sure to include the *complete* name of the first author or editor, unlike in a parenthetical citation. (See §7.7.) For example:

Spencer, Quayshawn. "Are Folk Races Like Dingoes, Dimes, or Dodos?" *The Norton Introduction to Philosophy*, edited by Gideon Rosen et al., 2nd ed., W. W. Norton and Company, 2018, pp. 571–78.

7.4.2 Titles

In your list of works cited, as in your prose, titles of longer or larger sources (books, journals, films, musicals, etc.) should be italicized, and titles of shorter or smaller sources (chapters, journal articles, short stories, songs, etc.) should be placed in quotation marks. This is true regardless of how the title appears in the source (ALL CAPS, all lowercase, *italicized*, etc.). If you are unsure about a particular case, consult an authoritative guide, such as the *MLA Handbook*, the *Chicago Manual of Style*, or your instructor.

All titles should appear in "title style" or "up style" (no matter how they appear in their sources): The first and last words of the title are capitalized, and every other word is also capitalized except for prepositions (e.g., *to*, *for*, *against*), conjunctions (e.g., *and*, *but*, *or*), articles (e.g., *a*, *an*, *the*), and the "to" in an infinitive verb (e.g., *The Way to Act*). As with people's names, any accents or diacritics should be preserved (e.g., *Noûs*).

7.4.3 Numbers

When giving page ranges, always give the complete initial page number, then a hyphen or en dash (with no space on either side), and then enough of the last digits of the final page number to remove any ambiguity.[2] For instance: 46–9, 46–59, 546–9, 546–59, 546–659. However, you should always include the "1" in "teen" numbers. For instance: 546–7, but 516–17.

The page numbers of "front matter," such as a preface or introduction, often appear as lowercase Roman numerals (e.g., ii, iv, xliii). You should follow your source in this. For all other numbers in your citations (volume and issue numbers of journals, section numbers, etc.), use Arabic numerals (1, 2, 3, etc.), even if they appear otherwise in the source (e.g., in Roman numerals).

The letters in ordinal numbers (1st, 3rd, 8th, etc.) should *not* appear in superscript (e.g., 2nd), though your word processor may try to force this formatting on you.

2 We depart slightly from MLA style here for the sake of simplicity.

7.5 Common Kinds of Print Sources

7.5.1 A Continuous Book

What we'll call a **continuous book** is a stand-alone volume on a unified topic, written continuously from front to back (as opposed to a collection of independent essays). A novel is a continuous book, as are many famous books in the history of philosophy (e.g., Kant's *Critique of Pure Reason*) and many textbooks (e.g., Alyssa Ney's *Metaphysics: An Introduction*). The book you are reading right now is a continuous book by two authors. When the same book is republished with changes (e.g., to update information), it is called a new *edition* of the book. Editions are typically numbered. For instance, you are currently reading the sixth edition of *Writing Philosophy Papers*.

To include a continuous book in your list of works cited, you will need the following information:

- the author's (or authors') names,
- the title of the book,
- the publisher, and
- the year of publication.[3]

If you're using any but the first edition of the book, you'll need to know which one. If the book has a translator or editor (as historical texts often do), you'll also need that information.

The cover and title page of a book usually have much—but not all—of the information you need. Figure 7.1 shows the cover and title page of a continuous book. The title (*The Philosophy of Art*), author (Stephen Davies), and publisher (Blackwell Publishing) are all clearly laid out. For the remaining publication information, you'll have to look at the copyright page (Figure 7.2).

Copyright pages often contain a lot of potentially confusing information, but after looking at a few, you'll get used to where to look for what you need. The year of publication is pretty straightforward in this case—it appears in four different places. Sometimes, though, it will appear only once. If more than one year is given, the most recent year is usually the one you're looking for. (This is often an indication that you're using a second or later edition.)

Template and Examples

Author's Last Name, First Name. *Title*. Publisher, year.

Davies, Stephen. *The Philosophy of Art*. Blackwell Publishing, 2006.

Kant, Immanuel. *Critique of the Power of Judgment*. Translated by Paul Guyer and Eric Matthews, edited by Paul Guyer, Cambridge University Press, 2000.

Note that even if you have only read one part of a continuous book (e.g., one chapter), *you must list the book as a whole*. Do not give chapter titles or page numbers, for instance. Your in-text citations will direct your reader to the particular parts of the book that you've used.

3 In some common citation styles, such as Chicago style and earlier versions of MLA style, you also need the place of publication, typically a city and (for U.S. cities) a state.

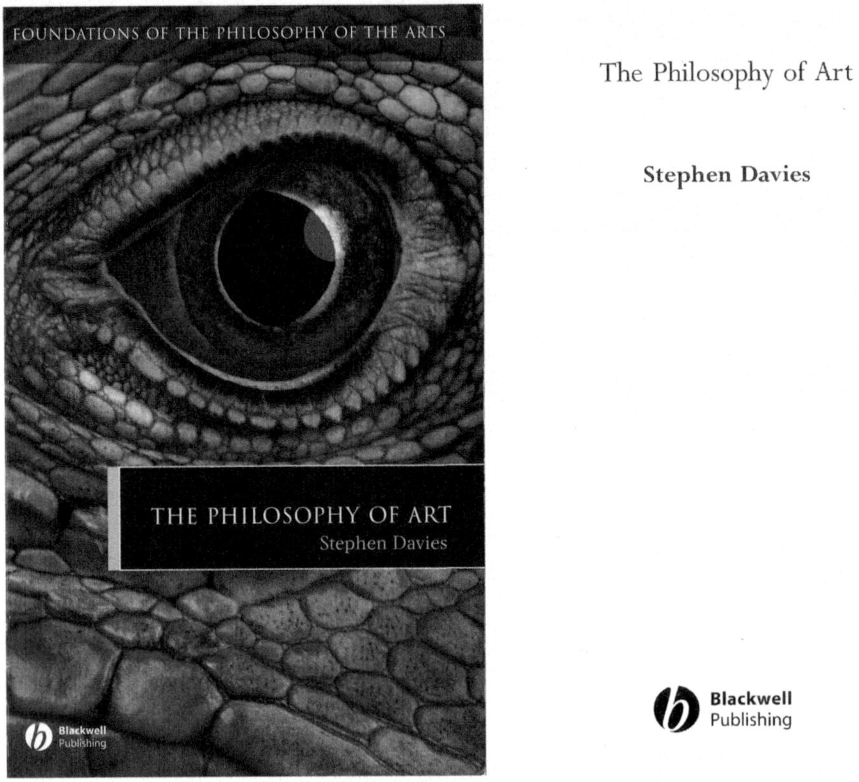

Figure 7.1 The cover and title page of a continuous book.

7.5.2 An Item in an Edited Collection

An *edited collection*, for our purposes, is a stand-alone volume that includes many essays or entries written by different people. The *editor* of such a volume is not the copy editor (who does the proofreading) but rather the person who has decided what items the book should include. Many different kinds of books are edited collections—for example, introductory anthologies (e.g., *The Norton Introduction to Philosophy*), collections of classic texts on a topic (e.g., *Metaphysics: An Anthology*), collections of new essays on a topic (e.g., *New Essays on the A Priori*), and many reference works (e.g., *The Routledge Companion to Philosophy and Music*). Just as a book may have more than one author, a collection may have more than one editor, and the editors' names typically appear on the book's cover. You will almost always be citing a particular **item in an edited collection** rather than the collection as a whole. You thus need two sets of information to include such an item in your list of works cited:

1. information about the individual item:
   - author(s),
   - title, and
   - page range; and

© 2006 by Stephen Davies

BLACKWELL PUBLISHING
350 Main Street, Malden, MA 02148-5020, USA
9600 Garsington Road, Oxford OX4 2DQ, UK
550 Swanston Street, Carlton, Victoria 3053, Australia

The right of Stephen Davies to be identified as the Author of this Work has been asserted in accordance with the UK Copyright, Designs, and Patents Act 1988.

All rights reserved. No part of this publication may be reproduced, stored in a retrieval system, or transmitted, in any form or by any means, electronic, mechanical, photocopying, recording or otherwise, except as permitted by the UK Copyright, Designs, and Patents Act 1988, without the prior permission of the publisher.

First published 2006 by Blackwell Publishing Ltd

1 2006

Library of Congress Cataloging-in-Publication Data

Davies, Stephen, 1950–
The philosophy of art / Stephen Davies.
p. cm.—(Foundations of the philosophy of the arts)
Includes index.
ISBN-13: 978-1-4051-2022-7 (alk. paper)
ISBN-10: 1-4051-2022-3 (alk. paper)
ISBN-13: 978-1-4051-2023-4 (pbk. : alk. paper)
ISBN-10: 1-4051-2023-1 (pbk. : alk. paper) 1. Art—Philosophy. 2. Aesthetics. I. Title. II. Series.

N66 D32 2006
701—dc22

2005010994

A catalogue record for this title is available from the British Library.

Set in 11.5pt Perpetua
by SPI Publisher Services, Pondicherry, India
Printed and bound in Great Britain
by TJ International Ltd, Padstow, Cornwall

The publisher's policy is to use permanent paper from mills that operate a sustainable forestry policy, and which has been manufactured from pulp processed using acid-free and elementary chlorine-free practices. Furthermore, the publisher ensures that the text paper and cover board used have met acceptable environmental accreditation standards.

For further information on
Blackwell Publishing, visit our website:
www.blackwellpublishing.com

Figure 7.2 The copyright page of the same book.

2. information about the collection as a whole:
   - title,
   - editor(s),
   - publisher, and
   - year of publication.

If you're using any but the first edition of the book, you'll need to know the edition number.

The author, title, and page range of the item should be clear from the item itself. In Figure 7.3, you can see the author and title of the item (Quayshawn Spencer, "Are Folk Races Like Dingoes, Dimes, or Dodos?") and that it runs from pages 571 to 578.

As with a continuous book, the cover and title page of an edited collection usually have much of the information you need about the collection as a whole. In Figure 7.4, you can see the title (*The Norton Introduction to Philosophy*), editors (Gideon Rosen, Alex Byrne, Joshua Cohen, Elizabeth Harman, and Seana Shiffrin), and publisher (W. W. Norton and Company), as well as that this is the second edition of the book. For

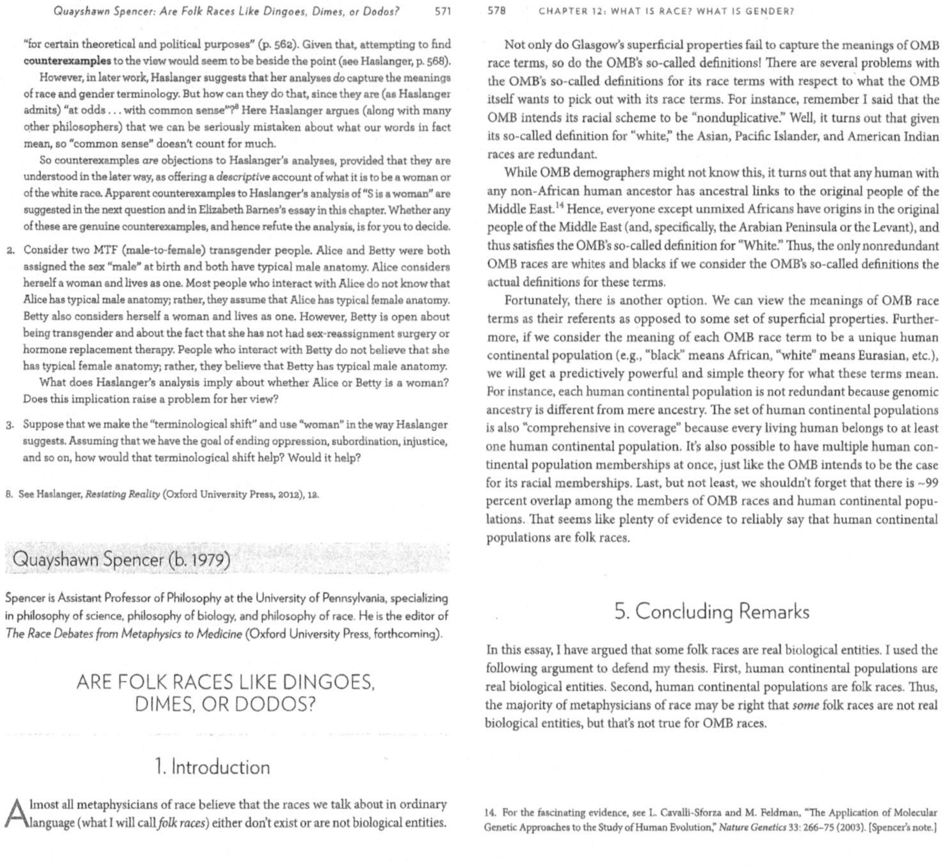

Quayshawn Spencer: Are Folk Races Like Dingoes, Dimes, or Dodos? 571

"for certain theoretical and political purposes" (p. 562). Given that, attempting to find **counterexamples** to the view would seem to be beside the point (see Haslanger, p. 568).

However, in later work, Haslanger suggests that her analyses *do* capture the meanings of race and gender terminology. But how can they do that, since they are (as Haslanger admits) "at odds . . . with common sense"?[8] Here Haslanger argues (along with many other philosophers) that we can be seriously mistaken about what our words in fact mean, so "common sense" doesn't count for much.

So counterexamples *are* objections to Haslanger's analyses, provided that they are understood in the later way, as offering a *descriptive* account of what it is to be a woman or of the white race. Apparent counterexamples to Haslanger's analysis of "S is a woman" are suggested in the next question and in Elizabeth Barnes's essay in this chapter. Whether any of these are genuine counterexamples, and hence refute the analysis, is for you to decide.

2. Consider two MTF (male-to-female) transgender people. Alice and Betty were both assigned the sex "male" at birth and both have typical male anatomy. Alice considers herself a woman and lives as one. Most people who interact with Alice do not know that Alice has typical male anatomy; rather, they assume that Alice has typical female anatomy. Betty also considers herself a woman and lives as one. However, Betty is open about being transgender and about the fact that she has not had sex-reassignment surgery or hormone replacement therapy. People who interact with Betty do not believe that she has typical female anatomy; rather, they believe that Betty has typical male anatomy.

   What does Haslanger's analysis imply about whether Alice or Betty is a woman? Does this implication raise a problem for her view?

3. Suppose that we make the "terminological shift" and use "woman" in the way Haslanger suggests. Assuming that we have the goal of ending oppression, subordination, injustice, and so on, how would that terminological shift help? Would it help?

8. See Haslanger, *Resisting Reality* (Oxford University Press, 2012), 12.

Quayshawn Spencer (b. 1979)

Spencer is Assistant Professor of Philosophy at the University of Pennsylvania, specializing in philosophy of science, philosophy of biology, and philosophy of race. He is the editor of *The Race Debates from Metaphysics to Medicine* (Oxford University Press, forthcoming).

ARE FOLK RACES LIKE DINGOES, DIMES, OR DODOS?

1. Introduction

Almost all metaphysicians of race believe that the races we talk about in ordinary language (what I will call *folk races*) either don't exist or are not biological entities.

578 CHAPTER 12: WHAT IS RACE? WHAT IS GENDER?

Not only do Glasgow's superficial properties fail to capture the meanings of OMB race terms, so do the OMB's so-called definitions! There are several problems with the OMB's so-called definitions for its race terms with respect to what the OMB itself wants to pick out with its race terms. For instance, remember I said that the OMB intends its racial scheme to be "nonduplicative." Well, it turns out that given its so-called definition for "white," the Asian, Pacific Islander, and American Indian races are redundant.

While OMB demographers might not know this, it turns out that any human with any non-African human ancestor has ancestral links to the original people of the Middle East.[14] Hence, everyone except unmixed Africans have origins in the original people of the Middle East (and, specifically, the Arabian Peninsula or the Levant), and thus satisfies the OMB's so-called definition for "White." Thus, the only nonredundant OMB races are whites and blacks if we consider the OMB's so-called definitions the actual definitions for these terms.

Fortunately, there is another option. We can view the meanings of OMB race terms as their referents as opposed to some set of superficial properties. Furthermore, if we consider the meaning of each OMB race term to be a unique human continental population (e.g., "black" means African, "white" means Eurasian, etc.), we will get a predictively powerful and simple theory for what these terms mean. For instance, each human continental population is not redundant because genomic ancestry is different from mere ancestry. The set of human continental populations is also "comprehensive in coverage" because every living human belongs to at least one human continental population. It's also possible to have multiple human continental population memberships at once, just like the OMB intends to be the case for its racial memberships. Last, but not least, we shouldn't forget that there is ~99 percent overlap among the members of OMB races and human continental populations. That seems like plenty of evidence to reliably say that human continental populations are folk races.

5. Concluding Remarks

In this essay, I have argued that some folk races are real biological entities. I used the following argument to defend my thesis. First, human continental populations are real biological entities. Second, human continental populations are folk races. Thus, the majority of metaphysicians of race may be right that *some* folk races are not real biological entities, but that's not true for OMB races.

14. For the fascinating evidence, see L. Cavalli-Sforza and M. Feldman, "The Application of Molecular Genetic Approaches to the Study of Human Evolution," *Nature Genetics* 33: 266–75 (2003). [Spencer's note.]

Figure 7.3 The first and last pages of an item in an edited collection.

the final piece of information you need (the year of publication), you'll again have to look at the copyright page (Figure 7.5).

Again, the copyright page has a lot of potentially confusing information. For one thing, it explicitly lists Ken Barton as the editor. But don't be fooled! It's very clear from the cover and title page that the editors—in the relevant sense—of this collection are the five people listed there. (Ken Barton, like the other people listed here, is a member of the production staff.) As for the publication year, there are two candidates: 2018 and 2015. Following our guideline (§7.5.1), you should use the most recent year. (2015 is listed because it is when the first edition was published.)

Many items in edited collections have been previously published elsewhere. Editors republish them because they think such items are worth sharing with a different audience. As good scholars, they indicate where the piece was originally published (e.g., in a different book or a scholarly journal). You might be tempted to use *this* information when citing the item in your own work—but that would be a mistake. You must cite the source *you* have read. One reason is that when an item is republished in an edited collection, it is often shortened or updated in various ways. So the ideas or words you're citing may not occur in the original publication. Another reason is that the page numbers you use in your in-text citations to point your reader to a particular passage will be the pages of the edited collection—not those of wherever the item was originally published. So your

The Norton Introduction to

PHILOSOPHY

Second Edition

GIDEON ROSEN
Princeton University

ALEX BYRNE
Massachusetts Institute of Technology

JOSHUA COHEN
Apple University; University of California, Berkeley

ELIZABETH HARMAN
Princeton University

SEANA SHIFFRIN
University of California, Los Angeles

W. W. NORTON & COMPANY, INC.
New York • London

Figure 7.4 The cover and title page of the same edited collection.

W. W. Norton & Company has been independent since its founding in 1923, when William Warder Norton and Mary D. Herter Norton first published lectures delivered at the People's Institute, the adult education division of New York City's Cooper Union. The firm soon expanded its program beyond the Institute, publishing books by celebrated academics from America and abroad. By midcentury, the two major pillars of Norton's publishing program—trade books and college texts—were firmly established. In the 1950s, the Norton family transferred control of the company to its employees, and today—with a staff of four hundred and a comparable number of trade, college, and professional titles published each year—W. W. Norton & Company stands as the largest and oldest publishing house owned wholly by its employees.

Copyright © 2018, 2015 by W. W. Norton & Company, Inc.
All rights reserved
Printed in the United States of America

Editor: Ken Barton
Assistant Editor: Shannon Jilek
Project Editor: Sujin Hong
Managing Editor, College Digital Media: Kim Yi
Production Manager: Eric Pier-Hocking
Media Editor: Erica Wnek
Media Assistant Editor: Ava Bramson
Marketing Manager, Philosophy: Michael Moss
Design Director: Hope Miller Goodell
Permissions Associate: Elizabeth Trammell
Permissions Manager: Megan Schindel
Composition: S4Carlisle Publishing Services
Manufacturing: LSC Communications—Crawfordsville

Permission to use copyrighted material is included in the Credits.

ISBN 978-0-393-62442-7

W. W. Norton & Company, Inc., 500 Fifth Avenue, New York, NY 10110
wwnorton.com

W. W. Norton & Company Ltd., 15 Carlisle Street, London W1D 3BS
1 2 3 4 5 6 7 8 9 0

Figure 7.5 The copyright page of the same edited collection.

reader will be unable to follow up your citations unless you cite the particular source you have read.

Template and Examples

Author's Last Name, First Name. "Item Title." *Collection Title*, **edited by** Editor's Name, Publisher, year, **pp.** item page range.

Spencer, Quayshawn. "Are Folk Races Like Dingoes, Dimes, or Dodos?" *The Norton Introduction to Philosophy*, edited by Gideon Rosen et al., 2nd ed., W. W. Norton and Company, 2018, pp. 571–78.

(In the example above, the question mark that ends the title of the item replaces the more usual period.)

Nicholls, Moira. "The Influences of Eastern Thought on Schopenhauer's Doctrine of the Thing-in-Itself." *The Cambridge Companion to Schopenhauer*, edited by Christopher Janaway, Cambridge University Press, 1999, pp. 171–212.

7.5.3 A Journal Article

Periodicals are published in *issues* or *numbers* that appear "periodically"—that is, at regular intervals (e.g., weekly or monthly). Newspapers and magazines are thus periodicals, and philosophy papers in areas such as practical ethics or public policy may cite these kinds of periodicals as sources. *Scholarly journals* (which we'll simply call *journals*) are periodicals containing articles by professional scholars whose primary audience is other scholars in their field. In addition to "regular" articles, journals may contain short "discussion" pieces on articles recently published in the same journal, reviews of books recently published in the field, and "symposia" or other collections of articles on a specific topic. Philosophy journals are often published in monthly or quarterly issues. Each issue is nominally part of a "volume" (usually a year's worth of issues) since, in the old days, libraries would physically bind a year's worth of issues into a single volume. As a result, the page numbers of journals often run continuously from one issue to another within a single year. (This convention persists even though few libraries still keep physical copies of journals.)

You will almost always be citing a **journal article**, not the journal as a whole, nor even a whole volume or issue. To include a journal article in your list of works cited, you'll need:

1. the title of the journal;
2. information about the article:
    - author(s),
    - title, and
    - page range; and
3. information about the particular issue in which the article appears:
    - volume number,
    - issue number (if applicable), and
    - date.

The date will include at least a year (for the volume). It will often (but not always) include a season or month (for the issue). Seasons are formatted in lowercase (e.g., "spring 2016"). Months are capitalized but abbreviated (except for May, June, and July) (e.g., "Mar. 1983").

When you access a journal article, you won't usually find a cover, title page, or copyright page. Fortunately, all the information you're looking for should appear on the first and last pages of the article. In the example in Figure 7.6, for instance, the title of the article ("Real Talk on the Metaphysics of Gender") is in the largest font, and the author's name (Robin Dembroff) appears below it. (In some journals, the author's name appears at the end of the article.) For the page range, you just need to note the numbers of the first and last pages of the article.

All the other information you need is in the top left corner of the page (in this example): journal title (*Philosophical Topics*), volume and issue number (46, 2), and date of publication (fall 2018). In some journals, the volume and issue number will be less explicitly labeled, appearing in something like one of the following formats: 46.2, 46(2), or 46/2. They may also appear as Roman numerals, as with the volume number in Figure 7.7.

PHILOSOPHICAL TOPICS
VOL. 46, NO. 2, FALL 2018

Real Talk on the Metaphysics of Gender

Robin Dembroff
Yale University

ABSTRACT. Gender classifications often are controversial. These controversies typically focus on whether gender classifications align with facts about gender kind membership: *Could someone really be nonbinary? Is Chris Mosier (a trans man) really a man?* I think this is a bad approach. Consider the possibility of ontological oppression, which arises when social kinds operating in a context unjustly constrain the behaviors, con**cepts, or affect of certain groups. Gender kinds operating in dominant** contexts, I argue, oppress trans and nonbinary persons in this way: they marginalize trans men and women, and exclude nonbinary persons. As a result, facts about membership in dominant gender kinds should not **settle gender classification practices.**

1. INTRODUCTION

In 2016, North Carolina embroiled itself in controversy by passing the "Public Facilities Privacy and Security Act." According to this law, someone could not legally enter a men's restroom or locker room unless they were assigned the sex *male* at birth, nor could they legally enter a women's restroom or locker room

21

Figure 7.6 The first page of a journal article.

Philosophy and
Phenomenological Research

Philosophy and Phenomenological Research
Vol. XCV No. 2, September 2017
doi: 10.1111/phpr.12273
© 2016 Philosophy and Phenomenological Research, LLC

How Is Wishful Seeing Like
Wishful Thinking?

SUSANNA SIEGEL
Harvard University

Figure 7.7 From the first page of a journal article.

Notice also that in the example in Figure 7.7, the copyright year is different from the volume year. You should use the volume year in such cases.

Sometimes, frustratingly, the information you need is not included in the article or is impossible to understand unless you are intimately familiar with the journal in question. In such cases, you should look up the article in a scholarly database for the information you need. We discuss how to do this in Sections 9.3.2 and 9.4.2.

Template and Examples

Author's Last Name, First Name. "Article Title." *Journal Title*, **vol.** volume number, **no.** issue number, month or season (if applicable) year, **pp.** article page range.

Dembroff, Robin. "Real Talk on the Metaphysics of Gender." *Philosophical Topics*, vol. 46, no. 2, fall 2018, pp. 21–50.

Siegel, Susanna. "How Is Wishful Seeing Like Wishful Thinking?" *Philosophy and Phenomenological Research*, vol. 95, no. 2, Sept. 2017, pp. 408–35.

7.6 Common Kinds of Online-Only Sources

Scholarly conventions for citing sources were developed long before the internet existed and were refined over many years; the conventions for citing online sources are recent and rapidly evolving. For instance, until quite recently there was a convention to include in your list of works cited the date you accessed an online source. The reasoning was that material on the web is constantly subject to change. But the current convention is to include this date only for sources that have no publication date or are likely to change (e.g., *Wikipedia* entries) and to omit it for sources that are relatively stable (e.g., online journals and reference works). Since citation systems are constantly playing catch-up with developing technology, you may have to use your judgment in citing new kinds of sources. You should be guided by the basic principle that the purpose of your citation is to enable your reader to locate the source you are citing.

One thing you will need in order to cite any source that is available *only* online is a **persistent identifier.** This is a piece of information that will point your reader (or her web browser) to the particular item you are citing. The two most widely used kinds of persistent identifiers are URLs (Uniform Resource Locators, commonly known as web addresses) and, more recently, DOIs (Digital Object Identifiers). If you include a URL in your citation, these guidelines should help you make sure you use the right one:

1. If the item you are citing is open-access—that is, freely available to anyone with an internet connection (not only to those with a subscription)—make sure you supply the URL for the *particular item* you are citing (e.g., an *article* in a journal, rather than the journal as a whole). For instance, the URL for the sample entry in an online-only reference work that we discuss below is https://plato.stanford.edu/archives/win2023/entries/faith. You can often simply copy this information from the address bar of your browser while you are at the site. Beware of three common pitfalls, however:
   a. First, be sure not to give the URL for the home page of the entire work (e.g., https://plato.stanford.edu/).
   b. Second, do not accidentally give the URL for one particular part of an entry. This can happen when you've used internal links to navigate the entry. You haven't ended up on a different webpage, but the URL in your browser address bar has changed (e.g., https://plato.stanford.edu/entries/faith/#FaiDoxVen). If you use this URL, then when your reader clicks on the link to follow up your citation, she will be plunged into the middle of the article rather than taken to the beginning.
   c. Third, the address in your browser may be a generic one rather than the address of the particular version of the item you are citing. For instance, the URL https://plato.stanford.edu/entries/faith/ will take your reader to the *current* version of that entry, which may be substantially different from the version you used as a source. In such cases, there should be information on the page about how to cite the particular version. In this case, you have to click the "Author and Citation Info" link, as we discuss below.
2. If the item you are citing is *not* open-access, you *should* use the URL of the (openly accessible) home page of the entire work (e.g., www.rep.routledge.com). This lets your reader see where you found this source and to proceed to it if she has access to the work, yet prevents her from immediately hitting an error page or paywall if she doesn't have access to it. Note that if you have accessed a source while logged into your library's resources, it may only be available to you because your library has a subscription.

What about a source that is available in print but which you accessed online, such as a PDF of a journal article you found in a database (e.g., *JSTOR*)? You should be guided by the principle that your citation should indicate *the kind of source* you are citing, not *how you accessed it.* On that basis, we recommend the following general guidelines. (As always, your instructor's requirements trump anything we say here.)

1. Do not use labels such as "print," "web," or "online" in your list of works cited. This adds no information to the citation that will help your reader locate the item.
2. If a source is available *both* online *and* in print (e.g., it's a journal article with page numbers), you should cite it as a print source, however you accessed it. Do not include

(for example) the URL of the site where you accessed it (e.g., *JSTOR*).[4] (You may include the DOI, if there is one, since this may help your reader locate your source.)

3. If a source is *only* available online (e.g., a blog or an online encyclopedia), your citation must include a persistent identifier, such as a URL or DOI. If you are submitting your paper electronically, this identifier should be a clickable link. (Make sure you test the link before submitting your paper.)

One situation can cause problems for following the second guideline: You may need to cite a source that you have access to only as an electronic document (e.g., a PDF) but which is clearly taken from a print source (e.g., it's been scanned from a book), yet doesn't contain enough information to construct a complete citation (e.g., it doesn't include the copyright page). In such cases, you should do your best to find the missing information. If your instructor supplied you with the source, ask her for the relevant information. Alternatively, you may have enough information to be able to find the rest using the resources we discuss in Sections 9.3.2–9.3.3. If all else fails, you can indicate where online you found the source and add a note explaining the problem.

7.6.1 An Entry in an Online-Only Reference Work

A *reference work* provides short introductions to topics. Some are written by a single person (or small team), but they are typically collections of specially commissioned pieces by many different authors. You will almost certainly be citing a particular entry in such a work rather than the work as a whole. Such an entry is essentially an item in an edited collection. To cite an entry in a *print* reference work, then, you can follow the guidelines in Section 7.5.2. But many useful philosophical reference works are available only online (e.g., the *Stanford Encyclopedia of Philosophy*, the *Internet Encyclopedia of Philosophy*, and recent editions of the *Routledge Encyclopedia of Philosophy*). To cite an **entry in an online-only reference work**, you won't need the page range of the item (because there isn't one), but you will need all the other information for an item in an edited collection, plus a persistent identifier (URL or DOI). That is, you'll need:

1. information about the individual item:
    - author(s),
    - title, and
    - persistent identifier; and
2. information about the collection as a whole:
    - title,
    - editor(s),
    - publisher, and
    - date of publication.

4 This is where we depart furthest from official MLA style. The MLA makes a very useful distinction between "containers" of sources (e.g., a journal or edited collection) and mere modes of access to sources (e.g., a course management system, such as Blackboard or Canvas). But where the MLA considers a database such as *JSTOR* to be a container, we believe it is better considered a mode of access.

In online reference works, sometimes the date of publication will be of the entry rather than the whole work, but that doesn't affect where the date goes in your citation. If there is no date of publication (as is currently the case with the *Internet Encyclopedia of Philosophy*, for example), you should record the date you accessed the entry. As with other kinds of sources, if there's more than one edition (as there is for the *Stanford Encyclopedia of Philosophy*), you'll need to know which one you're using.

Figure 7.8 shows the top and bottom of an entry in an online-only reference work. The titles of both the work (*Stanford Encyclopedia of Philosophy*) and the entry ("Faith"), along with the date of the most recent "substantive revision" (December 9, 2023), are clearly shown at the top, and the authors (John Bishop and Daniel J. McKaughan) at the bottom.

Like many others, this online-only reference work has a handy "Author and Citation Info" link on the left of the page. If you click on this, you'll get the following useful information:

> Bishop, John and Daniel J. McKaughan, "Faith", *The Stanford Encyclopedia of Philosophy* (Winter 2023 Edition), Edward N. Zalta & Uri Nodelman (eds.), URL https://plato.stanford.edu/archives/win2023/entries/faith/.

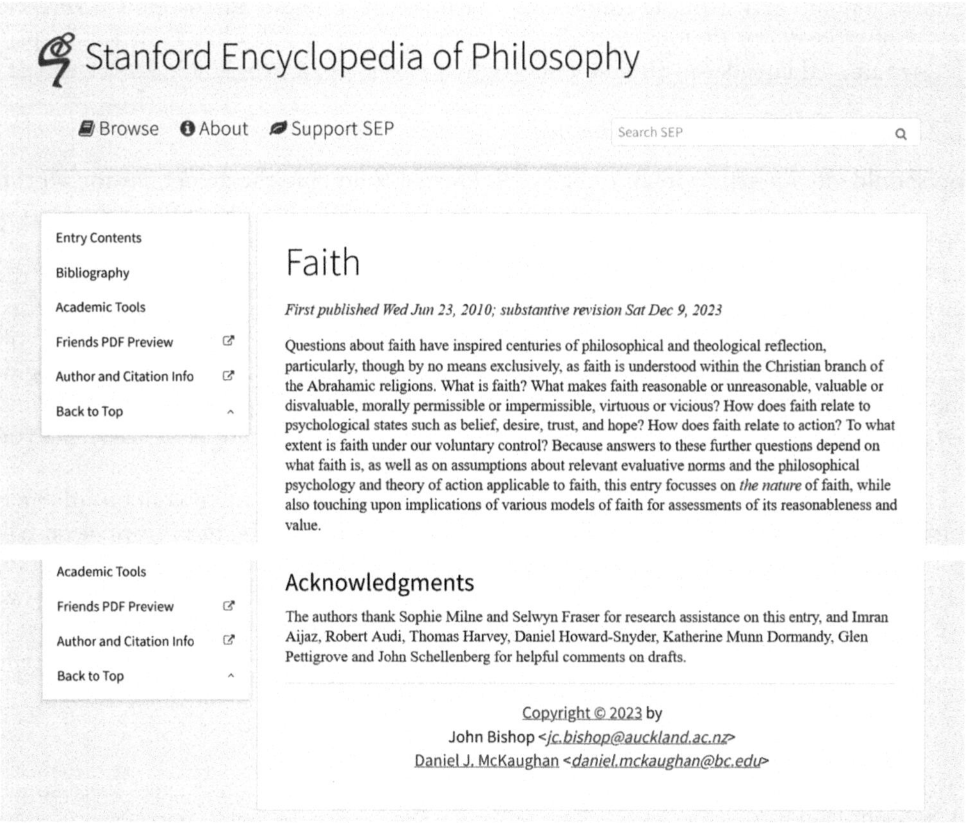

Figure 7.8 The top and bottom of an entry in an online-only reference work.

This contains all the information you'll need to construct a full bibliographic reference—but do not simply copy and paste it into your list of works cited! It is not formatted according to any of the standard citation systems for philosophy. Note also that the date given here (winter 2023) is different from the one at the top of the entry. Since this is the official citation information, we consider this the publication date. (As it happens, entries in the *Stanford Encyclopedia of Philosophy* are often revised between "substantive" revisions. So the edition you're using and citing may well be different from the most recent substantive revision.)

Template and Examples

Author's Last Name, First Name. "Entry Title." *Reference-Work Title*, **edited by** Editor's Name, edition, publication date (if available), persistent identifier, date accessed (if no publication date).

Bishop, John and Daniel J. McKaughan. "Faith." *The Stanford Encyclopedia of Philosophy*, edited by Edward N. Zalta and Uri Nodelman, winter 2023 ed., https://plato.stanford.edu/archives/win2023/entries/faith.

(Because editions of the *Stanford Encyclopedia of Philosophy* are identified by date, there is no need to supply a separate publication date.)

Shen, Lijuan and Paul D'Ambrosio. "Gender in Chinese Philosophy." *Internet Encyclopedia of Philosophy*, edited by James Fieser and Bradley Dowden, https://iep.utm.edu/gender-in-chinese-philosophy/. Accessed 28 Feb. 2023.

7.6.2 An Article in an Online-Only Journal

You should cite an article in an online-only journal following the guidelines for a print journal article in Section 7.5.3, departing where necessary for the peculiarities of the particular journal and supplying a persistent identifier (URL or DOI).

Figure 7.9 shows the beginning of an article in an online-only journal. The titles of the journal (*Contemporary Aesthetics*) and article ("Aesthetics from the Visual Artists' Viewpoint") are clearly indicated, as is the author's name (Dena Shottenkirk).[5] The volume number could be more clearly indicated, but clicking on the words in the line beginning "Volume" clarifies that this article is indeed in volume 19, published in 2021, and that the volumes of this journal are not divided into issues. There is no DOI, so you should copy the URL from your browser's address bar.

Like online-only reference works, online-only journal articles often contain information on how they should be cited. But, as with the reference works, this information will probably not be formatted according to the citation system you are using. (See Figure 7.10, for example.) So be sure to reformat the information according to the guidelines we give in this section. (In this case, notice that only the initial of the author's first name is supplied. But the author publishes using her full first name, as is clear from the article itself.)

5 The title of this article appears to contain a punctuation error: It should read "... the Visual Artist's Viewpoint." In such cases, you can include the title as it actually appears or silently correct the error, as we have done in our sample citation.

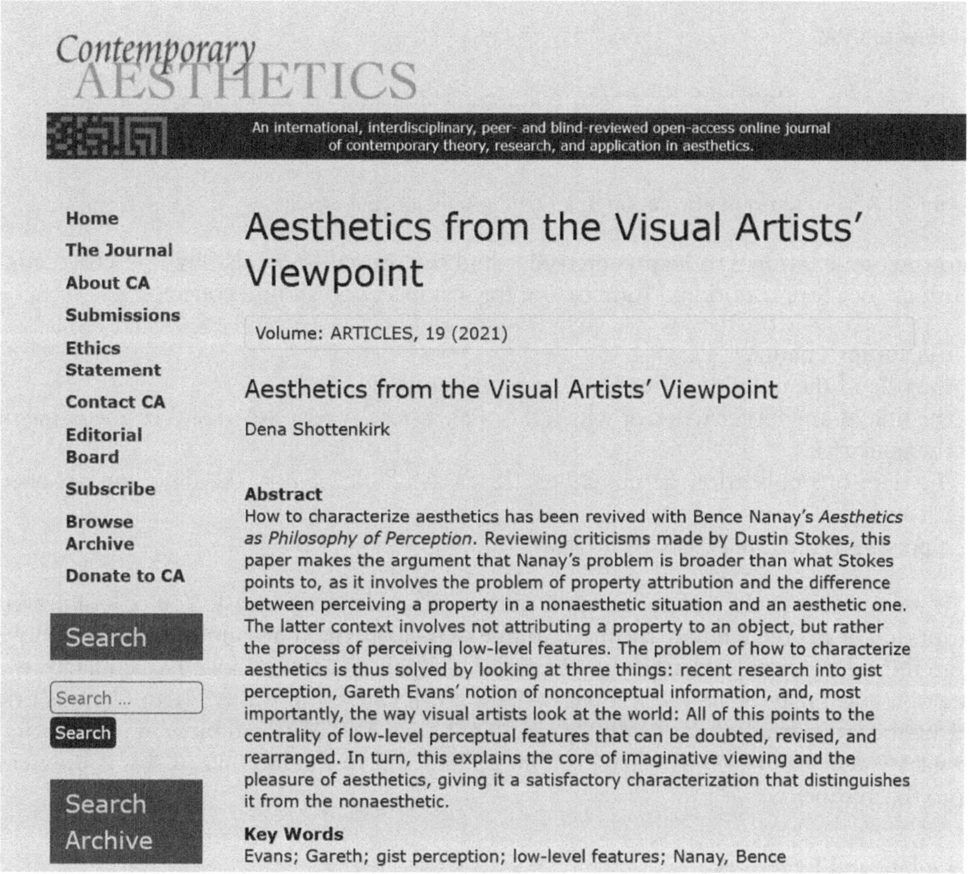

Contemporary
AESTHETICS

An international, interdisciplinary, peer- and blind-reviewed open-access online journal of contemporary theory, research, and application in aesthetics.

Home
The Journal
About CA
Submissions
Ethics Statement
Contact CA
Editorial Board
Subscribe
Browse Archive
Donate to CA

Search

Search ...

Search

Search Archive

Aesthetics from the Visual Artists' Viewpoint

Volume: ARTICLES, 19 (2021)

Aesthetics from the Visual Artists' Viewpoint

Dena Shottenkirk

Abstract
How to characterize aesthetics has been revived with Bence Nanay's *Aesthetics as Philosophy of Perception*. Reviewing criticisms made by Dustin Stokes, this paper makes the argument that Nanay's problem is broader than what Stokes points to, as it involves the problem of property attribution and the difference between perceiving a property in a nonaesthetic situation and an aesthetic one. The latter context involves not attributing a property to an object, but rather the process of perceiving low-level features. The problem of how to characterize aesthetics is thus solved by looking at three things: recent research into gist perception, Gareth Evans' notion of nonconceptual information, and, most importantly, the way visual artists look at the world: All of this points to the centrality of low-level perceptual features that can be doubted, revised, and rearranged. In turn, this explains the core of imaginative viewing and the pleasure of aesthetics, giving it a satisfactory characterization that distinguishes it from the nonaesthetic.

Key Words
Evans; Gareth; gist perception; low-level features; Nanay, Bence

Figure 7.9 The beginning of an article in an online-only journal.

Template and Examples

Author's Last Name, First Name. "Article Title." *Journal Title*, **vol.** volume number, **no.** issue number, year, persistent identifier.

Shottenkirk, Dena. "Aesthetics from the Visual Artist's Viewpoint." *Contemporary Aesthetics*, vol. 19, 2021, https://contempaesthetics.org/2021/03/04/aesthetics-from-the-visual-artists-viewpoint/.

De Toffoli, Silvia. "Who's Afraid of Mathematical Diagrams?" *Philosophers' Imprint*, vol. 23, no. 9, 2023, https://doi.org/10.3998/phimp.1348.

7.6.3 An Online Video or Podcast

The conventions for citing "digitally native" sources, such as a video on a website (e.g., YouTube) or a podcast episode, are still evolving. You should be guided, as always, by the

How to Cite:

De Toffoli, S., (2023) "Who's Afraid of Mathematical Diagrams?", ***Philosophers' Imprint*** 23: 9. doi: https://doi.org/10.3998/phimp.1348

Figure 7.10 The citation information in an online-only journal article.

purpose of a citation—to help your reader find the source—and also by the settled conventions for more traditional sources. So, for instance, you should collect:

- the author's name,
- the title of the individual item (e.g., video or episode),
- the title of any larger work of which it is a part (e.g., a series of videos or the name of the podcast),
- the date of publication or uploading (if it's available; if not, the date you accessed it), and
- a persistent identifier (usually a URL).

It's sometimes tricky to figure out the author of a video or podcast. You're looking for the person or people who are the main source of the content. This might be more obvious from the video or podcast itself than from the webpage where it is located. Similarly, the title of a video may be on the webpage where it is located, but if there is an obvious title within the video itself, that's probably a better choice. An additional piece of information about a video that you might need is who uploaded it to the internet (if this is different from the author).

Template and Examples

Author's Last Name, First Name. "Item Title." Channel or Series Title, episode number, publication date, persistent identifier.

Kim, Hannah, and Brandon Polite. "Korean Aesthetics: Past, Present, and Future." *Philosophers Discussing Art*, episode 26, 7 April 2022, https://www.youtube.com/watch?v=Zd_93PfrYag.

Chambers, Clare and David Edmonds. "Clare Chambers on the Unmodified Body." *Philosophy Bites*, 1 July 2022, https://philosophybites.com/2022/07/clare-chambers-on-the-unmodified-body.html.

7.7 In-Text Citations

7.7.1 The Basics

An in-text citation in MLA style appears in parentheses, usually right after the closing quotation mark (if you're citing a quotation) or right before the period at the end of a sentence (in most other cases). It includes the minimum amount of information necessary for your reader to identify (1) which particular source in your list of works cited you're citing and (2) where precisely in that source the specific material you're citing occurs. This means that in-text citations can look somewhat different, depending on their contexts. Consider the following examples:

(a) Davies considers a further argument that photographs are representations (186–8).

(b) Here is another argument that photographs are representations (Davies 186–8).

(c) Here is another argument that photographs are representations (Davies, *Philosophy of Art* 186–8).

All these examples cite the same part of the same source. So why are they all different? First, note that they are all the same in including the specific page range (186–8) where the argument being cited occurs. The differences are in how the author directs the reader to the source in the list of works cited that contains these pages. Because the list of works cited is arranged alphabetically by author's last name, the reader needs the author's last name to find the item. In example (a), the author's last name occurs unambiguously in the same sentence as the parenthetical citation, so it doesn't need to be included in the citation. In example (b), the author's name doesn't appear in the sentence, so it does need to be included in the citation. (Note that there is no punctuation inside the parentheses.)

Example (c) adds the **short-form title** of the source to the citation. This is necessary if there is **more than one item by the same author** in the list of works cited. Otherwise, the reader won't know which source by that author is being cited. (Note the comma between the author's name and the short-form title.) The short-form title is a single short phrase that captures the essence of the title. If the title is already short, as in the example above, just use the full title, dropping any initial article (e.g., *A*, *An*, *The*). There is no rule for generating every short-form title; just aim for a short phrase that includes the most important words from the full title. Below are some examples.

Full title	*Short-form title*
"Faith"	"Faith"
The Philosophy of Art	*Philosophy of Art*
"Korean Aesthetics: Past, Present, and Future"	"Korean Aesthetics"
"Are Folk Races Like Dingoes, Dimes, or Dodos?"	"Folk Races"

Consider two more sample citations of the same material:

(d) Here is another argument that photographs are representations (S. Davies 186–8).

(e) Here is another argument that photographs are representations (S. Davies, *Philosophy of Art* 186–8).

In example (d), the initial of the author's first name has been added to the citation. This is necessary if your list of works cited contains sources by **two authors with the same last name.** In example (e), the short-form title has been added since the list of works cited contains not only a source by a different Davies (hence the first initial) but also **more than one source by the same author** (hence the title of the source).

7.7.2 Citing More than One Source

If you need to cite two sources in a single in-text citation, simply separate them with a semicolon:

(f) There are five such human continental populations (Rosen et al. 544–45; Spencer 575).

If two in-text citations relate to different parts of a single sentence, place each at the end of the text expressing the idea cited and before any punctuation (e.g., comma or semicolon) separating that text from the rest of the sentence—but never inside quotation marks:

(g) There are five such human continental populations (Spencer 575), complicating claims that race is a "biological fiction" (Haslanger 43).

If a source has no page numbers (as is commonly the case with online-only sources), use some other division of the source if it will enable your reader to easily locate the particular material you're citing. For instance, many articles in online journals and reference works are divided into sections (see example (h)); for videos and podcasts, you can provide a "time stamp" (see example (i)):

(h) Several philosophers have argued that faith does not require belief (Bishop and McKaughan §8).[6]

(i) Kim points out that this argument is very similar to European notions of "art for art's sake" (Kim and Polite 9:30–10:33).

7.7.3 Some Complications in Citing Quotations

The only difference in formatting a citation for a **block quotation** is that the citation comes *after* the final period and is separated from it by a space. (See the example in §7.3.1.)

You may find yourself **quoting a quotation.** That is, a source you have read (X) quotes from another source (Y) that you have not read. You want to use the words quoted from Y. How do you cite them? You need to cite the text you have read (X) but indicate that the words you've quoted are a quotation within X from another source. You do this by adding the abbreviation "qtd. in" (short for "quoted in") in your citation. For instance,

6 Official MLA style requires a comma after the author's name in this example since there is a symbol between that name and the section number. We think this unnecessarily complicates the system, and thus omit such commas.

suppose you have read a text by Bertrand Russell in which he quotes Julian Huxley, and you want to use those quoted words of Huxley's. You would indicate this as follows:

(j) Julian Huxley claims that the mind–body problem must be approached from what he calls "the evolutionary angle" (qtd. in Russell 249).

Note that to cite a text of Huxley's in the above context would technically be plagiarism, since that would imply that you have read the Huxley text that Russell quotes. Among other things, indicating that you're quoting a quotation absolves you of any responsibility for errors that the quoter (in this case, Russell) might have made.

7.7.4 Citing an Entire Source

We have emphasized the importance of including an in-text citation with a page number (or small page range) for every idea you've taken from a published source. But sometimes you may need to cite an entire source. This can be done without a parenthetical citation. Consider the following sentence:

(k) Quayshawn Spencer argues that some folk races, at least, are biologically real.

If there is only one source by Spencer in the list of works cited, using his name clearly directs the reader to that source. So this counts as a citation. If you don't use the author's name in the sentence, you can refer to an entire source in a parenthetical citation, as follows:

(l) At least one philosopher argues that *some* folk races are biologically real (Spencer).

However, although examples (k) and (l) are acceptable, we still encourage you to provide a specific page number (or small page range) if you can. Even if these sentences are intended to summarize the thesis of the entire source cited, there is probably a particular page on which the author expresses this thesis. Providing that page number in a citation may well help your reader locate the idea in the source.

8 Taking Notes and Writing Shorter Papers

Thesis-defense papers allow you to demonstrate the sorts of reasoning skills that are at the heart of philosophy. But they are not the only kind of written work assigned in philosophy courses. It would be impossible to cover in this short book the huge variety of written work assigned in philosophy courses, but in this chapter and the next, we examine a few other common kinds of assignments. In this chapter, we discuss three kinds of papers that are often relatively short: **summary papers**, **response papers**, and **compare-and-contrast papers**. In the next chapter, we discuss **annotated bibliographies** and **research papers**.

Much of the material we've covered in the preceding seven chapters is just as relevant to the assignments we discuss in this chapter and the next as it is to thesis-defense papers. Indeed, response papers, compare-and-contrast papers, and research papers share many important features with thesis-defense papers. Even in summary papers, though you do not defend a thesis of your own, you will typically have to identify the thesis and argumentation of the text you are summarizing.

Your instructor may not use the same labels we do (e.g., "summary paper") for the kinds of assignments we discuss in this chapter and the next. That doesn't matter. What matters is what an assignment requires you to do. You should pay attention to the verbs used in the description of your task, such as *explain*, *analyze*, *identify*, *compare*, *contrast*, *illustrate*, *summarize*, *locate*, *arrange*, *justify*, *define*, *prove*, *describe*, and *recount*. Some of these terms are sometimes used interchangeably, but each may be used to ask you to do something different. And, of course, a single assignment may require you to do more than one thing. You must read the assignment carefully to determine what particular tasks you are being given and then perform each of them. As always, if you are unsure what precisely is being required of you, you should clarify it with your instructor.

8.1 How to Take Notes in Philosophy

Many philosophical writing assignments require you to summarize the ideas and arguments of other philosophers. But nobody can write a clear, accurate summary of someone else's philosophical ideas on the first try, and the more philosophy you take in, the more difficult it becomes to remember it all clearly. After several weeks of philosophy classes (not to mention classes in other subjects and the activities of everyday life), you are unlikely to remember all the arguments, objections, terms, and so on that have been covered, let alone the content of every text you've read. Taking good notes from philosophical materials and in class is thus extremely important. In this section, we give you some

DOI: 10.4324/9781003512318-8

tips for how to begin taking good notes. You'll doubtless develop your own system, but you shouldn't lose sight of these basics of good note-taking.

Philosophers are primarily interested in *arguments*—that is, a conclusion together with reasons that are intended to show its truth. Thus, when you take notes, your primary task is to *clarify* for yourself the arguments of others. Your secondary task in note-taking is to record your own thoughts about these arguments that will doubtless occur to you. Some of your thoughts may be questions about aspects of the material you do not understand. Others may be evaluations of the arguments you encounter—how convincing you find them and, crucially, why. It is very important to keep these two note-taking tasks distinct—in your mind and in your notes. Confusing your own ideas with those of another philosopher will at best make your notes misleading, and thus any work based on them potentially inaccurate. At worst, confusing your own ideas with those of others can result in unintended plagiarism.

8.1.1 Taking Notes from a Text

Philosophical texts are typically quite dense; that is, there tends to be more information per page than in much other writing. That's why you might find you are assigned fewer pages of reading for a philosophy course than for other reading-heavy courses. But this density means that you have to read philosophical texts *slowly*, *carefully*, and *repeatedly*. Good philosophers don't waste words and are very careful about which words they use; if there's something about a text you don't understand (a word, a sentence, or a paragraph), you're probably missing something important. This is why you should read with a dictionary by your side. (See §6.3 for advice on choosing and using a dictionary.) If you are reading carefully, you should find yourself constantly asking questions such as "How does this sentence relate to the previous one?" and "What is the author trying to communicate with this long sentence packed with so many clauses?" You should find yourself pausing regularly to ask yourself if you still understand what the author is trying to prove and how one point is related to another.

It's helpful to take notes on your first time through a philosophical text, but you'll usually have a better grasp of it once you've read the whole thing (and, indeed, after you've read other texts on the same topic). The opening sentences and paragraphs may be very important, but sometimes they are incidental to the main argument. The thesis may not be stated until the end of the text. The structure of the argument may not be explicitly mapped out. All of this can make it difficult to follow the argument the first time through. So you shouldn't expect to have satisfactory notes on a text after only one reading. You should plan on reading each text at least twice, and whenever you revisit a text, you should have your notes at hand so you can revise them as your understanding of the text deepens.

Many people find it helpful to mark up the text—underlining or highlighting important conclusions, making marginal notes, and so on. But marking up the text is no substitute for taking notes. You *must* explain the content of each text *in your own words*. Only then will you really discover to what extent you understand it. If you find that you are writing in the original author's voice (using his idiosyncratic vocabulary or sentence structure) or virtually copying individual sentences (merely changing turns of phrase and substituting synonyms), it is a sign that you do not yet understand the material you are summarizing. You should return to the text or seek help from your classmates or instructor.

Your notes should be shorter than the original text. You can pack the author's ideas into much less space because you are presenting only their essentials. However, *you should take notes in complete sentences*. Bullet points and incomplete sentences often record a topic or idea but not the author's *attitude toward* that topic or idea, or the *role it plays* in the author's argument. These may seem obvious when you're taking your notes, but they will likely be less clear when you return to them to write a paper or study for an exam.

We noted in Section 2.2.1 that a paragraph is the unit of thought in a thesis-defense paper. Any philosophical text longer than a single paragraph thus has at least two distinct parts. Most philosophical texts have several larger parts, each consisting of several paragraphs. In some texts, these parts are explicitly indicated by headings or numbers; in others, there are no explicit divisions. In your notes from a text with headings, you should reproduce those headings and offer a summary of what the author does under each. For a text whose parts are only numbered, you should supply headings of your own that would be helpful to a reader of the text. (Imagine yourself editing the piece for inclusion in an introductory anthology.) When you encounter a text with no explicit divisions at all, you should still divide your notes on it into sections and provide helpful headings for each. (You can mark these section breaks in the text and record their page numbers in your notes.) One way to begin dividing a text into sections is to think of it as an extended argument. What is the ultimate conclusion of the piece? What major premises are argued for along the way? Each of these might well be covered in its own part of the text. Then there might be parts devoted to defining new terms or explaining technical points, digressive subsections, introductory and concluding sections, and so on. The more familiar with the text you become, the more detailed your conception of its structure, and hence your notes, will become.

Your notes should record not just what the author says but also what you think about it. Imagine yourself in conversation with the author. Is there something you would ask the author to clarify? Write this down as a question. Does an objection to the author's argument occur to you? Write this down, too, and then write down how you think the author might respond to your objection. However, *be sure to indicate clearly which notes record your thoughts and which notes record those of the author*. Depending on whether you take notes by hand or electronically, you can do this by enclosing your own thoughts in square brackets, indenting them like a block quotation, or using a different font color for them. Otherwise, it will be surprisingly easy, once you've been away from the text for a while, to forget which of your notes record what you found in the text and which record original thoughts of your own. It's also important to indicate clearly any material you copy into your notes verbatim. The most obvious way to do this is to put it in quotation marks. Failure to do this can lead to inadvertent plagiarism.

You should bring your notes on a text to any class on the same topic since they'll help you jump quickly to thoughts you had about the reading when they come up in a lecture or discussion and give you some indication of where in the text the idea you're thinking of is located.

8.1.2 Taking Notes from a Talk

You may be required to attend a philosophical lecture in person or online, or you may be assigned a philosophical video to watch. You should take notes from these in much the same way you take notes from a text. If you are taking notes from a recording, you have the advantage of being able to experience it more than once, as with a text. If you are taking notes at a live event, you do not have that advantage. You can only do your best, then, to record as much content and structure as you can while the event unfolds. (If you would like to record such an event, make sure you get permission from the speaker first, who may well ask for assurances that you will not share the recording and will delete it once you are done with it.)

If there is a discussion period after a talk, be sure to stay for it. It is remarkable how much more clearly and concisely many philosophers explain their main ideas in response to questions than in their prepared lectures. Of course, this is also an opportunity to ask the speaker a question yourself. Doing so can be a bit daunting, but most philosophers love to discuss their work and thus appreciate questions. There are many different kinds of questions you can ask, but it always helps to begin by thanking the speaker for giving the talk and complimenting some aspect of it, if possible. That's polite, and it helps reassure the speaker. (You might be surprised by how nervous even seasoned speakers can be about giving a talk to people they don't know well.)

To ask a good question of *clarification*, try to identify as clearly as possible the point you want clarified. (Was it an argument, a premise within an argument, the conclusion of an argument, an example, ...?) You should begin by explaining to the speaker what you *do* understand (the rest of the argument, say, or the point of the example). For instance:

> Thanks for the interesting talk. When you were discussing the possibility of time travel, I thought the point of the example from the film *12 Monkeys* was to show that time travel cannot be coherently imagined. But I wasn't sure what you thought was incoherent about the film. Could you say a little more about that?

Raising an *objection* is a staple of philosophical discourse—but you should, of course, be polite about it.

> I really enjoyed your talk—thanks. I'd never thought about how difficult it might be to define a well-known art form such as film. I think you suggested that *motion* was a necessary condition for being a film. But aren't there actual films, such as Derek Jarman's *Blue*, that contain no moving images?

Application questions suggest extending what the speaker has said to further examples or domains. Sometimes you may just want to point out such an application, but it's polite to phrase such suggestions as questions to give the speaker an opening to reply.

> Thanks. I found your discussion of narrative strategies in film very compelling. It seems to me that you might say the same things about other narrative works, such as novels. Would you be prepared to extend your arguments about flashbacks to works other than films?

Lacuna questions suggest that there is something missing from the speaker's argument. ("Lacuna" is Latin for "hole.") Sometimes a lacuna can be presented as an objection, but it can usually be phrased as a request for more information.

> Thanks for your talk, which I found very compelling. You argued that we don't have free will because determinism is true, but I don't think you offered a positive argument *for* determinism. How would you respond to someone who questioned the truth of determinism?

8.1.3 Taking Class Notes

Taking class notes is a two-stage process. First, in class, you should write down as much as you can of what is said by everyone—your instructor, your classmates, and yourself—in addition to what is displayed on the board, screen, and the like. Do not make the mistake of writing down *only* what is displayed visually. That material is often little more than headings and keywords. The true content of the course is what your instructor and classmates *say* under those headings and about those keywords.

You should impose as much structure as you can on these notes as you go, labeling arguments, objections, replies, and so on. There will not be enough time to do this adequately in class, however, nor is it always obvious what is happening in a discussion while it is occurring. So you should revise your notes *as soon as possible after each class*. (If you take notes by hand, this is a good opportunity to transfer them into an electronic document.) At this second stage of your note-taking, you can make corrections, reorder and revise what you've written, amplify things you didn't have time to write down fully in class while you still remember them, and so on. If something is unclear, you should ask your instructor or classmates about it.

If you miss a class, make sure you get access as soon as possible to the notes of a classmate who takes good notes. Even if these notes are in an electronic format, do not simply copy and paste them into your own class notes. *Write them out yourself*, and then read through them carefully. If (as is highly likely) there is anything you don't understand, ask your classmate about it. If that doesn't clarify the matter sufficiently, talk to your instructor. Indeed, if your instructor is willing, it would be very helpful to visit her during office hours to talk through the material you missed. Make sure, however, that you take the lead in explaining what you've gathered from any assigned reading and the notes you've borrowed. It is not your instructor's responsibility to catch you up on material you have missed, even if there was a good reason for your absence.

You should consider asking your instructor if she would be willing to review a sample of your (revised and tidied-up) class notes early in a course, especially if you are new to philosophy. If she is willing, your instructor should be able to give you some pointers about whether you're taking enough notes, getting the right things down, and organizing the material in a way that makes sense.

8.2 Summary Papers

If you are asked only to *summarize*, *describe*, or *explain* a text, passage, or talk, your instructor probably intends to evaluate your understanding of the arguments it contains rather than your ability to critically discuss those arguments. We call such assignments **summary papers**. (Because such summaries are often relatively brief, your instructor may not call them "papers" at all.)

If you have taken good notes from a text or talk, you are well on your way to a summary paper. But while your notes likely follow the structure of the material you are summarizing, your summary should not necessarily do so. A summary is certainly not intended to be a sentence-by-sentence or even paragraph-by-paragraph rewriting of the original. Your task is to explain the material to a reader who is unfamiliar with the topic. Such a reader likely differs from the intended audience of the material you are summarizing, and thus your approach will differ from that of the person whose work you are summarizing.

There is no template that you can follow for every text, passage, or talk you may be asked to summarize, but you should consider starting with a paragraph in which you state and explain the main thesis or conclusion of the material, followed by a series of paragraphs each devoted to one of the reasons or premises given for that thesis or conclusion. If your summary paper is short (say, two pages or less), you need not include an opening or closing paragraph (of the kind we discuss in §2.2.3) since your reader should be able to hold the entire structure of your paper in her mind.

As with your notes, idiosyncrasies of the author's writing style should not appear in your summary. You should be explaining the material in your own words. You may sometimes feel that you must quote directly from the text to convey the content clearly. As we said in Section 4.3, however, you should err on the side of *not* doing this. Indeed, a summary paper is probably where you should resist this temptation most strongly since the whole point of the assignment is to explain the material in your own words. If you do decide to quote directly, you must clearly indicate that you are doing so and acknowledge the quotation's source. (See §7.3.1.)

Unless your instructor directs you otherwise, you do not have to limit yourself exclusively to concepts in the text that you are summarizing. For instance, you might explain the author's reasoning and views by an analogy, as in this example:

> Descartes, in his *Meditations*, resolves to find a single point of certainty and then to draw conclusions, one at a time, that follow necessarily from the preceding points. This is similar to the inferential process of geometrical proofs, in which we move from what we know or postulate to other claims that must necessarily be true if the initial ones are.

The analogy to geometry does not appear in the *Meditations*, but if it helps to illuminate Descartes's project, why not use it? (Of course, if you learned of this analogy from a particular source, you must acknowledge it. See Chapter 7.)

You might similarly employ an original example to illustrate a point:

> In Plato's *Republic*, the character Socrates claims that there are conflicts between the elements of an unjust or unhealthy soul—for example, between a person's reason and appetite. To envision such internal strife, we might think of meals at which we are tempted to have an extra helping, when our reason tells us we shouldn't because of the extra calories or bloated feeling that will result.

In a more sophisticated summary, you might help your reader understand the material you are summarizing by describing its relations to other material by the same philosopher or by comparing it with another philosopher's work. References to the life or cultural context of the philosopher may also be useful—as long as they contribute to your reader's understanding of the specific material you are summarizing.

We have discussed summary papers as assignments, but good notes taken from multiple readings of a single text over time will approach the structure of a summary paper. And you may find that writing a summary paper on some material you must master is helpful even when you are not required to do so. It will clarify the author's argument in your own mind and provide a tool for recalling and reviewing the material after the passage of time. You might also mine such summaries for relatively polished prose that can contribute to a longer paper that discusses the material you have summarized.

8.3 Response Papers

In a **response paper**, you give your reasoned, usually evaluative, commentary on some material (a text, talk, film, etc.). Such assignments might more accurately be called *critical-summary papers* since they combine the kind of summary you find in a summary paper with a critical response. Here, as elsewhere, "critical" does not necessarily mean *negative* but rather *thoughtful and evaluative*. Such responses can be positive or negative (or a mixture of both). Kinds of critical discussion include:

(a) criticizing an argument (e.g., showing that a particular premise is false or that the argument is invalid),
(b) critically discussing an example (e.g., arguing that it does not show what the author intends it to),
(c) providing a counterexample to a claim or argument,
(d) extending an argument in the reading (e.g., arguing that the author could have defended an even stronger thesis than she has),
(e) supplying a different argument for a thesis defended in the reading, and
(f) arguing for a relevant position not covered in the reading.

Sometimes a value-neutral response is acceptable—for instance, the nonevaluative *application* of a theory or argument in the material you are discussing to a new example or area.

If you are not given detailed instructions about what to include in your response paper, we offer the following advice. First, it is better to cover one point in some depth than several points superficially. For instance, rather than offering a list of objections to an author's argument, decide which you think is the strongest and discuss it in some detail. (Compare §4.1.) Second, aim for a structure that "zooms in" on your critical discussion. Suppose you are required to write a two-page response paper on a journal article. Two pages is about 600 words. Aim to begin with a short summary of the article as a whole (one paragraph of about 100 words): What is the author's thesis? How does she argue for it? You can then explain in more detail (one paragraph of about 200 words) *one aspect* of the text: the argument, claim, or example that you will critically respond to. That leaves you about half the paper (one or two paragraphs totaling 300 words) for your critical discussion.

As with summary papers, if a response paper is short, it doesn't need an opening or closing paragraph—your reader should be able to follow the structure of a one- or two-page paper without a preview. Unlike a summary paper, a response paper does have a thesis: the main critical point you make about the target material. This thesis should be clear to your reader by the end of the paper. But remember that this is a *response* paper (as opposed to a thesis-defense paper) because the instructor wants to evaluate your ability to critically respond to another philosopher's work. The more interested you are in the topic, the more likely you will want to defend a substantial thesis of your own about it, independent of the material to which you are responding. But that would inevitably reduce the space available to provide your critical response. Also, the paper is likely too short for you to defend a substantial thesis of your own. Resist the temptation! Save your larger ideas for a thesis-defense paper.

A word of clarification: Sometimes "response paper" refers to a paper in which you express your subjective reactions to the material that you have read. You may report on any personal reaction, emotional or intellectual; justification is usually not required. This is *not* the kind of paper we have discussed in this section. Like journals or notebooks, which are also assigned in some philosophy courses, the required format and content of subjective-response papers vary so widely that there is little advice we can offer. Your instructor should provide instructions on these kinds of assignments. If she does not, you should ask for guidance.

8.4 Compare-and-Contrast Papers

The final kind of paper we discuss in this chapter is the **compare-and-contrast paper.** You may be asked to compare and contrast a wide range of things, such as (1) the ideas of specific philosophers, (2) the ideas of any philosophers in a particular philosophical movement, (3) philosophical movements or schools of thought themselves, (4) works by different authors, (5) works by the same author, or (6) the ways that one concept is developed in different contexts. The particular philosophers, ideas, and so on may be specified in the assignment, or you may have some freedom to choose what you compare. Here are some sample compare-and-contrast paper prompts:

> Compare and contrast the political views of John Locke and Thomas Hobbes.
> Compare and contrast the ethical thought of one utilitarian and one intuitionist.
> Compare and contrast Akan and Yoruba ethics.
> Compare and contrast *The Trial* by Franz Kafka and *The Fall* by Albert Camus.
> Compare and contrast Plato's *Charmides* and his *Laches*.
> Compare and contrast the concept of liberation as developed by Gustavo Gutiérrez and by Frantz Fanon.

(Note that if you are asked simply to *compare* two things, you are probably still expected to discuss both similarities and differences. As you can confirm by consulting a dictionary, it is not true that comparing things involves considering only similarities. That notion seems, somewhat ironically, to have become entrenched through the widespread use of the phrase "compare and contrast" in writing assignments.)

The more specific the comparison required by the assignment, the less work you will have to do to decide what to cover. For instance, the last sample prompt above is arguably the easiest to address because it specifies both the topic and the thinkers, thus limiting the range of material you must synthesize and analyze. If you are given a broad prompt, such as the first example above, you should consider narrowing it down yourself—assuming this is acceptable, given the terms of your assignment. (If in doubt, check with your instructor.) For instance, after some preparatory work, you may decide to address this narrower version of the prompt:

> Compare and contrast the concept of a social or political "state of nature" as developed by John Locke and Thomas Hobbes.

The search for comparisons and contrasts is, of course, nothing more than an attempt to find what is similar and what is different about the two things being compared. Many of the dissimilarities will be obvious. If you are familiar with the things to be compared, you will almost certainly notice some things that can be said of one but not the other. If you do not discern any differences, you probably need to return to the material or seek help from your instructor or classmates.

The similarities may be more difficult to recognize. If the two things you have to compare seem to have little in common, try thinking about very general aspects of them. Perhaps the thinkers or philosophies that are being compared share at least some unstated assumptions about human motivation, political rights, mental capacities, language, emotion, personal fulfillment, or some other important notions relevant to the comparison. The things being compared almost always have *something* in common.

A compare-and-contrast paper should be a unified essay, not a mere list of various similarities and dissimilarities. So what will provide a focus for your paper? One way of achieving such unity is to begin with a short account of the general ways that the compared things are the same and the general ways that they are different. When you do this, you almost transform your paper into a thesis-defense paper. You might profitably complete the transformation and present a thesis in which you state, generally speaking, how the two things being compared are similar and how they differ. Consider these examples of compare-and-contrast thesis statements:

> Plato's ideal society as presented in the *Republic* and Edward Bellamy's as presented in *Looking Backward* share several definitive assumptions about the character of good citizens and healthy relations between social groups, but they diverge significantly on desirable political structures and styles of living.

> Plato and Bellamy agree that social conditions greatly influence the character of interactions in a society, but they disagree on the extent to which divergent individual traits can be changed.

> Plato and Bellamy share the belief that personal wealth and acquisitiveness must be controlled in any society that is to avoid corruption, but they differ on which social policies could bring about such a change in people and on whether such a change could be universal.

The remainder of the paper's opening paragraph may preview the sorts of evidence to be offered. Then the philosophers' general positions and specific passages from their writings can be offered as evidence for each of these claims.

Whether or not you structure your compare-and-contrast paper as a thesis defense, there is another organizational issue to consider. Should you (1) deal with one of the two things to be compared in the first half of the paper and then compare and contrast as you present the parallel aspects of the second? Or should you (2) move back and forth between the two, comparing one aspect of each at a time?

Generally, the second approach is better. For one thing, with the first approach, you don't immerse the reader immediately in the activity of comparing and contrasting, which is both the purpose of the paper and inherently engaging. The first approach may also force some readers to return repeatedly to the first part of the paper to remind themselves of what you wrote there about each aspect that is being considered in the second part. This is awkward and irksome. If, in order to avoid this problem, you do lots of reminding in the second part, you become repetitive. That can bother your reader, too, and waste valuable space. (This is essentially the same reason that we recommend, in §3.5, responding to one objection before explaining another.)

One hybrid approach begins with a short summary of each of the two things to be compared, followed by a comparative section. But it is hard to do this well. Short summaries do not give a basis for an in-depth comparison, and long summaries are tedious and require deferring the heart of the paper even longer than on the first approach considered above.

Despite the generalizations we've made here, each of these structures for a compare-and-contrast paper may be the most suitable for certain topics. Do not make a final decision on the paper's structure until you consider what it will take to deal with the particular points you want to make about the specific material you are discussing.

9 Doing Philosophical Research

Up to this point, we have assumed that the sources you use in your philosophy papers are readily available—for instance, as required reading for a course. In this chapter we discuss how to go about finding materials on a philosophical topic yourself—that is, how to do **philosophical research**. We begin by discussing two common kinds of assignments requiring such research: the annotated bibliography and the research paper. We then turn to resources and techniques for doing philosophical research.

9.1 Research Assignments

9.1.1 Annotated Bibliographies

An **annotated bibliography** is a list of sources (hence "bibliography"), each accompanied by a short passage describing and perhaps evaluating its content (the "annotations"). Annotated bibliographies are published by scholars as resources for others doing research on particular topics. (See §9.3.1.) Authors of such bibliographies typically aim to include the most helpful and important materials on their topics. When you are required to create an annotated bibliography as an assignment in a philosophy course, your instructor typically wants to assess your ability to find, summarize, and perhaps evaluate philosophical sources relevant to some topic. An annotated bibliography may be required as an independent assignment, or you may be required to submit one in advance of, or together with, a research paper.

The most commonly required kind of annotation is an **abstract**—that is, a brief summary of the source stating the thesis and main lines of argument. Abstracts can range in length from a single sentence (or even sentence fragment) to several paragraphs. Most common, however, is the single-paragraph abstract. One way to go about producing such an abstract is to write a detailed formal opening paragraph for the text (see §2.2.3), but in the third-person (e.g., "Appiah argues ...").

In addition to a descriptive abstract, you may be asked to evaluate your sources. Pay attention to the perspective from which you are asked to evaluate them. Are you supposed to evaluate the strength of the arguments in each source or how useful it would be for a research paper on a particular topic? If the assignment is unclear on this, seek clarification from your instructor. Make sure you keep your descriptive summary and any evaluation of each source separate. The easiest way to do this is to write two paragraphs on each source: one descriptive and one evaluative. If you are required to write a single paragraph combining both, complete your descriptive summary before turning to your evaluation—and signpost that turn clearly. (See §2.2.2.)

DOI: 10.4324/9781003512318-9

9.1.2 Research Papers

Unless directed otherwise by your instructor, you should think of a research paper as simply a thesis-defense paper that includes sources you have found yourself. All of the advice we have given in Chapters 1–7 thus applies to writing a research paper. But research papers in particular can tempt you to make a couple of mistakes that we address here.

Perhaps the biggest danger when writing a research paper is merely summarizing the various sources you have discovered in your research instead of writing an original defense of your own thesis, drawing on helpful sources you've discovered through your research. If this is what your instructor wanted, she would have assigned an annotated bibliography. Falling into this trap of writing summaries instead of a thesis-defense paper is a sign that you have not fully digested the materials you have uncovered in your research and used them to come to your own conclusion—your own thesis to defend—about the topic you are addressing. If you find yourself in this situation, review our discussion of how to develop a thesis (§3.4).

A second research-paper pitfall is trying to squeeze into your paper a discussion of every single source you've read in the course of your research. This will unhelpfully complicate your paper. As with any thesis-defense paper, you should decide what to include on the basis of what will enable you to make the strongest case for your thesis. (See §4.1.) The point of the research is simply to discover helpful material—arguments, concepts, and examples that will help you come to your own conclusion about the topic you are considering. Later in this chapter, we discuss how to find materials that are most likely to be helpful in this way. Unfortunately, however, you can never be sure in advance whether a source will contain something helpful to you. There is little you can do about this except develop a "philosophical" attitude toward the research process. You cannot hope to find nuggets of philosophical gold without poring through some philosophical dross.

Choosing a Topic

The advice we have already given about choosing a topic (§3.3) is just as relevant to research papers as to other thesis-defense papers: You should choose a topic that genuinely interests you since that tends to result in a better paper. You should also be careful to pick a *philosophical* topic. Nonphilosophical sources may be highly relevant to certain philosophical topics (see §9.2.1), but if the question your thesis answers would best be answered by conducting a survey or doing an experiment, then it is unlikely to be a philosophical topic.

One consideration for choosing a topic for a research paper in particular is how much material has been published on your topic. If you choose a well-established topic in philosophy, such as John Locke's theory of property, you will easily discover thousands of books and articles on the topic. That's an advantage in that you'll have no trouble finding material, but it's a disadvantage in that you'll face the difficult task of choosing which few pieces to read out of that wealth of material. (We discuss strategies for making such choices in §9.3.) One solution to this problem is to narrow your topic—for instance, to Locke's claim that we own our bodies. Naturally, only a fraction of the material on Locke's theory of property will be devoted to this particular issue.

If, on the other hand, you choose a topic that philosophers have only recently begun thinking about, such as the value of video games, it will be more difficult to find material devoted to it. The advantage of this situation is that you will not have to make so many decisions about which materials you will actually read. It is also easier, of course, to get an overview of a smaller amount of material. The related disadvantage is that you may not find as much useful material as you would with a more established topic. One solution to this problem is to come up with your own arguments about the topic. But that can be difficult, and it won't help to the extent that you are being assessed on your ability to do philosophical research. Another solution is to broaden your search for materials without broadening your topic. For instance, if you think that video games are artworks, then you could search for materials on the value of art (a more established topic) and apply the arguments you find in that literature to video games. If done well, this can demonstrate your ability both to do philosophical research and to use others' work in creating your own philosophical arguments.

Developing a Thesis

Again, the advice we have already given on developing a thesis (§3.4) is just as relevant for research papers as for other thesis-defense papers. When writing a research paper, however, it is perhaps even more important to keep an open mind about your thesis. In the course of your research, you may discover arguments about your topic that are entirely new to you. If you find them convincing, you may end up with a view on your topic that directly contradicts the thesis you initially planned to defend. If you stick to your original thesis, the resulting paper may be less convincing than if you had defended the thesis you now believe. One way to keep an open mind about your topic is to let your research be guided by a question (e.g., *Do we own our bodies?*) rather than a topic (e.g., *ownership of bodies*) or claim (e.g., *We do not own our bodies.*). You should be able to articulate at least two plausible, mutually exclusive answers to your question. As we said at the beginning of Chapter 2, if there is no plausible alternative to your thesis, then there is no point in writing a paper defending it. Returning throughout your research to the question you are considering, and plausible alternative answers to it, should help you keep an open mind.

9.2 Scholarly Philosophical Sources

9.2.1 The Basics of Scholarly Philosophical Sources

Before we consider resources and techniques for doing your own philosophical research, it's worth discussing the kinds of sources you'll be looking for. Philosophical papers sometimes draw on materials from disciplines outside philosophy itself. For example, a paper on the ethics of capital punishment might include information on the costs of incarcerating and executing people or evidence about the effectiveness of capital punishment as a deterrent; a paper on the nature of consciousness might draw on empirical research by scholars in biochemistry, neuroscience, and psychology; and a paper on musical understanding might draw on research in music theory. This kind of empirical information is carefully gathered by scholars and published in scholarly venues that specialize in these disciplines. While some of the information in the remainder of this chapter may help you seek out such empirical information, we cannot introduce you to resources and techniques for doing research in every scholarly field. We focus on resources and techniques for finding scholarly *philosophical* sources. For help finding sources in other disciplines that are relevant to your paper, consult your instructor or a librarian.

What makes a source **scholarly**, and why should you care? You should care because you want, in your research, to discover the sources that will be most helpful to you in coming to a conclusion about some philosophical question or problem. Lots of people doubtless have opinions about your topic, but scholars have years of training and experience using techniques that enable them to understand what has been achieved in their area of expertise and (hopefully) to make novel contributions of their own. None of this makes scholars infallible, of course—after all, they frequently disagree with one another, whether they are experts in philosophy, physics, or musicology. But they are much more likely than others to have better informed, more carefully thought-out, and more clearly expressed views about topics in their areas of expertise.

Scholarly publications are characteristically peer-reviewed. The basic idea of **peer review** is that nothing is published in a scholarly venue without being vetted by other scholars with expertise in the topic. So, for instance, to get her essay published as an article in a scholarly journal, a philosopher must submit it to the editors of the journal (themselves professional philosophers), who will send it to two or more "referees," "readers," or "reviewers"—other professional philosophers with expertise in the topic of the essay (the author's "peers"). Each referee writes a "report" on the essay for the editors, somewhat like a response paper (see §8.3), summarizing the essay, critically discussing its argument, and making a judgment about whether it is an original and valuable contribution to the field. On the basis of those reports, the editors decide whether to accept the essay for publication, reject it, or invite the author to submit a version revised in light of the referees' reports. A similar process occurs when someone seeks to publish a book with a scholarly publisher.

Importantly, most peer review happens anonymously: The system is set up so that neither the author nor the referees know one another's identities. Sometimes even the editors do not know the identity of the author. This anonymity is intended to remove potential bias against or in favor of particular individuals or groups.

So, how can you tell if a publication is peer-reviewed and hence scholarly? Unfortunately, it's often quite difficult to figure out whether a particular source has been peer-reviewed. If the source *is* peer-reviewed, that information is probably on (or inferable from) the website of the publisher, journal, or source itself—though it may require some digging. But if the source *isn't* peer-reviewed, the only evidence will probably be the *absence* of such evidence (and confirming that absence will likely require even more digging). Happily, the techniques we discuss in the following sections should lead you almost exclusively to scholarly material, so if you use those techniques, you don't have to worry about checking whether each source you find is peer-reviewed.

It's worth noting that material can be scholarly *without* being peer-reviewed. Theoretically, a self-taught amateur without any academic qualifications might post on his social media account a scrupulously researched and powerfully written philosophical essay. In practice, however, this is unlikely to happen. It is more likely that someone with an advanced degree in philosophy and peer-reviewed publications to their name will publish something in her area of expertise that has not gone through the peer-review process. Examples might include a podcast or YouTube episode in an established series run by another professional philosopher or a "think piece" in a newspaper, magazine, or blog. It is also increasingly common for philosophers to post drafts of their works-in-progress on personal websites or in databases such as *PhilPapers*. (See §9.3.2.) The more evidence you have that the author of such material is a scholar of philosophy, the more confident you can be that the material can appropriately be cited in your research assignment. Relevant evidence includes the author's having a Ph.D. in philosophy, having published in peer-reviewed venues on the same topic, and having had work on the topic cited by other scholars in peer-reviewed venues. (You can discover some of this evidence using resources and techniques we discuss in §9.3.)

As you may already have inferred, scholarliness is not an all-or-nothing affair and probably not a completely objective matter. But that doesn't mean it's unimportant. As we said above, scholarly sources will be the most helpful to you in coming to a conclusion about some philosophical question or problem. Moreover, your instructor may require that you use only scholarly—or even peer-reviewed—sources in your paper or annotated bibliography. If you are unsure about a particular source or the assignment's requirements, check with your instructor before making substantial progress using the source or on the assignment.

9.2.2 *Primary and Secondary Sources*

A distinction is sometimes made between *primary sources* and *secondary sources.* In philosophy, it is most likely to be relevant to research in the history of philosophy. The distinction is drawn differently in different disciplines, but in philosophy a primary source is material (e.g., a book) by a philosopher whose work is a focus of your paper. A secondary source is material (e.g., a book or journal article) *about* a primary source or its author. For example, Mary Wollstonecraft published her influential *Vindication of the Rights of Woman* in 1792. If you are writing a paper on Wollstonecraft's views, or the history of feminist thought, this book would be a primary source (even if you're using a modern edition). But you may also use philosophical materials *about* Wollstonecraft's book in your paper—for example, Nancy Kendrick's essay "Marriage, Love, and Friendship" in the 2019 book *The Wollstonecraftian Mind.* This would be a secondary source.

Notice that the distinction between primary and secondary sources is contextual. In a paper on Wollstonecraft's *Vindication*, Simone de Beauvoir's *The Second Sex* (1949), in which she comments on Wollstonecraft, might count as a secondary source, while in a paper on the history of feminist thought, both Wollstonecraft's *Vindication* and de Beauvoir's *Second Sex* might count as primary sources. If your instructor requires you to use a certain number of primary or secondary sources and you're unsure about a particular example, ask for clarification.

For some assignments, particularly those framed topically rather than historically, the distinction between primary and secondary sources may be irrelevant. In a paper on the ethics of playing violent video games, for instance, you may draw on a range of sources without any being primary or secondary. Even if you cite, say, Aristotle's *Nicomachean Ethics* in the course of your argument, it isn't a primary source—even though it's a foundational text in Western philosophy—since it's not the focus of your paper.

9.3 Discovering Scholarly Philosophical Sources

The hardest parts of writing a philosophical research paper are understanding what others have already said about your topic, using that to help figure out what you think about the topic, and expressing your considered view clearly and concisely. For an annotated bibliography, you only (!) have to understand the sources you've found and summarize (and perhaps evaluate) them clearly and concisely. But you can't even begin to do any of this until you've *found* what other people have said about your topic.

There are two distinct stages to "finding" such sources. We call them **discovery** and **access**. You *discover* a source when you learn that it exists; you *access* that source when you track down a copy so that you can read it. Doing research on the internet can make these two stages feel seamless: You can enter some terms in a search box, click on a result, and find yourself reading a journal article you've never heard of before, having discovered and accessed it virtually simultaneously. But if you want to read the most helpful sources for arriving at your own views about a philosophical topic—or if you are being evaluated on the quality of sources you find—this method will yield disappointing results. You'll likely end up reading a random selection of material that is barely related to your topic and thus not very useful in helping you answer the specific question you are addressing. In this section, we introduce you to a range of resources and techniques—ordered from the most to least helpful—for discovering the most useful sources on your topic. In Section 9.4, we turn to accessing the sources you discover.

9.3.1 Mining Bibliographies

You might have thought we would start with advice for improving your internet searches. We do discuss internet searches below, but even well-designed searches can get you an unhelpfully large number of results with no indication of how useful each source will be. A better place to start is the list of works cited or bibliography of a scholarly source on the topic you are researching. The bibliographies of various kinds of sources can be helpful.

Reference Works

As we explained in Section 7.6.1, a **reference work** provides short introductions to topics. Most reference works are collections of specially commissioned pieces by many different authors. One of the roles of the entries in such works is to cite the sources that scholars have found most helpful with respect to a given topic. So they are a good place to start your research.

There are different kinds of reference works. Though the terminology is not always used consistently, a **dictionary** typically contains shorter entries on a wider range of topics (definitions of terms, profiles of famous philosophers, and so on). Good philosophical dictionaries include *The Cambridge Dictionary of Philosophy*, *The Oxford Companion to Philosophy*, and *The Concise Routledge Encyclopedia of Philosophy*. Not all philosophical dictionaries include bibliographies in their entries, however.

An **encyclopedia** typically contains longer entries than a dictionary. Good general philosophical encyclopedias include *The Internet Encyclopedia of Philosophy* (https://iep.utm.edu/), *The Stanford Encyclopedia of Philosophy* (https://plato.stanford.edu/), and *The Routledge Encyclopedia of Philosophy Online* (https://www.rep.routledge.com/). The entries in all these encyclopedias have useful bibliographies. There are also reference works on specific areas within philosophy. These go by various names, including "handbook," "companion," "guide," and so on. There are far too many such works for us to give even a representative sample here, but this short list gives a sense of the kinds of titles they have: *The Blackwell Guide to Feminist Philosophy*, *The Oxford Handbook of Epicurus and Epicureanism*, *A Companion to African Philosophy*. To discover a reference work in the area to which your research topic belongs, use the resources and techniques we cover in the following subsections.

To mine a bibliography for your research, you first have to find an entry as closely related to your topic as possible. You should thus start with more specific reference works, if possible. For example, if you are working on a paper on the ethics of animal experimentation, a reference work on animal ethics will be more helpful than a reference work on ethics in general, which will in turn be more helpful than a general philosophical reference work. For the same reasons, once you've located a reference work, you should use fairly specific terms (e.g., "video game" or "Beauvoir") to search within it. If you don't find anything relevant, use broader terms (e.g., "fiction" or "feminism"). (If you are using a print copy, look for such keywords in the table of contents and the index.) You should look in a range of reference works for two reasons. First, some may have entries on topics more closely related to your research topic than others. Second, comparing results from different entries can show you which sources are most commonly cited and thus most likely to be helpful.

Once you've found a relevant entry, skim through it, taking note of the headings and subheadings. If possible, identify specific sections of the entry that look most relevant to your topic. Read these sections, and record the sources that are cited in connection with the issues most relevant to your topic. If you notice the same source being cited in different entries related to your topic (in the same reference work or in different ones), it's a good sign that the source will be helpful for your research.

A cautionary note on *Wikipedia*: This open-access, online encyclopedia is the first port of call for many students when it comes to academic research. Many scholars regard it with suspicion, however—and your instructor may be among them. Bear in mind that *anyone* may author or alter a *Wikipedia* entry. Although attentive editing by *Wikipedia* staff and other contributors makes many entries useful starting points for learning about a new topic, *Wikipedia* is not peer-reviewed. It is not a scholarly source.

Journals

There is one philosophical **journal**—*Philosophy Compass*—that is essentially a reference work. It contains only articles that are introductions to specific topics in philosophy, many of which are more specific than you would find in even the most specialized of other reference works. It is thus a great source of bibliographies to mine for your own research. *Philosophy Compass* is not open-access, but your library may have a subscription. If not, you can search for articles on the journal's website (https://compass.onlinelibrary.wiley.com/journal/17479991) and interloan the article you want. (See §9.4.1.)

Textbooks and Edited Collections

For the purpose of mining bibliographies, you can treat **textbooks** and **edited collections of new work** much like reference works. A textbook, like a reference work, is designed to introduce you to a subject by giving you an overview of its most important topics and literature. Some edited collections contain only classic texts on a topic, covering decades or centuries of scholarship; others contain only work newly written for those particular collections. Some are a mixture of both. Only new work is useful for bibliography mining—the more recent the better—since any bibliography gives you a snapshot of what were considered the most useful sources on a topic *when the work was published*.

There are textbooks and edited collections on philosophy in general, but for mining bibliographies, you'll be much better off finding a textbook or collection on a specific topic as close to your research topic as possible. Unfortunately, it is not easy to search specifically for textbooks or edited collections. You can try searching your library catalog or *WorldCat* (see §9.3.3) using keywords such as "introduction" (which appears in many textbook titles) or "anthology" (which appears in the titles of some edited collections), but there's no guarantee of success. Entries in reference works sometimes list other helpful overviews in their opening paragraphs or bibliographies. Alternatively, you might consider simply asking your instructor or a librarian for recommendations.

Other Scholarly Sources

As we mentioned in Section 9.1.1, there are **bibliographies** published by scholars with the sole purpose of being used by other researchers who want to find the most useful sources on a topic. Some bibliographies are published as books (e.g., *Women Philosophers: A Bibliography of Books Through 1990*), but many are now published online. Particularly helpful are the online Oxford Bibliographies (https://www.oxfordbibliographies.com/page/philosophy), which cover a wide range of philosophical topics. These are not open-access, but your library may have a subscription, or you could try interloaning the relevant bibliography. (See §9.4.1.)

You can, of course, mine the bibliographies of much other scholarship, such as **books** and **journal articles**. The reason we don't recommend *starting* with these bibliographies is that they do not typically attempt to give an overview of a topic. Thus what is cited is only what the author found useful for defending her particular thesis. Nonetheless, a good scholar writing on a given topic will cite only sources that (in her opinion) are worth reading on the topic. So if a source is cited *in close connection with a discussion relevant to your topic*, it's a sign that it may be of use to you.

Two Final Thoughts on Mining Bibliographies

As you mine more bibliographies, you'll get a better sense of the sources that are considered central to your topic from how often and in what contexts they are cited. That doesn't necessarily mean you should read all or only those most central sources. Maybe you'll have a sense of the content of a source from discussions of it in materials you've already read and be able to tell that reading it won't be helpful for your project. But by mining bibliographies, you'll end up with a much better list of potentially helpful sources—and a better sense of how they relate to your research project—than if you had simply started with a web search.

We should end with one unavoidable shortcoming of mining bibliographies. When discussing edited collections, we noted that you will only discover sources *older* than the bibliography you're mining. This is, of course, true of any bibliography you mine. To discover more recent material on your topic, then, you will have to look elsewhere—for example, in a database.

9.3.2 Searching Databases

What we will call a **database** is a collection of information about publications, a bit like a library catalog. It can tell you what has been published and may contain copies of or links to published material or information about where to find it. (A site that contains copies of sources is sometimes called a *repository*.)

An important database for philosophical research is *Philosopher's Index*. It indexes (i.e., collects information about) a wide range of reputable philosophical journals, many chapters in edited collections, and some whole books. It is not open-access, but most academic libraries have a subscription. (If you can't find it through your library's website, ask a librarian.) To discover items, use search terms related to your topic. If you get too many results, you will need to narrow your search. One way to do this is by adding search terms and linking them with "AND." For instance, a search for "Locke" returns around 5,000 results (as we write this), while a search for "Locke" AND "property" returns about 500. To narrow the results still further, click on a couple of the results that look most relevant to your topic and look at the keywords listed under "subjects." These are terms that *Philosopher's Index* uses to categorize materials. Using these terms will thus help you find relevant material. For instance, one such keyword is "property rights." Searching for "Locke" (in any field) AND "property rights" (in the "Subjects" field) returns about 50 results. That's still a lot of material to work through, especially since you have no indication of the quality or relevance of each item. That's why we recommend mining bibliographies first. If you've mined bibliographies on this topic for older sources and thus further restrict your search to materials published in the last ten years, you'll get about 20 results.

If you are researching a topic on which little has been written, you may need to *broaden* your search. You can do this by using more general search terms, or by linking them with "OR." For instance, searching for "video games" AND "violence" returns just one result (as we write this). Searching "video games" OR "violence" returns around 2,500 results, but that's far too many to work with and will include lots of material that has nothing to do with video games. (The "OR" search will find any record containing the term "violence," whether or not it has anything to do with video games.) The details of the result of the first ("AND") search, however, show that "gaming" is another keyword that *Philosopher's Index* uses. Searching for "video games" OR "gaming" AND "ethics" returns around 20 results, which is far more manageable (especially when you can quickly eliminate several results because they're obviously about "gaming the system" rather than video games).

Another excellent database for discovering sources is *PhilPapers* (https://philpapers.org/). It is open-access and even more comprehensive than *Philosopher's Index*. For instance, it indexes *forthcoming* material—that is, material that has been peer-reviewed and accepted for publication in a scholarly venue but that has not yet been published—and it sometimes gives you access to a **preprint** or manuscript version of the material. The site also includes **works-in-progress**—that is, draft material that the author is still working on. Both preprints and works-in-progress (by reputable scholars) are cutting-edge scholarly material, though that is no guarantee of their quality or relevance to your topic. You should use the "Advanced Search" feature to focus your search. It functions much like searching in *Philosopher's Index*, so follow our suggestions above to narrow or broaden your search.

A **full-text database** contains not just bibliographic information, such as title, author, and keywords, but also the full text of the sources it indexes, allowing for "deeper" searches. *JSTOR* and *Project MUSE* are two good full-text databases that index materials in philosophy (among other disciplines). However, they index less material than the databases we discuss above, and *Philosopher's Index* and *PhilPapers* are now partially full text, anyway (i.e., they contain the full texts of *some* of the materials they index). So we recommend using *Philosopher's Index* and *PhilPapers* for discovering scholarly philosophical sources.

9.3.3 Searching Library Catalogs

Traditionally, each library had its own **catalog**, which indexed only physical materials that the library owned. With more and more material available online, library catalogs are increasingly integrated with databases that include material not owned by the library. But you can still often access a catalog that indexes only your own library's materials, which can be useful for discovering books on your research topic. For instance, if you want to begin your research, as we recommend, by mining the bibliographies of reference works, you'll want to start with reference works that you can access immediately. Some of those may be available online, whether they are open-access or available through your library's subscriptions. But some may be available only physically, in the **stacks** (a librarian's term for bookshelves).

The stacks are organized by the unique **call numbers** assigned to each book. Most academic libraries use the Library of Congress call-number system, in which each book is assigned a call number on the basis of its topic. In this system, most philosophy books have a call number beginning with the letter B, but many are classified in other areas. For instance, a book on the philosophy of law may be grouped with other books on law rather than other books on philosophy.

Whether or not you find a reference work relevant to your topic in the catalog, it might be worth browsing the library stacks devoted to your topic. To find those stacks, simply look up in the catalog the call numbers of two or three books that are squarely on your topic, and browse the shelves around those call numbers. You might happen across something helpful to your research. (It must be said that the Library of Congress system is not very intuitive; if you are having trouble finding something on the basis of a call number or finding the call numbers most relevant to your topic, consult a librarian.)

Remember that the library catalog, if distinct from other databases, indexes only materials that the library has access to. Another serious limitation is that while traditional library catalogs index scholarly journals, they do not index the articles within the journals, which is not very helpful for research on a specific topic. For these reasons, the library catalog should be only one resource you use among many, and it will probably not be the most useful resource.

WorldCat (https://www.worldcat.org/) essentially integrates the catalogs of libraries all over the world. It indexes books (and other media) on *everything*, not just philosophy, but can sometimes be useful for finding books and individual chapters on your topic. If your library has an agreement with *WorldCat*, you may be able to click from a search result to the item in your library or to your library's interloan service. (See §9.4.1.) As with the databases discussed above, we recommend using the "Advanced Search" feature to focus your search.

9.3.4 Asking People with Experience and Expertise

If you have been given a research assignment, you may have received some instruction on how to do philosophical research—and, of course, you're reading this very helpful chapter! Nonetheless, doing philosophical research is a skill that takes time and practice to learn, so if you encounter problems, you should not hesitate to reach out to people with experience in doing philosophical research or expertise in research skills. One obvious candidate is your instructor. Even if she does not specialize in the subject of the course you are taking with her, she will have general expertise in doing philosophical research. If you come to her with a question that shows you have already used the resources she has provided you with and made an effort to figure out the answer yourself, she should be happy to help. You might also consult classmates or acquaintances who have done philosophical research projects before and other philosophy faculty at your institution.

You should also consider seeking help from librarians, especially if you're having trouble with something in the library's domain, such as a database. Many college libraries have staff dedicated to helping students with research assignments, and some have staff with particular expertise in philosophy. To see if your library has such staff, look on the library website, contact the library, or drop in and ask a librarian.

9.4 Accessing Scholarly Philosophical Sources

Suppose you have discovered a source you think would be helpful for your research assignment. Now you need to **access** it—that is, get hold of a copy so that you can read (or watch, or listen to) it.

If the source is freely available on the internet, this should be easy; any citation of it should include a permanent identifier, such as a URL or DOI, which you can click, copy and paste into your browser, or type into your browser. (See §7.6 for information about permanent identifiers.) If you don't have the permanent identifier or (despite its name) it no longer works, you may be able to find the source by doing a web search using the information you do have, such as author and title. If that doesn't work, you might try the Internet Archive (https://archive.org/web/), which archives copies of web pages that are no longer active.

If the source is not freely available on the internet, it will most likely belong to one of two kinds: books (including individual chapters) and journal articles. Accessing each of these kinds of sources can require different techniques; we thus discuss them in turn.

9.4.1 Accessing Books and Book Chapters

What we here call **books** is a large category, including continuous books, edited collections, reference works, textbooks, and so on. Sometimes you will want to access an entire book, sometimes just a single chapter.

The first way you should attempt to access a book (or book chapter) you have discovered is through your library catalog. You may be able to click through links on the book's page in *PhilPapers* or *WorldCat* to the record in your library catalog. Otherwise, you'll simply search the catalog using the book's title or author's name. If the library owns an electronic copy of the book, you should be able to click on a link in the record and start reading. If the library owns a hard copy, and it is available, record the call number and go to the corresponding place in the library to retrieve the book. If the book is not there, inform a librarian that it is missing—librarians can often locate missing items within a couple of days and alert you when they find it. If the library owns a hard copy but it is checked out, you can usually "request" or "recall" it by clicking a button in its record in the catalog. Academic libraries often require that an item be returned early if it is requested by another person.

If your library does not have a copy of the book, you can try accessing an electronic copy on the internet. *PhilPapers* offers various potential links from a book's record. Otherwise, *Google Books* (https://books.google.com/) and the *Internet Archive* (https://archive.org/details/texts and https://openlibrary.org/) are good places to start. Be aware that, for reasons of copyright, you are more likely to find older books on these sites than more recent scholarship. This applies to translations of historical works, too. It may be worth seeking out a more recent translation of, say, Plato's dialogues than making do with a more readily available but outdated 19th-century translation.

Another method for accessing books and book chapters is **interlibrary loan** (or **interloan**). Basically, your library borrows the item you seek from another library—potentially anywhere in the world—for your use. What students can interloan differs from library to library (in part because shipping is expensive), but the method is usually the same: You fill out a web form with information about the item you want, and a librarian handles the rest, informing you when the item is available (or that it cannot be interloaned). The more information you can supply, the more likely the librarian will be able to find it for you. Thus, we suggest looking up the book on *WorldCat* (https://www.worldcat.org/), which will contain information about it that may be required in the interloan form but which does not appear in the citation you have (e.g., the ISBN—a number unique to each published book).

You may have more success interloaning a single chapter than an entire book since such items are now often interloaned electronically: Someone at the library that owns the book scans the chapter as a PDF and emails it to your library (which is a lot cheaper and faster than shipping a book). We thus highly recommend that if you need only a chapter from a book, you request only that chapter. (Note that this may mean filling out a different web form than the one for a complete book.) This should be easy if you've discovered an item in an edited collection, but if you've discovered, say, a "continuous book" (see §7.5.1), it may not be obvious which chapter(s) will be most helpful for your research. There may be no way around this problem, but you should try looking at the table of contents of the book. You can find this in some cases on the publisher's website, in your library's catalog, *WorldCat* (https://www.worldcat.org/), *Google Books* (https://books.google.com/), or the "look inside" previews on *Amazon* (https://www.amazon.com/).

If all else fails, you might consider emailing the author (assuming the author is a living scholar!), explaining that you do not have access to the book through your library, and asking for a preprint copy of the relevant chapter. (Asking for a whole book would be considered presumptuous by some authors.) Most authors are happy to hear that students want to read their work and understand the difficulties some face in accessing it. We can offer no guarantees, but you might be surprised by the enthusiasm of the author's response.

9.4.2 Accessing Journal Articles

Apart from books (and book chapters), the kind of source you will most often want to access is likely a **journal article**. As we discussed in Section 7.5.3, scholarly journals are periodicals (that is, published in issues that appear at regular intervals, often monthly or quarterly) containing articles by professional scholars whose primary audience is other scholars in their field.

These days, most articles available directly through your library are available electronically. If you have familiarized yourself with *Philosopher's Index*, perhaps the easiest way to access a particular article is to click on the "PDF Full Text" link in the article's record. Similarly, the "External links" and "Through your library" links in records on *PhilPapers* can take you to PDFs of some articles. Alternatively, you can look up the journal in the library catalog and click through a series of links to get to the particular volume and issue containing the article you seek, and finally to the article itself. This may take you through some intermediate websites—a database such as *Philosopher's Index* or a repository such as *JSTOR*. Once you've accessed the article in electronic form, you should save a copy where you will easily be able to find it again (e.g., in a folder of sources inside a folder devoted to your research project).

If you do not have access to an article through your library, you can try other resources such as *Google Scholar* (https://scholar.google.com/; look for the PDF or HTML links to the right of the search results) or *PhilPapers* (https://philpapers.org/). As we mentioned in Section 9.3.2, in addition to links to open-access articles and works-in-progress, *PhilPapers* contains many preprints of journal articles, which are usually very close to the published article in terms of content, though they differ in terms of formatting and pagination. However, current scholarly convention is to cite the official published version of a published source; if you are considering citing a preprint, first check with your instructor that this is acceptable.

Libraries used to keep physical copies of journals bound into volumes, sometimes dating back decades. If your library has such **bound volumes of a journal** in which an article you've discovered appears, it may not be available electronically. In that case, unless you can find it electronically in one of the ways we have already discussed, you will have to look up the journal in the library catalog, note its call number, go to the stacks where that journal resides, and look for the volume that contains the article. Bound journal volumes are often noncirculating—that is, you can't check them out of the library—in which case you will have to read or make a copy of the article in the library.

If you cannot access an article in any of the ways we have covered thus far, you should interloan it. (See §9.4.1.) The information in a full bibliographic reference for the article should be enough to complete the relevant interloan form. There may be a link to your library's interloan service within the database in which you've discovered the article. As with an interloaned book chapter, you may conveniently receive such interloans as PDFs.

Finally, as with books and book chapters, if all else fails, you might consider emailing the author, explaining that your library does not have access to the article, and asking for a preprint copy. You never know—the author might even send you a copy of the published article.

10 Good Reasoning

Throughout this book, we have emphasized the importance of providing clear and convincing arguments in favor of the view you defend in your philosophy paper. **Logic** and **critical thinking** are the fields of philosophy devoted to studying arguments. Philosophers in these fields study what different kinds of arguments there are and what distinguishes good arguments from bad ones. In this chapter, we introduce you to some basic concepts, terms, and techniques that should help you to *identify* the kinds of arguments you are making in your paper and encountering in the work of others and to *evaluate* those arguments.[1]

An **argument** is a set of reasons, called **premises**, together with a **conclusion** those premises are intended to support. When someone presents you with an argument, she typically intends to get you to make an **inference**—that is, to come to believe something on the basis of some reasons. Similarly, when you present your reader with an argument in your thesis-defense paper, you suggest that because the argument's premises are true, your reader ought, as a rational person, to *infer* your conclusion—that is, to come to believe it on the basis of your premises. (In everyday conversation, people generally talk about "inferring" something when they're less than completely confident about the inference in question. In philosophy, however, "inference" refers to *any* psychological process of coming to believe something on the basis of reasons.)

10.1 The Content and Structure of Arguments

To determine how good or bad an argument is, you need to evaluate two aspects of it. One is the truth or falsity of its premises. We will refer to this as a matter of the *content* of the argument. The other is the inference that the argument invites you to make—the relationship between the premises and the conclusion that supposedly justifies your believing the conclusion on the basis of the premises. We will refer to this as a matter of the *structure* of the argument.[2]

1 We are indebted, throughout this chapter, to materials we have used to teach introductory reasoning and argumentation over the years, especially Elliott Sober's *Core Questions in Philosophy* (9–35) and Gideon Rosen et al.'s *Norton Introduction to Philosophy* (xxxiii–li).

2 For readers who already know some logic: As we use the term, "structure" is a broader concept than that of logical form. Logical form is one kind of argument structure. We use the term (and concept) "form" below, when we consider deductive arguments in particular.

DOI: 10.4324/9781003512318-10

Let us illustrate these two aspects with a couple of absurd arguments.[3] Suppose someone presented you with the following argument:

> The President of the United States is a unicorn, and all unicorns are fish. So the President of the United States must be a fish.

The conclusion of the argument is stated last, signaled by the conclusion indicator "so": *The President of the United States must be a fish.* The remaining two claims (linked by "and") are the premises. (For a discussion of premise and conclusion indicators, see §5.4.)

This is a terrible argument. You would never believe the conclusion on the basis of the premises, since you know that the premises are false. But you can probably see that there's *something* good about the argument. The conclusion is closely related to the premises. In fact, the premises and conclusion are related in such a way that *if* the premises *were* true, then a reasonable person would *have* to believe the conclusion on the basis of those premises. The *structure* of this argument is logically impeccable; nonetheless, because that structure is filled with false *content*, the argument gives you no reason to believe its conclusion.

Now consider the following argument:

> More than one person lives in Australia, and coffee is a popular drink in the United States. So cell phones were invented in the twentieth century.

The premises of this argument, unlike those of the previous argument, are both true. Nonetheless, this is also a terrible argument. You would never believe the conclusion on the basis of the premises since you can see that the premises—although true—are unrelated to the conclusion. The number of people living in Australia and the popularity of coffee in the United States are completely irrelevant to when cell phones were invented. This argument is a kind of mirror image of the previous one: The *content* of this argument is impeccable, but because of the way that content is structured, the argument gives you no reason to believe its conclusion.

You may have noticed that we have ignored whether the *conclusions* of these arguments are true or false. That's because evaluating an argument *only* requires examining the truth or falsity of the *premises* (the argument's content) and the *relationship between* the premises and conclusion (the argument's structure). Ultimately, we are interested in arguments because if an argument has good content and structure, then it gives us reason to believe its conclusion. If we could assess the truth or falsity of the conclusion without assessing the argument, we wouldn't need the argument in the first place.

There are different kinds of rational inference—that is, different ways in which a rational person can come to believe something on the basis of reasons. As a result, there are different ways in which an argument can be well structured. The three major kinds of arguments we discuss in this chapter are distinguished by the different kinds of inferences you call on your reader to make when you employ one of them. In Sections 10.2–10.4, we discuss what philosophers call *deductive* reasoning. In Section 10.2.5, we discuss two kinds of nondeductive reasoning: *inductive* and *abductive* reasoning. We devote most of our discussion to the *structure* of each kind of argument—that is, to the distinctive way

3 All of our examples in this chapter have only one or two premises. That is just to keep the examples simple; an argument can have any number of premises.

in which the premises are related to the conclusion. But we also discuss the way in which the truth or falsity of the premises—the argument's *content*—is related to its strength.

10.2 Deductive Reasoning: Validity and Soundness

A **deductive** argument is one in which the premises are designed to *guarantee* the truth of the conclusion without any possibility of error. Deductive reasoning is relatively well understood. In this section, we introduce two central concepts of deductive logic. In each of the following two sections, we introduce one common family of deductive arguments.

10.2.1 Validity

Sometimes a writer suggests that if you were to accept the premises that have been offered, then you would have no rational alternative to accepting the conclusion also—you would be logically compelled to believe the conclusion. Such a writer believes that he has given what logicians call a **valid** argument, that is, one in which the premises—if true—*necessarily* imply the truth of the conclusion.

In ordinary conversation, when one describes a person's views as "valid," one often means that those views are reasonable, even if one does not oneself agree with them. In philosophy, "valid" is a very important technical term and should not be used in the ordinary conversational sense. You should use the word "valid" in your philosophy paper *only* when you mean the logical concept we discuss in this section.

To assess whether an argument is valid (in the logical sense), we can—indeed, we *must*—put aside the question of whether the premises are in fact true. Validity is a matter of the *structure* or *form* of an argument, not its content:[4]

> To say that an argument is valid is to say that *if the premises were true, then the conclusion would have to be true.*

In other words, to determine whether an argument is valid, you should ignore whatever you think about the truth or falsity of the premises and ask: "*If* the premises were true, would the conclusion then *have* to be true?" A *yes* answer to this question indicates that the argument is valid. An answer of *no*, *maybe*, *probably*, or even *almost certainly* indicates that the argument is **invalid** (i.e., not valid).

Consider two more definitions of validity. They present the preceding point in different words.

> A valid argument is one in which the truth of the premises would guarantee the truth of the conclusion.

> An argument is valid if and only if it is *absolutely impossible* for its premises to be true and its conclusion false. (Rosen et al. xxxv; bold formatting removed)

Notice two crucial similarities between all three of these quite differently worded definitions. The first similarity is that each definition expresses the idea that *the validity*

4 For reasons that are beyond the scope of this chapter, we will (as noted above) refer to the *form* rather than *structure* of deductive arguments.

of an argument has nothing to do with whether the premises are actually true or false. That is, validity is a matter of the *form* of an argument, not its content. In the first and second definitions, this is indicated with the words "if" and "would." In the third definition, it is implicit in the notion of impossibility—we are considering what *would* be the case *if* the premises were true.

The second similarity is that each definition expresses the *strength* of validity. If the premises of a valid argument were true, the conclusion would *have* to be true; its truth would be *guaranteed*; the alternative is *absolutely impossible.*

To illustrate the notion of validity, let's consider some examples. Recall our first example from Section 10.1:

> The President of the United States is a unicorn, and all unicorns are fish. So the President of the United States must be a fish.

This argument is valid because *if* the premises were true, then the conclusion would *have* to be true.

Sometimes philosophers write arguments in what we might call "standard format," putting each premise and the conclusion on a separate line and numbering them. This can make it easier to see the structure of the argument, and to refer to individual premises without having to restate them. Here, for instance, is the previous argument in standard format:

1. The President of the United States is a unicorn.
2. All unicorns are fish.
3. So the President of the United States is a fish.

In standard format, the conclusion is always stated last. Sometimes, it is further indicated by a conclusion indicator (in this case "so"). Sometimes, a line is drawn after the last premise to indicate that the conclusion follows:

1. The President of the United States is a unicorn.
2. <u>All unicorns are fish</u>.
3. So the President of the United States is a fish.

Notice that in our standard-format versions of the original argument we have used slightly different words to state the conclusion, changing "must be" to "is." It is worth recalling from Chapters 5 and 6 that the same idea can be expressed in different words. Philosophers sometimes put this by saying that two different sentences can *express the same proposition.* That is, a **proposition**, in the philosophical sense, is something like the *meaning* of a sentence—the content of the sentence that could be expressed in other words. For example, the two sentences "All dogs have four legs" and "Every dog has four legs" express the same proposition; they're two different ways of saying the same thing. Crucially, for our purposes in this chapter, this means that both sentences must have the same **truth value**; that is, both sentences must be true, or both sentences must be false. If they really express the same proposition, it would be impossible for one sentence to be true and the other false. This means that there's nothing wrong with rewording a premise or conclusion, provided that the reworded sentence really does express the same proposition as the original sentence.

It might seem that our rewording of the conclusion of the unicorn argument is not so innocent. Doesn't the original conclusion "the President of the United States *must be* a fish" say something stronger than our rewording: "the President of the United States *is* a fish"? Taken in isolation, these sentences do express different propositions. But in the context of the original argument, the word "must" is not so much part of the conclusion as an indication that the author of the argument intends it to have the strength of validity—in other words, that the argument is deductive.

Consider another argument:

> The reason the moon orbits the Earth is that the moon is made of green cheese—and most things made of green cheese orbit the Earth.

In standard format:

4. The moon is made of green cheese.
5. Most things made of green cheese orbit the Earth.
6. So the moon orbits the Earth.

This argument is *invalid* because the premises would not *guarantee* the conclusion, even if they were true. Even if the moon were made of green cheese, and even if most things made of green cheese orbited the Earth, this would leave open the *possibility* that the moon is one of the few things made of green cheese that do not orbit the Earth. In this case, of course, you know independently of this argument that the conclusion is true. You would still have to admit that the argument presented here is invalid since validity concerns *not* the truth of the premises or conclusion of an argument but *only* the logical relationship between its premises and conclusion.

Logicians have developed sophisticated formal methods for evaluating the validity of arguments. Such methods, which you would learn in an introductory logic course, are beyond the scope of this chapter.[5] But one informal way to test for the validity of an argument is to try to imagine a situation in which the premises are true and the conclusion is false. If you *can* imagine such a situation, then the argument is *invalid*. After all, if the argument were valid, then in *any* situation in which the premises were true, the conclusion would *have* to be true. Your imagined situation is a **counterexample** to the validity of the argument (i.e., it's an example that shows the *invalidity* of the argument).

Take, for instance, the preceding argument. Can you imagine a situation in which (5) most things made of green cheese orbit the Earth, and (4) the moon is made of green cheese, yet in which the moon does not orbit the Earth (i.e., the negation of the conclusion)? You should be able to: You just need to imagine a world in which *most* things made of green cheese orbit the Earth, but the moon isn't one of them (even though it's made of green cheese in this imaginary situation). For instance, you could imagine that the moon orbits Mars or doesn't move at all. Since you can imagine a situation in which the premises are true but the conclusion false, you know that this argument is invalid.

By contrast, take our first example argument. Imagine a situation in which (2) all unicorns are fish, and (1) the President of the United States is a unicorn. Can you imagine that, in this situation, the President might not be a fish (the negation of the argument's

5 There are many good introductions to formal logic, including Barker-Plummer, Barwise, and Etchemendy's *Language, Proof, and Logic* and Smith's *Introduction to Formal Logic*.

conclusion)? No—that would be impossible, given the two things you've already imagined of the situation. So the argument is valid.

Be careful, though—this method is helpful but not infallible. If you can imagine a counterexample to an argument's validity, then you should conclude that it's invalid. However, if you *can't* imagine a counterexample, that doesn't show that there isn't one. Perhaps you simply haven't managed to think of one. A counterexample to a serious philosophical argument on an abstract topic can be especially difficult to come up with.

10.2.2 Soundness

Validity is a matter of the *form* of an argument, and good form alone cannot give you good reason to believe a particular conclusion, as our unicorn argument (1–3) shows. We thus turn now to the *content* of deductive arguments: how the truth or falsity of their premises affects what you should rationally believe on the basis of those premises.

Deductive arguments are potentially powerful because of the strength of validity. The conclusion of a valid argument is *guaranteed* to be true—it can't possibly be false—*if* its premises are true. But that's a big "if." We can divide valid arguments into two groups: Those whose premises are *all* true, and those whose premises are *not* all true (i.e., those with at least one false premise). If a valid argument's premises are all true, then its conclusion is guaranteed to be true—a rational person must accept its conclusion. By contrast, if even a single premise of a valid argument is false, then the argument gives you *no reason whatsoever* to believe its conclusion.[6]

So when someone offers a deductive argument, she intends not only that it be valid but also that each of its premises is true. Philosophers describe an argument that meets both these criteria as **sound**. That is, an argument is sound if—and only if—it meets *both* of the following conditions:

(i) the argument is valid, and
(ii) each of its premises is true.

If an argument fails to meet *either one* of these two conditions, it is **unsound** and, to repeat, gives you *no reason whatsoever* to believe its conclusion. (Notice that soundness concerns *both* the form *and* content of an argument.)

Recall the first argument we considered when explaining validity:

1. The President of the United States is a unicorn.
2. All unicorns are fish.
3. So the President of the United States is a fish.

The argument passes the first test for soundness: Its conclusion would have to be true if its premises were true. That is, it is valid. However, at least one of the premises is false. So the argument fails the second test for soundness; the argument is unsound. (Premise 1 is obviously false. Philosophers disagree about whether we know the truth value of premise 2. What do you think?) As we said in Section 10.1, the *structure* or *form* of this argument

6 That is, it gives you no reason whatsoever to infer its conclusion *deductively*. This qualification should be taken to apply throughout our discussion of deduction. An unsound argument may give some reason—even very good reason—to infer its conclusion inductively or abductively. See Section 10.2.5.

is logically impeccable (it is valid), but the *content* of the argument (it has at least one false premise) renders it useless. It gives you no reason whatsoever to believe its conclusion.

The following argument, by contrast, is sound:

> Anyone who can understand the sentences in this book has a good grasp of the English language. You can understand the sentences in this book. Thus, you have a good grasp of the English language.

In standard format:

7. Anyone who can understand the sentences in this book has a good grasp of the English language.
8. You can understand the sentences in this book.
9. Thus, you have a good grasp of the English language.

To check its validity, we ask: *If* anyone who can understand the sentences in this book has a good grasp of English, *and if* you can understand the sentences in this book, *then* would it *have* to be true that you have a good grasp of English? The answer is *yes*, so the argument is valid; it passes the first test for soundness. The other question to be asked is: Are all the premises true? Again, the answer is *yes*. Since the argument passes both tests, it is sound, and the conclusion must be true.

Notice that an unsound argument will not necessarily have a false conclusion. Consider our moon argument once more:

4. The moon is made of green cheese.
5. Most things made of green cheese orbit the Earth.
6. So the moon orbits the Earth.

This argument is invalid, and both its premises are false, yet it has a true conclusion. Despite having a true conclusion, this is a terrible argument because it is unsound—it gives you *no reason whatsoever* to believe its conclusion. The point of an argument is not simply to *have* a true conclusion; the point of an argument is to *give you good reasons to believe* its conclusion.

Even if an argument's premises *and* conclusion are true, it could still be unsound because it could be invalid. The cell-phone argument in Section 10.1 is of this kind. Here is a subtler example:

10. You are reading this book.
11. No one deserves to be tortured for reading a book.
12. So, you are not being tortured for reading this book.

Unlike with our absurd cell-phone argument, the same concepts appear in the premises and conclusion of this argument in a way that might at first seem rationally compelling. But the argument is invalid. Even though you don't deserve to be tortured for reading this book, it's *possible* that someone might torture you for reading it. Yet validity, and thus soundness, requires that it be *impossible* for the premises to be true and the conclusion false. This argument does not meet that stringent requirement. So the argument is invalid and thus unsound—despite having true premises and a true conclusion. Such arguments can be especially beguiling if you are disposed to believe the conclusion. But they give you no reason to believe their conclusions.

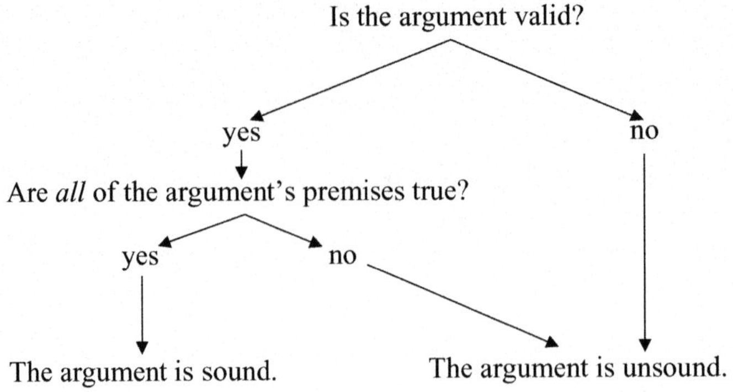

Figure 10.1 The relationships between validity, truth, and soundness.

Figure 10.1 and the table below may help you to see the relationships between validity, truth, and soundness. Notice that it is possible for an argument to be valid and sound (e.g., our reading-with-understanding example, 7–9), valid and unsound (e.g., our unicorn example, 1–3), or invalid and unsound (e.g., our moon example, 4–6). However, it is impossible for an argument to be invalid and sound since in order to be sound, an argument must be valid—that's part of the concept of soundness.

Inference	Premises	Argument
Valid	All true	Sound
	One or more false	Unsound
Invalid	All true	Unsound
	One or more false	Unsound

10.2.3 Circularity

It is worth revisiting the fallacy of *begging the question* in the context of deductive reasoning. Recall from Section 4.7 that you "beg the question" when you argue in a circle—stating or implying your conclusion in one of your premises. Consider the following straightforward example:

13. You are reading a book about how to write philosophy papers.
14. So, you are reading a book about how to write philosophy papers.

You probably see that *something* is wrong with this argument. But notice that it is sound: *if* its single premise were true, then the conclusion would *have* to be true. And the premise *is* true. So the argument is valid. The argument thus meets both the conditions for being sound. Why, then, is this a bad argument? The purpose of an argument is to rationally compel you to believe something (the conclusion) on the basis of *another* claim or claims that you already believe (the premises). But, obviously, if you already believe the premise of this particular argument, you thereby already believe the conclusion since they say exactly the same thing. So the argument cannot rationally compel you to believe that conclusion.

It's difficult to imagine someone seriously offering an argument as obviously circular as this one. But when it comes to actual philosophical arguments, circularity can be fiendishly difficult to detect. You must simply do your best, then, to consider whether a given argument—your own or someone else's—implicitly assumes the truth of its conclusion in one of its premises.

10.2.4 Validity, Soundness, and the Limits of Knowledge

Suppose that you are assessing an argument, and you've confirmed that it is valid and that all but one of its premises are true. You're not sure about the remaining premise. You've done your best to figure out whether it is true or false, but you just don't know. Is the argument sound or unsound? The answer is that *you do not know*. An argument's soundness does not depend on your beliefs, knowledge, or personal perspective. If the argument is valid and all its premises are true, then the argument is sound—whether you know it or not. If you don't know whether the argument is valid, or whether all of its premises are true, then you won't know whether it is sound. Furthermore, if you *incorrectly* judge an argument's validity or the truth value of one or more of its premises, you may well assess its soundness incorrectly.

10.2.5 Logical Terminology

Because of the importance of the quality of arguments in philosophical writing, you should use the words "valid," "invalid," "sound," and "unsound" *only* to describe *arguments* (and only in the logical senses we have been discussing). Because validity and invalidity are particular logical relationships between more than one claim (at least one premise and a conclusion), it makes no sense to describe a single claim or a theory—anything other than an argument or inference, in fact—as valid or invalid. And because validity is part of the concept of soundness, it makes no sense to describe anything other than an argument or inference as sound or unsound, either. The other side of this coin is that you should never describe an individual sentence, claim, or proposition as valid or invalid, sound or unsound. Individual claims are *true* or *false* (never valid or invalid, sound or unsound).

We have used "toy" arguments to illustrate the concepts of soundness and validity—arguments that are so obviously valid or invalid or whose premises are so obviously true or false that no one would seriously offer them. Assessing actual philosophical arguments, whether your own or others', can be much more difficult. However, certain kinds of deductive argument, both valid and invalid, are commonly found in all areas of philosophy—indeed, in all human reasoning. In the next two sections, we consider some of the most common such kinds of arguments.

10.3 Deductive Reasoning: Conditional Arguments

How many times do you use the word "if" in an average day? *If I take that course, then .... If the car could be fixed by tomorrow morning, then .... If you had changed your approach, then ....* Because this little word is so familiar, we are not especially alert to its logical implications. We should be. The word "if" often introduces a sentence expressing a conditional proposition, and conditional propositions are used frequently in both everyday and philosophical reasoning. Yet people consistently make mistakes when assessing the validity of arguments with conditional premises. It is thus important that we take a special look at this kind of argument.

10.3.1 Conditional Propositions

A **conditional proposition** (or "conditional" for short) has two parts linked in an if–then structure. For example:

> If you're in London, then you're in England.

A conditional says that if one thing is true (i.e., if a certain "condition" is fulfilled), then something else is true. In this example, the author is claiming that if it's true that you're in London, then it's true that you're in England. This sample conditional is true. It doesn't say that you're in London. Nor does it say that you're in England. What it says is that *if* the first part is true, *then* the second part is also true. And because anyone in London is thereby in England, the conditional as a whole is true (whether or not you're in London).[7]

The part of a conditional proposition between the words "if" and "then" is called the **antecedent.** The part that follows the word "then" is called the **consequent.** (See Figure 10.2.) Conditional propositions are useful precisely because they link two other propositions (the antecedent and consequent) whose truth can be assessed independently. It is thus important to remember that the antecedent does not include the word "if," and the consequent does not include the word "then." These small but crucial words are, rather, the logical glue holding the antecedent and the consequent together. You probably know whether the following proposition is true or false: *You're in London.* But ask yourself whether the following is true or false: *If you're in London.* The question doesn't make sense. "If you're in London" doesn't express a proposition; it's not a complete sentence. So it can't be the antecedent or consequent of a conditional proposition.

If you switch the antecedent and consequent, the result is a different conditional. Consider the following two conditionals:

> If you're in London, then you're in England.
> If you're in England, then you're in London.

Suppose you are in Manchester (another city in England). The first conditional is still true. What about the second conditional? It is clearly false. It says that if you're in

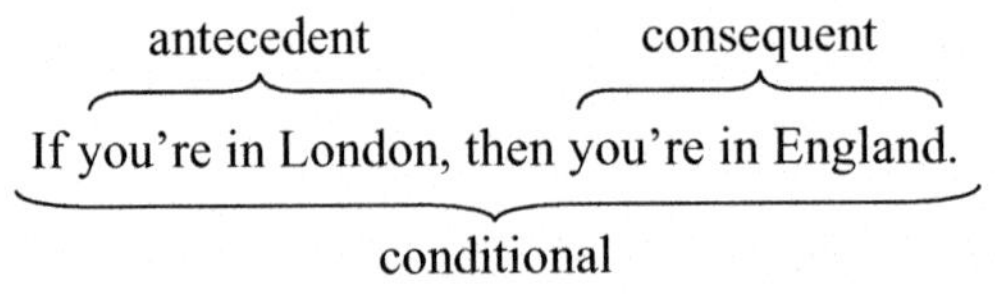

Figure 10.2 The parts of a conditional proposition.

7 You might worry that we haven't specified what "London" means in this example. If it's London, Ontario, then the conditional is false. This is a good worry for a philosopher to have; it's one reason that defining your terms can be so important. (See §5.6.) For the purposes of the examples in this chapter, however, rest assured that by "London" we mean the city that is the capital of the United Kingdom, where the Thames flows past Big Ben, and so on.

England, then you're in London, but you *are* in England (because you're in Manchester), and you're *not* in London. Since one of these conditionals can be true and the other false, they express different propositions. The moral of this story is that you should be very careful never to switch the antecedent and consequent of a conditional.

A sentence can express a conditional proposition without using the words "if" and "then." Here are three common variations:

1. The word "then" may be omitted. The following sentences express the same proposition:

   If you're in London, then you're in England.
   If you're in London, you're in England.

2. Other words, such as "when" or "whenever," sometimes introduce the antecedent instead of "if." For instance, the following sentences all express the same proposition:

   If you're in London, you're in England.
   When you're in London, you're in England.
   Whenever you're in London, you're in England.

3. The order of the antecedent and consequent *in the sentence* does not affect what *proposition* is expressed. For instance, the following two sentences express the same proposition:

   If you're in London, you're in England.
   You're in England if you're in London.

   The antecedent of the second sentence is still "you're in London." What makes it the antecedent is the *logical role* it plays in the proposition as a whole (indicated here by the word "if"), not where it falls on the page. This is one reason we use the technical terms "antecedent" and "consequent" rather than, say, "first part" or "second half." The antecedent may come before or after the consequent in a sentence expressing a conditional proposition.

It's important to realize that all a conditional says is that *if* the antecedent is *true*, then the consequent is *true*.[8] It does not claim any temporal, causal, or necessary relationship between the antecedent and the consequent. Let's consider these topics in turn.

Because conditional sentences often contain the words "when" or "then," it's easy to slip into thinking that what the consequent describes must happen *after* what the antecedent describes and is *caused* by it. But a conditional proposition says nothing about temporal order or causation. Consider our original example once more: *If you're in London, then you're in England.* This conditional proposition is true, but it doesn't imply that *first* you arrived in London and then, a little later, you were in England. (In fact, that would be

8 At least, that's all it says for our purposes in this chapter. The logic of conditionals is a deep and difficult subject. For an accessible introduction, see the two chapters on conditionals in Peter Smith's *Introduction to Formal Logic* (148–71).

impossible: If you're in London, you're already in England!) And it's not as if being in London *caused* you to be in England. Perhaps an invitation to visit relatives in Manchester caused you to be in England. Of course, there *can* be temporal and causal relations between the antecedent and consequent of a conditional proposition. Perhaps *if you drop the glass, then it will break*. If so, the dropping occurs before the breaking and causes it. But all that conditional proposition says is that if the antecedent is true, then the consequent is true; it doesn't imply anything about the temporal or causal relations between the dropping and the breaking. After all, the following is also a perfectly fine (but quite different) conditional proposition: *If the glass is broken, then it was dropped*. But in this case, what the *consequent* describes comes before and causes what the *antecedent* describes.

It's also easy to think that a conditional implies some *necessary connection* between its antecedent and consequent. But this is not the case. If everyone turns up to a party in jeans, then it's true that *if you're at the party, then you're wearing jeans*. But there's no necessary connection between the antecedent and consequent of this conditional. People could easily have worn different clothes to the party. As with temporal and causal connections, there *might* be a necessary connection between an antecedent and consequent (e.g., *if something is square, then it has four sides*). But you can't infer that necessary connection from the mere fact that this is a true conditional.

A final thing to remember about conditional sentences is that "if" and "only if" mean quite different things. People sometimes think that when they say "only if," they are merely being emphatic about their "if" statement. Actually, however, replacing "if" with "only if" results in a completely different claim. Consider the following two sentences:

X. You passed the final exam if you passed the midterm exam.
Y. You passed the final exam only if you passed the midterm exam.

They may look very similar, but they express quite different propositions. Sentence X is good news if you passed the midterm, because it implies that you passed the final. If you *didn't* pass the midterm, you can't infer anything about your performance on the final from just that fact and sentence X. But sentence Y says that you didn't pass the final *unless* you passed the midterm. Perhaps you've already realized that sentence Y is equivalent to the following:

Z. You passed the midterm exam if you passed the final exam.

That is, merely by adding the word "only" to sentence X, sentence Y essentially swaps the antecedent and consequent of sentence X. And as we've already seen, swapping the antecedent and consequent of a conditional proposition results in a quite different proposition.

As we'll soon see, conditional arguments cause enough confusion without the added complications of the phrase "only if." If you encounter (or draft) a conditional statement containing the phrase "only if," we recommend that you consider reformulating it so that it's a straightforward if–then claim.[9]

9 A caveat: Philosophers often use the phrase "if and only if" (often abbreviated to "iff"). Because this phrase contains *both* logical connectives "if" and "only if," a statement containing it is not a conditional claim, and our advice above does not apply to it. Such statements are *biconditionals*. That is, they claim that the conditional relationship goes both ways between the two parts of the statement. In other words, "A if, and only if, B" is equivalent to "If A, then B; and if B, then A."

10.3.2 Conditional Arguments

As we use the term, a **conditional argument** is simply an argument with a conditional premise. Despite constantly using conditional reasoning and encountering the conditional arguments of others, people often evaluate the validity of such reasoning incorrectly. Let's consider how these mistakes are made. This should help you to recognize your own faulty conditional reasoning and to revise your paper to eliminate it. It should also help you to identify and critically discuss the conditional arguments of others.

Examine the following four arguments in turn, deciding in each case whether the argument is valid or invalid.

A: 13. Whenever a Cambridge philosopher writes an essay, its thesis is well supported.
14. A Cambridge philosopher wrote this essay.
15. So the thesis of this essay is well supported.

B: 16. Whenever a Cambridge philosopher writes an essay, its thesis is well supported.
17. The thesis of this essay is well supported.
18. So a Cambridge philosopher wrote this essay.

C: 19. Whenever a Cambridge philosopher writes an essay, its thesis is well supported.
20. The thesis of this essay is not well supported.
21. So a Cambridge philosopher did not write this essay.

D: 22. Whenever a Cambridge philosopher writes an essay, its thesis is well supported.
23. A Cambridge philosopher did not write this essay.
24. So the thesis of this essay is not well supported.

Stop here. Do not read on unless you have already determined, to your own satisfaction, whether each of the preceding arguments is valid or invalid.

Now, consider four more arguments. Once more, decide whether each is valid or invalid.

A*: 25. Whenever you're in London, you're in England.
26. You're in London.
27. So you're in England.

B*: 28. Whenever you're in London, you're in England.
29. You're in England.
30. So you're in London.

C*: 31. Whenever you're in London, you're in England.
32. You're not in England.
33. So you're not in London.

D*: 34. Whenever you're in London, you're in England.
35. You're not in London.
36. So you're not in England.

However well you did assessing the validity of the original arguments A through D (we'll get to the answers soon!), you probably found it easier to do so for the parallel arguments A* through D*. That's because it's often the subject matter or content of an argument that makes it confusing. But recall that validity has nothing to do with an argument's content; it is entirely a matter of an argument's *form*. If you carefully compare arguments A though D with arguments A* through D*, you should be able to see that A and A* have the same form, as do B and B*, and so on. All we have done is replace each instance of "a Cambridge philosopher writes an essay" with "you're in London" and each instance of "the essay's thesis is well supported" with "you're in England." Because the geographical propositions are less confusing than the propositions about Cambridge philosophers, most people are better able to focus on the form of the second set of arguments.

The beauty of this is that—since validity is all about an argument's form, having nothing to do with its content—if you can see that, say, B* is invalid, you know that the original argument B must be invalid because it has exactly the same form. (Soundness is another matter—an argument's content is *crucial* to its soundness. So, for instance, though both A and A* are valid arguments, it might well be the case that one is sound and the other unsound since the premises of one may all be true while the other has a false premise.)

This replacement technique is one method you can use to help you ignore an argument's content and see its form, enabling you to judge its validity more easily. However, when using this method, you must be very careful always to replace the same phrase with its corresponding phrase, and to pay attention to negations. (For instance, "the thesis of this essay is *not* well supported" must be replaced with "you're *not* in England.")

We'll look at another replacement technique for focusing on the form of an argument soon, but first, let's consider each of our four argument forms in turn to see which are valid and which are invalid. Each begins with the same conditional premise, then has a premise that affirms or denies the antecedent or consequent of the conditional premise, and concludes by affirming or denying the other part of the conditional premise. (These similarities contribute to the ease with which these quite different forms of argument can be confused.)

The form of arguments A and A* is valid. *Any* argument with this form will be valid, regardless of its content. After all, the conditional premise says that *if* the antecedent is true, *then* the consequent is true, and the other premise says that the antecedent *is* true. So if both the premises are true, the consequent *must* be true—and that is indeed the conclusion of this argument form. Because this form of argument has been recognized as common and valid for many centuries, it still bears a Latin name. It is called ***modus ponens***, which means "the method of affirming," since the nonconditional premise affirms the antecedent of the conditional premise.

The form of arguments B and B* is invalid. *Any* argument with this form will be invalid, regardless of its content. The conditional premise says that if the antecedent is true, then the consequent is true; the other premise says that the consequent is true. But nothing about the antecedent follows from these two premises (despite what's claimed in the conclusion). Just because you're in England if you're in London, it doesn't follow that you're in London if you're in England. (You could be in Manchester.) So even if the premises of argument B* are true, its conclusion could be false—that is, the argument is invalid. The same applies to argument B: Even if both premises are true, the essay in question could have been written by a Texan philosopher. This kind of argument is a *formal fallacy*—that is, a common error that is due to the form of an argument.[10] It also has its own name: **affirming the consequent** (because that's what the nonconditional premise does).

The form of arguments C and C* is valid. *Any* argument with this form will be valid, regardless of its content. The conditional premise says that if the antecedent is true, then the consequent is true; the other premise denies the consequent. Now, if the conditional premise is true, but the consequent is not true, then the antecedent can't possibly be true. After all, the conditional premise says precisely that if the antecedent is true, then the consequent is true; so if the consequent isn't true, the antecedent can't be either. (If being in London implies you're in England, and you're *not* in England, then you can't be in London.) And that's just what the conclusion says. Like arguments of form A, this form of argument has long been recognized as common and valid, and thus has a Latin name: ***modus tollens***, which means "the method of denying," since the nonconditional premise denies the consequent of the conditional premise.

Finally, the form of arguments D and D* is invalid. *Any* argument with this form will be invalid, regardless of its content. The conditional premise says that if the antecedent is true, then the consequent is true; the other premise says that the antecedent is false. But nothing about the consequent follows from these two premises (despite what's claimed in the conclusion). Just because being in London implies being in England, it doesn't follow that if you're *not* in London, you're *not* in England. (Again, you could be in Manchester.) So even if the premises of argument D* are true, its conclusion could be false—that is, the argument is invalid. The same applies to argument D: Even if both premises are true, the essay in question could have been written by a Texan *and* have a well-supported thesis. This kind of argument is another formal fallacy.[11] It also has its own name: **denying the antecedent** (because that's what the nonconditional premise does).[12]

The second replacement technique for focusing on an argument's form to assess its validity *entirely eliminates* the argument's content, exposing its bare form. Using this method, taking arguments A though D once more, you might replace each instance of "a Cambridge philosopher writes an essay" with "P" and each instance of "the essay's thesis is well supported" with "Q." (As with the first method, you must be very careful to do the replacements consistently and pay attention to negations.) Using this second method, we get the following versions of arguments A through D. (We've also replaced "whenever" with "if" and explicitly supplied a "then" in each conditional premise since we think that makes the form of each argument even easier to see.)

10 In two studies, 67% and 53% of subjects judged arguments affirming the consequent to be valid. In the same studies, 100% and 78% of subjects judged *modus ponens* arguments as valid (Evans, "Selective Processes in Reasoning" 148).

11 In two studies, 38% and 54% of subjects judged arguments denying the antecedent to be valid. In both studies, 42% of subjects judged *modus tollens* arguments to be valid (Evans, "Selective Processes in Reasoning" 148). (Notice that, in one study, more subjects thought the *invalid* reasoning was valid than thought the *valid* reasoning was valid!)

12 We could refer to *modus ponens* and *modus tollens* as "affirming the antecedent" and "denying the consequent." However, the Latin names are widely used in philosophy, and it is perhaps helpful to have different kinds of names for the valid and invalid argument forms.

A′: If P, then Q.
P.
So Q.

B′: If P, then Q.
Q.
So P.

C′: If P, then Q.
Not Q.
So not P.

D′: If P, then Q.
Not P.
So not Q.

Some people find the pure, abstract argument forms laid bare in examples A′ through D′ even easier to assess for validity than arguments A* through D*. Others find the replacement of ordinary language with symbols mystifying. You should use whichever method you find most helpful for focusing on an argument's form to assess its validity.

10.4 Deductive Reasoning: Syllogisms

Like "if," the little words "all," "no," and "some" are used casually and often. In a philosophy paper, you might find yourself drafting sentences such as "All events have a cause," "No abortion is morally acceptable," or "Some beliefs count as knowledge." Think carefully when you draft sentences like these. Beginning a statement with "all" or "no" can easily result in overstatement. (See §§4.4 & 5.3.) More relevant to our concerns in this chapter is that some arguments containing a premise beginning with "all" can be as misleading as the conditional fallacies we considered above—they can appear to be valid when they are in fact invalid.

In this section, we examine **syllogisms**. A syllogism is an argument with two premises and a conclusion, where each of these three claims relates two categories of things and can be worded to begin with "all," "no," or "some."

When assessing syllogistic reasoning, it's sometimes useful to reword a claim to clarify that it is an "all," "some," or "none" claim about two categories of things, even if the result is stylistically awkward. For instance, there are many different words that express the ideas of "all" ("every," "without exception," ...) and "none" ("no," "nobody," ...). Rewording such claims to use just "all" and "no" can clarify the form of the argument. For instance, the claim "Dogs are, without exception, mammals" might be reworded as "All dogs are mammals."

It is also important to realize that when philosophers use the word "some," especially in logical contexts, it is often a technical term. In ordinary English, the word "some" typically means "a few." But in logical contexts, "some" means *one or more*. For instance, the claim that "some cats have six toes per paw" is true if *at least one* cat has six toes per paw. The reason for this usage is that philosophers are interested in the truth value of claims that *no* members of one category belong in another category (e.g., "No abortion is morally acceptable"). If just a single member (i.e., "some") of the first category belongs to the second category, the "no" claim is false. So it's helpful to have a short way of saying "at least one," and philosophers use "some" for that.

Finally, it can help to make explicit what two categories are being related. For instance, the claim that "All events have a cause" might be reworded as "All events are things that are caused" to make explicit that the claim describes a relationship between the categories *events* and *things that are caused.* Similarly, "No abortion is morally acceptable" might be reworded as "No abortion is a morally acceptable action."

10.4.1 The Universal Syllogism and Its Counterfeit Fallacies

Consider the following argument:

37. All English philosophers are empiricists.
38. All empiricists are logicians.
39. Therefore, all English philosophers are logicians.

This argument is valid. If both premises were true, then the conclusion would have to be true. (The argument is unsound because neither premise is true, but we continue to focus on validity.) *Any* argument with this form is valid. The form is called the **universal syllogism** since it features three universal ("all") claims. Make up your own example. Here is the pattern:

All As are Bs.
All Bs are Cs.
Therefore, all As are Cs.

If you choose obviously false premises, your argument will be silly because it will be obviously unsound. Still, it will be valid.

The universal syllogism is a common form of reasoning, and to many people its validity will be obvious. However, that obvious validity can itself be a problem. As with conditional arguments, a person may mistake a similar but invalid form for the valid one. Consider another argument form in which the premises and conclusion begin with "all":

All As are Bs.
All As are Cs.
Therefore, all Bs are Cs.

This form of reasoning is invalid; it is a formal fallacy. Here is an argument with that form:

40. All English philosophers are empiricists.
41. All English philosophers are logicians.
42. Therefore, all empiricists are logicians.

For all the premises say, there could be a French empiricist who is not a logician. That is, the premises could be true and the conclusion false, so the argument is invalid. If you were at all tempted to say that this argument is valid, consider the following argument with the same form:

43. All dogs are animals.
44. All dogs have four legs.
45. Therefore, all animals have four legs.

You are unlikely to be taken in by this argument because you know, on independent grounds, that the conclusion is false. But the conclusion of any serious philosophical argument will be more controversial, so you need to be able to assess the validity of the argument's form.

As with conditional arguments, the *content* of a syllogism can blind you to the invalidity of its *form*. So, as with conditional arguments, you should test the form of any syllogism you construct or encounter by either substituting simpler claims into the argument or exposing the form by replacing the content with variables (e.g., A, B, and C).

There is another formal fallacy that might be mistaken for the valid universal syllogism:

All As are Bs.
All Cs are Bs.
Therefore, all As are Cs.

As with the conditional fallacies we considered, you may be able to create an argument with this form that has true premises and a true conclusion. But no argument of this form can be sound—that is, no argument of this form can give you any reason whatsoever to believe its conclusion—because the form is always invalid, as the following counterexample shows:

46. All dogs are animals.
47. All cats are animals.
48. Therefore, all dogs are cats.

10.4.2 The Universal-to-Particular Syllogism and its Counterfeit Fallacies

The following argument is valid:

49. All of Plato's dialogues are philosophically significant writings.
50. Some of Plato's dialogues are characterized by humor and irony.
51. Therefore, some philosophically significant writings are characterized by humor and irony.

If you accept those premises, then you cannot consistently deny the conclusion; it would have to be true too. This argument form is called the **universal-to-particular syllogism** because it moves from a universal ("all") claim to a particular ("some") claim. There are two kinds of universal-to-particular syllogisms:

All As are Bs.	All As are Bs.
Some A is a C.	Some C is an A.
Therefore, some B is a C.	Therefore, some C is a B.

The premises and conclusions of the invalid counterfeits of this syllogism—further formal fallacies—have the same opening words: *all*, *some*, and *some*. However, the categories (A, B, and C) appear in different places. Here are the deceptive forms:

All As are Bs.	All As are Bs.
Some B is a C.	Some C is a B.
Therefore, some A is a C.	Therefore, some A is a C.

The following reasoning is an example of the first counterfeit form:

52. All of Plato's dialogues are philosophically significant writings.
53. Some philosophically significant writings are characterized by humor and irony.
54. Therefore, some of Plato's dialogues are characterized by humor and irony.

Although the conclusion is true, the argument is invalid—the premises do not guarantee the conclusion. The philosophically significant writings referred to in the second premise might all be by people other than Plato.

Once more, these forms' invalidity can be seen by producing versions with simple content. For instance:

55. All dogs are mammals.
56. Some mammals are whales.
57. Therefore, some dogs are whales.

10.5 Nondeductive Reasoning

Deductive reasoning is powerful in that a sound argument *guarantees* the truth of its conclusion. The other side of this coin, however, is that it is difficult to provide a convincing sound argument for a controversial philosophical claim. If an argument's validity and the truth of its premises are obvious, then everyone would already have drawn its conclusion—so that conclusion wouldn't be controversial. Like everyone else, then, philosophers also make use of other kinds of reasoning. Good nondeductive arguments do not *guarantee* the truth of their conclusions—they are invalid and thus unsound—but they nonetheless give us good reason for believing those conclusions.

Nondeductive reasoning is extremely common. When you go to the store to get something for dinner, you do so because you reasonably believe that there will be something at the store you can eat. But you cannot provide a sound argument for that belief. (Try it!) For all you know, it's *possible* that, for instance, the store has just gone out of business. Nonetheless, your belief that there will be something at the store you can eat is reasonable. Indeed, it would be irrational *not* to go to the store because of the mere possibility that it has just gone out of business.

Nondeductive reasoning is not as well understood as deductive reasoning. Nonetheless, logicians have developed some concepts that help us to describe and assess nondeductive arguments. In this section, we introduce two common kinds of nondeductive arguments, along with techniques for assessing how good such arguments are.

10.5.1 Inductive Reasoning

We often make generalizations. In everyday life, someone might say that *math majors are really smart*, even though he's met only a handful of math majors. If his reasoning is the following, then it's obviously invalid.

58. The seven math majors I've met are really smart.
59. So all math majors are really smart.

It's *possible* that at least a few math majors somewhere in the world are not really smart. So even if the premise is true, it doesn't guarantee the truth of the conclusion. Nonetheless, we frequently—and rationally—infer general claims from limited evidence. We rely on opinion polls not to learn, say, how many people *out of the handful interviewed* plan to vote for Medina but to learn what proportion *of all voters* plan to vote for Medina. We do scientific experiments to discover not just whether *these particular* grains of salt dissolve in water but whether *all* salt dissolves in water. Sometimes polls and experiments can mislead us, but they surely don't *necessarily* mislead us. Many polls and experiments give us valuable information that we couldn't get any other way. We can't, after all, interview every single citizen about their political views; we have limited resources. Nor can we run an experiment on every single grain of salt in the universe; we need to save some for our fries.

Logicians have given the name **induction** to the kind of reasoning where we make an inference *from* a claim about a sample (the premise) *to* a claim about a whole domain (the conclusion).[13] That is, an inductive argument draws a conclusion about an entire *domain* (e.g., all voters) on the basis of a *sample* from that domain (e.g., the voters we interviewed). In the chemistry-experiment example, the domain is all salt, and the sample is the salt we used in the experiment.

The gap between the sample mentioned in the premise and the domain mentioned in the conclusion explains the invalidity of inductive arguments. It's always *possible* that the people we interviewed included the *only* citizens who plan to vote for Medina in the upcoming election, or that *only* the specific salt molecules we put in the test tube today are water-soluble. Inductive reasoning can nonetheless be reliable because although these situations are *possible*, they are not *probable*.

So, inductive arguments are never valid; they are always invalid. Therefore, they are never sound, always unsound. It is thus almost never interesting or relevant that an inductive argument is invalid (and thus unsound). Inductive arguments aren't *intended* to be valid or sound. Nonetheless, inductive arguments can be better or worse. What, then, determines how good an inductive argument is?

Let's begin with the *structure* of an inductive argument. Assuming for the moment that we have a true claim about a sample, what makes for a good inference from that claim to a claim about the domain to which the sample belongs? That is, what takes the place of validity in the assessment of an inductive argument? The answer is that there are two factors. The first is **sample size**: The bigger the sample, the stronger the inductive inference. The more people you interview, the more trust we reasonably place in your conclusion that, say, 55% of people plan to vote for Medina. The more often we repeat the salt

13 This sense of "induction" is distinct from (though related to) the mathematical technique of the same name. In fact, mathematical induction is a form of deductive reasoning.

experiment and get the same results, the more confident we reasonably are that all salt dissolves in water.

A *deductive* argument is either valid or invalid; there's no middle ground. But because the strength of an *inductive* inference depends on the size of its sample, its strength is not an all-or-nothing affair. An inductive argument can be stronger or weaker. A larger sample always results in a stronger inductive argument, but inductive arguments always fall short of the strength of validity. You might have thought that you could construct a rock-solid, validity-strength inductive inference by including the entire domain in your "sample." If you interviewed *every single voter*, and 55% of them (truthfully) said that they planned to vote for Medina, you could be absolutely sure that 55% of voters plan to vote for Medina. But notice that your assertion is no longer the result of an inductive *inference*. You are no longer *generalizing* from a claim about a sample to a claim about a domain of which the sample is a part; instead, you have simply observed something about the entire domain.

The second factor that affects the strength of an inductive argument is **representativeness**. That is, a sample that is more representative of the whole domain (in the relevant respect, e.g., voting plans or solubility) will naturally give us a better basis for drawing conclusions about that domain; a biased, non-representative sample will skew our conclusion. There's a problem here, though: How are we supposed to know whether our sample is representative? If we knew that the sample of people we polled about their voting plans was perfectly representative of the population as a whole (with respect to their voting plans), we wouldn't need to do the poll in the first place—we would already know what proportion of the population plans to vote for Medina. As a result, attempts to attain representativeness are, practically speaking, attempts to eliminate potential sources of bias.

One well-known technique for eliminating bias is randomization. If you interview only college students about their voting plans, you may well get a biased sample of all voters. Perhaps students are better informed than most people, and thus tend to vote for particular kinds of candidates. You are more likely to get a representative sample, then, if you pick a random sample of all voters. This is easier said than done, but even if you manage it, this is no *guarantee* of a representative sample. The 55 voters out of the 100 you selected randomly might still just happen to be the *only* people who plan to vote for Medina. Unbeknownst to you, and through no fault of your own, your conclusion—that 55% of voters plan to vote for Medina—will be false, and your inductive inference weak because your sample is highly unrepresentative.

What about your chemistry experiment, though? When you put some salt in a test tube, add water, and stir, you confidently infer that *all salt dissolves in water*. Your premise concerns a *tiny* sample of all the salt and water there is, though, and you haven't selected grains of salt and drops of water randomly from as many different sources as you can. Shouldn't you be worried that you need a bigger and potentially less biased sample? Not really. First, there is an important difference between political views and chemical properties. We know that political views are not evenly distributed among the population, so our best chance at getting a representative sample is to take it randomly from the whole domain. By contrast, we know that chemical properties (e.g., solubility) *are* evenly distributed among molecules of the same kind (e.g., salt and water). So *any* sample of salt or water we find in a chemistry lab is very likely to be highly representative of *all* salt and water in the relevant respects.[14] Second, though it is true that a bigger sample would (as

14 Notice that we know these things (at least in part) on the basis of inductive reasoning!

always) increase the strength of your inductive inference, it is also true that—*given a large, uniform domain*—increasing the sample size increases the strength of an inductive inference by only a tiny amount.

As with all arguments, the strength of an inductive argument depends not only on its *structure* (i.e., the size and representativeness of the sample) but also on its *content*: the truth or falsity of its premises. If you draw a conclusion about the solubility of salt only to discover that your lab partner fabricated all the experimental data, you should abandon your conclusion. No matter how well reasoned it is, it is based (for all you know) on a false claim about the sample, and thus you have no reason to believe it. Things are a little more complicated with the content of inductive arguments than deductive arguments, however. A deductive argument is a *chain* of reasoning: If a single premise is false, then the chain is broken, and the argument gives you no reason whatsoever to believe the conclusion. An inductive argument is more like a rope made of many threads. If you discover that *one* person of the hundred you polled is not an eligible voter, the poll still gives you good reason to believe its results—just slightly less good reason than if you'd managed to poll 100 eligible voters.[15]

Finally, note that we often effortlessly combine different types of reasoning. Suppose we reason as follows:

> The store has been open every Thursday so far this year. So the store will be open next Thursday.

This is not a valid argument—it's *possible* that the store will be closed next Thursday. But on the face of it, it's not an inductive argument either. After all, the conclusion is about the store's hours on a particular Thursday; it's not a generalization about the store's hours every Thursday. What's implicitly going on here is probably an inductive inference followed by a deductive inference:

60. The store has been open every Thursday so far this year.
61. So, the store is open every Thursday.
62. So, the store will be open next Thursday.

The inference from (60) to (61) is inductive. How strong it is will depend on how far through the year we are (i.e., the sample size) and whether the Thursdays we've experienced are representative—with respect to the store's hours—of all Thursdays. (Perhaps the store closes on public holidays, but no public holidays fall on Thursdays early in the year.) The inference from (61) to (62) is deductive. Assuming only premise 60, the final conclusion (62) might be false. But assuming premise 61, there's no way the final conclusion could be false.

There's no harm in this kind of compression of reasoning in a casual conversation, but in your philosophy paper you should be aware—and ensure your reader is aware—of what kinds of inferences you're making at what points.

15 Another way of looking at this issue would be to insist that an inductive argument with a single false premise, just like a deductive argument with a single false premise, gives you *no reason whatsoever* to believe its conclusion. It's just that it's easier to convert an inductive argument with a single false premise into a different inductive argument of similar strength: Simply remove the offending claim.

10.5.2 Abductive Reasoning

When we reason inductively, we generalize about one kind of thing. We start with a claim about *some* things of that kind, and we draw a conclusion about *all* things of that kind. By contrast, we sometimes consider some information and—reasonably, though nondeductively—draw a conclusion about a completely different kind of thing. This kind of reasoning is a staple of detective fiction. The detective notices a peculiar smudge on the doorframe, a witness jumping in response to a particular question, and rumors of a rivalry between two siblings and infers that the missing painting has been not stolen but hidden in the attic. The premises of the detective's argument concern a smudge, a jump, and a rumor, but her conclusion concerns the location of a painting. This kind of reasoning is also common in the sciences. In the seventeenth century, Isaac Newton considered various facts about how things fall and the motion of the moon, planets, and comets and inferred that there is a force—gravity—that operates between all masses. Gravity didn't feature in his premises, but it played a starring role in his revolutionary conclusion.

Logicians have given the name **abduction** to this kind of reasoning. In abductive reasoning, we make an inference *from* some information (the premises) *to* an *explanation* of that information (the conclusion). (The "kidnapping" sense of the term can be distracting, but the connection between the two is that an abductive argument "leads us away" from the topic of its premises to a conclusion about something else.)

Abductive reasoning is often called *inference to the best explanation*, but we should note two things about this label. First, there's no guarantee that the conclusion of an abductive argument really is the *best* explanation. Just as deductive arguments are those *intended* to be sound but may be unsound, the conclusion of an abductive argument is *intended* to be the best explanation of the premises. But there are bad abductive arguments. These are those in which the reasoning goes wrong, and there is a better explanation (perhaps *many* better explanations) of the premises than the argument's conclusion.

Second, the explanation is "best" not in the sense that it is *true* (though that is certainly the hope) but in the sense that a rational person would prefer that explanation over all others. Abductive arguments are never valid because it is always possible that some other hypothesis *in fact* explains the information from which we infer our conclusion—even if we have properly reasoned to the (rationally) best explanation. In the detective example above, for instance, it's possible that the painting was sent to an art restorer, but everyone in the household has strangely forgotten this. In the scientific example, it's *possible* that an invisible, all-powerful demon is moving everything in the universe around so that it *looks* like there's a universal force of gravity when in fact there is no such thing. Abductive reasoning can nonetheless be reliable because although these alternative explanations are *possible*, they are not *probable*. (Compare inductive reasoning: The fact that, despite your best efforts, you might unluckily end up with an unrepresentative sample does not mean that induction is generally unreliable.)

As with inductive arguments, then, abductive arguments are never valid; they are always invalid. Therefore, they are never sound, always unsound. It is thus almost never interesting or relevant that an abductive argument is invalid (and thus unsound). Abductive arguments aren't *intended* to be valid or sound. Nonetheless, abductive arguments can be better or worse. What, then, determines how good an abductive argument is?

Let's begin with the *structure* of an abductive argument. Assume for the moment that the premises of the argument (that is, the claims about the information we're attempting to explain) are true. What makes for a good inference from that information to the explanation of it? That is, what takes the place of validity (for deduction) or sample size and representativeness (for induction) in the assessment of an abductive argument? In short: What makes an explanation of some information the *best* explanation? This is even less well understood than what makes for a good inductive argument. Rather than attempting to give a theory of abduction, then, we will explain four rules of thumb that will help you to assess whether a **hypothesis** (i.e., one possible explanation) is the best explanation of some information.

Suppose that your friend Sam comes home one day to discover that the valuable jewelry he inherited from his grandmother is missing. What could explain this? It's possible that someone was wandering by, decided to break into Sam's room, found the jewelry, and stole it. But you know that Sam has a roommate, Riley, who knows about the jewelry and has access to Sam's room.

Notice that you fairly automatically start considering alternative hypotheses. You'll never arrive at the *best* explanation of your information if it isn't among the hypotheses you're considering. Hence our first rule of thumb:

> Abductive rule of thumb #1: The greater the range of hypotheses considered, the stronger the inference.

Unfortunately, considering a range of hypotheses that includes the *best* explanation is easier said than done. There is a huge number of *possible* explanations of any information you're likely to be considering, and it is often very difficult to think of even the most plausible candidates. Consider fictional detectives, who are typically excellent at abductive reasoning.[16] At the end of a good crime novel, the detective typically surprises the reader (and other characters) by offering a rationally compelling explanation of evidence that has been made available to the reader in the course of the novel. Readers have all the clues; they just don't typically think of the hypothesis that turns out to be the best explanation of those clues. Similarly, Newton's conclusion that there must be a force of gravity operating between every mass in the universe was the result of brilliant abductive reasoning. The evidence was available to many intelligent, rational people who knew a lot about physics and astronomy, but it was not so easy to think of the hypothesis of a gravitational force.

Now suppose that, like a good detective, you test the hypothesis that Riley stole the jewelry by asking Riley where she was when the jewelry went missing. It turns out that Riley has an alibi: She was on campus, taking a chemistry exam the entire time Sam was out of his room. Alibis are examples of another abductive rule of thumb:

> Abductive rule of thumb #2: The more false implications a hypothesis has, the weaker the inference.

When people offer alibis, they are implicitly falsifying an implication of the hypothesis that they committed the crime. The basic form of an alibi is as follows:

63. If X committed the crime, then X was at the scene of the crime.
64. X was not at the scene of the crime.
65. So X did not commit the crime.

16 Sherlock Holmes famously refers to his reasoning as "deduction," but he is using the term differently from how philosophers use it.

Notice that this argument has the form of *modus tollens* (see §10.3.2), with the alibi serving to justify the second premise. That might suggest that a single false implication *guarantees* that the hypothesis is false. But when reasoning abductively, we typically don't have access to all the information we would need to confidently make a sound deductive inference that a hypothesis is false. It's typically *possible* that the conditional premise is false. In our example, it's *possible* that Riley stole the jewelry by programming a robot to shift it from Sam's room to hers while she was taking the chemistry exam. Nonetheless, we would ordinarily—and rightly—take Riley's alibi to significantly weaken our confidence in the hypothesis that she stole Sam's jewelry. More generally, the more (plausible) implications of a hypothesis there are that turn out to be false, the less confidence we should have that the hypothesis is true.

Many scientific experiments also rely on this abductive rule of thumb. For instance, the early modern theory that light is transmitted through a "luminiferous aether" implied that the speed of light would vary if measured in different directions. When physicists tested this prediction, however, they discovered that the speed of light did *not* vary as predicted. So the luminiferous-aether theory was abandoned.

You might have thought that this second rule of thumb implies that the *more true* implications a hypothesis has, the *stronger* the inference. But it's a little more complicated than that since *many true implications give us no reason at all to believe a hypothesis*. For instance, it would be reasonable to expect that if Riley stole the jewelry (the hypothesis), then Riley was alive while the jewelry was stolen (the implication). But suppose you test this implication and it turns out to be true: Riley was indeed alive while the jewelry was stolen. This doesn't give you any reason to believe the hypothesis that Riley stole the jewelry. Why? Because you'd expect her to be alive while the jewelry was stolen *whether or not* Riley stole it. What we need is an implication that would likely be *true if the hypothesis is true but false if the hypothesis is false*. In other words:

> Abductive rule of thumb #3: The more true implications a hypothesis has *that would likely be false if the hypothesis were false*, the stronger the inference.

One implication of this sort would be that *the jewelry is in Riley's possession*. We would expect her to have the jewelry if she stole it, but not if she didn't. Of course, it's *possible* the thief stashed the jewelry in Riley's room or that someone is trying to frame Riley, but her possession of the jewelry would still be *some* reasonable evidence that she stole it.

Similarly, Newton's theory of gravity was used to predict the existence and location of a planet beyond Uranus on the basis of Uranus's path through the sky—a prediction that would be surprising if the theory of gravity were false. When Neptune was discovered to exist just where it was predicted to be, that was taken to be strong evidence in favor of Newton's theory.[17]

Suppose you have concluded that Riley took Sam's jewelry (on the basis of evidence we are not at liberty to divulge here). Still, there are at least two possibilities. First, perhaps Riley stole the jewelry of her own free will. Second, perhaps Riley took the jewelry because her mind was being controlled by distant aliens using a technology undetectable by humans. How can we decide between these two hypotheses? Applying the first two rules of thumb, we might consider implications of the two hypotheses, such as *there are*

17 Our discussion of this rule is heavily influenced by Elliott Sober's "surprise principle" (*Core Questions in Philosophy* 28–30).

aliens or *there are alien technologies undetectable by humans*. The problem, however, is that we can't practically test these hypotheses. Fortunately, there is another rule of thumb we can apply in this case:

> Abductive rule of thumb #4: Given two hypotheses of equal explanatory power, we should prefer the simpler hypothesis.

In the absence of any evidence for the existence of aliens, we have reason to prefer our simple hypothesis that Riley stole the jewelry of her own free will.[18]

This fourth rule of thumb is explicitly comparative; it says that a simpler hypothesis is better than a more complicated hypothesis (other things being equal). But the second and third rules of thumb could also be considered comparative: A hypothesis with several false implications is worse (other things being equal) than a hypothesis with none (rule #2). And a hypothesis with more true implications that would otherwise likely be false is better than one with fewer such implications (rule #3). This is why the *first* rule of thumb is so important: Since you're typically comparing alternative hypotheses, you want to do your best to ensure that you're considering a wide range of hypotheses.

As with all arguments, the strength of an abductive argument depends not only on its *structure* (i.e., how it fares with respect to the rules of thumb) but also on its *content*: the truth or falsity of its premises. If the detective merely *dreamt* that there was a smudge on the doorframe, that a witness jumped in response to her question, and so on, then any inference the detective makes to an explanation of the smudge, the jumping, and so on is groundless. There is no explanation of things that are not the case.[19]

What if not all of the premises are false, however? Suppose the detective wasn't dreaming and that most of her clues were true facts but that there was no smudge on the doorframe. Rather, there was a cockroach crawling up the doorframe, which (because of her poor eyesight) the detective mistook for a smudge. It is difficult to generalize about the effects of such false premises on abductive arguments. An inductive argument is based on many pieces of evidence of a single kind (e.g., survey responses or experimental results). Remove one piece, and what remains is very similar, if slightly weaker, evidence for the conclusion. An abductive argument, however, is typically based on evidence of different kinds, and the strength of the inference depends on how well the conclusion explains the total set of evidence. Perhaps all we can say, then, is that if one premise of an abductive argument is false, you should eliminate it from the argument and consider how well the conclusion explains the evidence that remains.[20]

18 This rule of thumb is sometimes called *Ockham's razor*, after a medieval philosopher (William of Ockham) who influentially argued that we should not posit the existence of more than we have to. But the term "Ockham's razor" gets used in different ways by different philosophers.

19 In one sense, of course, there are explanations of what is not the case. For instance, you could explain why Alex is not in class today. (She is ill.) But this is an explanation of something that *is* the case (Alex's absence). What we mean is that (in this same situation, for instance) there can be no explanation of why Alex *is* in class—because she isn't.

20 As with inductive arguments, another way of looking at this issue would be to insist that an abductive argument with a single false premise, just like a deductive argument with a single false premise, gives you *no reason whatsoever* to believe its conclusion. As with inductive arguments, though, it's easy to convert an abductive argument with a single false premise into a similar abductive argument without a false premise: Simply remove the offending claim. *Unlike* the inductive case, there's no guarantee that the resulting argument will be similar in strength to the original argument.

10.6 Concluding Remarks

In this chapter, we have introduced some basic concepts, terms, and techniques of deductive and nondeductive reasoning. These are all aimed at helping you to assess the strength of arguments you encounter or create. Two basic aspects of any argument are relevant to an assessment of its strength. One is its *content*—whether its premises are true or false. Since when you give an argument you ask your audience to infer the conclusion from the premises, if any of the premises are false, then the strength of the inference will be affected. But, as we have seen, precisely how the inference is affected depends on the kind of argument it is. That brings us to the second aspect of an argument relevant to its strength—its *structure*. This is a matter of *how* the premises, if true, are supposed to support the truth of the conclusion. We have looked at three quite different ways in which premises can support a conclusion, each corresponding to a different kind of inference a rational person can make: deductive, inductive, and abductive inferences. The tools we have introduced in this chapter should help you assess the strength of many arguments you encounter and create, but you should also be willing to consider that a given argument may not fit any of the templates we have provided here.

Appendix A

Sample Drafts with Comments and Revisions

In Sections 3.7–3.9, we discuss the importance of revising your paper as you reread it and in response to the feedback of others. In this appendix, we provide three excerpts from drafts of various philosophy papers, marked up by a reader with an eye to improving the writing, along with a version of each excerpt revised in light of the reader's comments and an explanation of the revisions. You can imagine that the reader is someone the author has asked to provide comments on the draft or even the author herself. In many cases, there is more than one way to correct a specific writing problem; in such cases, the revised version given here illustrates just one of those ways.

First, consider this opening paragraph from a paper on the metaphysics of race and the revised version.

Put article titles in quotation marks

In his article *Are Folk Races Like Dingoes, Dimes, or Dodos?*, Quayshawn Spencer argues

wrong word? Where does this quotation end?

that race is a biologically construct Biological in the sense that "careful biology has

→ This isn't a complete sentence.

determined that the entity actually exists (573). I contend that allthough biological features

although

play some role in the construction of race, what race someone belongs to is ultimately a

Use lowercase here

social fact. To support this thesis, I will show (1) Show that Spencer's account of the origin of

i.e. ?

"folk races" (e.g., racial groups referred to in ordinary talk) is implausible, (2) By Spencer's

own admission, there are folk races that are not biologically real, so his theory that race is

biologically real can't be the whole story of the realness of race, and, finally, that the

too colloquial? awkward

biological groups Spencer identifies do not match up with folk races.

This series doesn't have parallel construction.

Can you make point #2 more concise?

In his article "Are Folk Races Like Dingoes, Dimes, or Dodos?", Quayshawn Spencer argues that race is biologically real; that is, "careful biology has determined that [it] actually exists" (573). I contend that although biological features play some role in the construction of race, what race someone belongs to is ultimately a social fact. To support this thesis, I will show (1) that Spencer's account of the origin of "folk races" (i.e., racial groups referred to in ordinary talk) is implausible, (2) that there are folk races that are not biologically real, and (3) that the biological groups Spencer identifies do not match up with folk races.

In the revised version, the author has correctly put the article title in quotation marks. (See §7.4.2.) She has also acknowledged that the noun "construct" refers to something made by people and thus is confusing if applied to biological entities, as in the draft. The second sentence (a sentence fragment in the first draft) has been incorporated into the first sentence (§6.4.2) using a semicolon (§6.8.3), and—after checking the quotation against the source—the closing quotation marks have been supplied (§6.8.6). The author has also taken the opportunity to simplify the quotation, indicating her changes with square brackets (§6.8.6). The spelling error ("all though")—one not picked up by the author's spellchecker—has been corrected (§3.9). The preview of points supporting the thesis has been reworded so that each point is grammatically parallel (§6.4.2). Now the expression of each point grammatically follows the introductory phrase ("To support this thesis, I will show ..."), and the repeated "show" (not caught by the reader) has been deleted. The abbreviation "e.g." has been corrected to "i.e." (§§6.6 & 6.10.2). Finally, the author has realized that she was trying to cram too much into the summary of the second point. Cutting it down to the central point has allowed her to remove the colloquial and awkward phrasing.

Now consider a passage from a paper on René Descartes's *Meditations* and its revision.

n

In the first Meditation, Descartes never claimed that a "evil genius not less powerful than

Be consistent with verb tense.

deceitful" (148) actually exists. He only claims that we cannot establish "one hundred

F Descartes

percent" that such a being does not exist, for ~~him~~ that is enough. He only need to establish

too colloquial

comma splice

ematics

the POSSIBILITY in order to throw into doubt even the seemingly certian truths of math.

Use italics for emphasis.

> In the first Meditation, Descartes never claims that an "evil genius not less powerful than deceitful" (148) actually exists. He only claims that we cannot establish with certainty that such a being does not exist. For Descartes, this is enough. He only needs to establish the *possibility* of this evil genius to throw into doubt even the seemingly certain truths of math.

The author has corrected the distracting shift in verb tense (see §6.7 on "Tenses"). She may already have sensed that the phrase "one hundred per cent" is too casual for an academic paper since she originally put it in quotation marks (§6.8.6). (The quotation marks may also have misled some readers into thinking that the phrase is a quotation from Descartes.) The phrase has now been replaced with the more formal "with certainty." The final comma in the second sentence (between the words "exist" and "for") incorrectly joins two complete sentences (§6.4.2); a period replaces the comma in the revision. The new sentence thus created now begins with a capital letter, and "him" is replaced with "Descartes," so there is no misunderstanding, even on first reading, about who is being referred to. The all-caps formatting of "POSSIBILITY" has been changed to italics (§6.9). Three other small changes have been made: "a" is changed to "an" in the first sentence of the passage, and two "typos" (typographical errors) in the last sentence have been corrected ("needs" and "certain"). Note that the author has declined to change the final word "math" to "mathematics." Even good writers may disagree about whether the abbreviation "math" is too informal for an academic paper, and, on reflection, this author has decided that it is acceptable (§3.8).

Finally, consider part of a paper about the political philosophy of John Locke.

No need for these quotation marks

Locke claims that people have "inalienable" rights: A right to life, A right to liberty, And a right to property. The rights to life and liberty are strong ones, as Locke describes them in his "The Second Treatise of Government." It is the third one, the to property, that get watered down by Locke. It turns out that self-interested Locke, of the propertied class, does not endorse giving up his own wealth and letting everyone actually have property, as the right implies. He ends up claiming only that no one may be deprived of their option of competing in the economic marketplace for property. Locke is not an eglitarian, when you really come down to it.

Use complete sentences.

vague

right

awkward

Italicize book titles.

unclear

Delete reference to Locke's character, or make precise, defensible claims about it.

The last half of this paragraph is colloquial & unclear. Rewrite for precision and concision.

> Locke claims that people have inalienable rights: a right to life, a right to liberty, and a right to property. The rights to life and liberty, as Locke describes them in *The Second Treatise of Government*, are substantial ones, guaranteeing us highly valued benefits, such as the right to self-defense and freedom of expression. The right to property, however, may at first appear to guarantee more than it ultimately does. Locke does not depart so radically from his background as a person of the propertied class as to become an economic egalitarian. His final position on the right to property is not that everyone is guaranteed actual possessions. The right is to compete for property in the economic marketplace; no one may deprive you, by statute or edict, of your place in the free market of economic rivals.

The term "inalienable" in the first sentence is a nontechnical English word used in its ordinary sense, so the quotation marks are unnecessary. (We include them in the previous sentence because we *mention*, rather than *use*, the term there. See §6.8.6.) The three sentence fragments that follow are now included in the opening sentence (§§6.4.2 & 6.8.3). In the next sentence, the book title is correctly italicized instead of being placed in quotation marks (§7.4.2), and "his" has been deleted to eliminate the awkwardness of "... his *The* ...." (The author could just as well have left "his" and deleted "*The*".) The vague word "strong" is deleted (§5.5); the point is clarified with the word "substantial" and an additional explanatory phrase. The second half of the paragraph is completely redrafted in response to the reader's comments (§3.8). More than simple editing was required in this case to eliminate the unpolished, imprecise style. Notice that in the revision, the semicolon (in the last sentence) is used correctly. An independent clause—a complete statement with subject and predicate, able to stand alone—both precedes and follows it (§6.8.3).

Appendix B
A Sample Paper

The following is a short thesis-defense paper written in response to the following prompt:

3. If determinism is true, can we be morally responsible for any of our actions?

There are not many explicit signposts in this paper, but can you identify the function of each paragraph (formal opening paragraph, objection, reply, etc.)?

Alex Kenosha
PHI 102: Introduction to Philosophy
Thesis-defense paper
Prompt 3
Word count: 1,235

How Our Actions Can Be Free in a Causal World

Suppose that you decide to donate a hundred dollars to a climate-change organization instead of buying the new shoes you would love but don't really need (cf. Strawson 600). Many people would say that you deserve moral praise for your selfless choice. But do you really? Some would argue that because human beings are physical organisms, subject to the laws of nature, they have no control over their actions and so do not deserve praise or blame for them.

In this paper, I argue that our actions can be free in a sense that gives us moral responsibility for them, even if we belong to a world entirely subject to the laws of nature. I defend this claim by, first, explaining the reasons why someone might deny we are morally responsible for our actions and, second, explaining where I think this reasoning goes wrong, thereby arguing that we are morally responsible for our actions. I end by considering the objection that my view ignores the moral implications of the ultimate causes of our actions. My reply is that, overall, my view accords better than the alternative with our ordinary notion of moral responsibility.

I assume throughout this paper that determinism is true—that is, that the state of the universe at any moment is entirely determined by the state of the universe at the previous moment together with the laws of nature (Pereboom 1). You, including your brain, are part of the universe, so whatever happens in your brain when you decide to donate your hundred dollars instead of buying the shoes (for instance) is entirely determined by the laws of nature acting upon what the universe was like in the previous moment.

Does determinism imply that your decision to donate the money was not free? On the one hand, you considered reasons for spending your money one way or another—weighing, for example, the pleasure the shoes would bring against your moral obligation to help combat climate change—and decided to donate the money. This seems, on the face of it, to be a free action. (No one held a gun to your head.) On the other hand, the pleasure you take in shoes, your beliefs about your moral obligations, and even the way in which you weigh reasons and come to decisions are all determined by the laws of nature acting on how the universe happens to be. So whatever state your brain is in was ultimately determined by factors outside your control, such as the genes you inherited from your parents and the environment in which you were raised and developed your beliefs, desires, and personality.

According to "hard determinists," these facts about the ultimate origins of your actions imply that you deserve no praise or blame for any of your actions. You deserve praise for an action only if the choice to perform it was truly yours, under your ultimate control. The hard determinist argues that because the ultimate causes of your actions are beyond your control—indeed, they occur before you even existed—you cannot be responsible for those actions (Timpe §3.c).

I believe that the hard determinist concludes too quickly that we are not responsible for our actions because she ignores an important distinction between kinds of causes. If a rock falls on a mouse, killing it, it would be absurd to consider the rock morally responsible for the mouse's death. But if a person kills a mouse with a rock, we rightly hold the person morally responsible for the mouse's death.[1] The crucial distinction between the two cases is that the person—unlike the rock—has a mind. People act for *reasons*, and we hold them responsible for their reasoned decisions. We praise you for donating your money to charity because we think that you are capable of weighing your moral obligations against your selfish desires in deciding what to do. If we discovered that you donated the money only because you had been "programmed" to do so by a hypnotist, then we would *not* praise your for your action.

In short, I am a "compatibilist" because I believe that determinism is compatible with at least some of our actions' being free in the sense that makes us morally responsible for them. An action is free, on my view, if it results from a *normal process of rational deliberation*. There is no space to develop an account of normal rational deliberation here, but the idea would be that the kinds of cases where we hesitate to hold people (fully) morally responsible for their actions—cases of hypnotism, drugging, mental illness, and so on—are plausibly not cases of normal rational deliberation (Ayer 622-3).

A hard determinist might object to my compatibilism by comparing two actions. Suppose that while you donated your hundred dollars, your friend spent their money on some shoes they didn't need. Suppose also that the donation is morally praiseworthy and the purchase morally blameworthy. The hard determinist will point to the fact that *something* explains the difference between these two people's decisions. Perhaps you have a better understanding of our moral obligations than your friend, or perhaps your friend is more strongly motivated by pleasure than

[1] Thanks to my sister, Bree, for suggesting this example.

you are. Unless you and your friend are responsible for these aspects of your characters, you are not responsible for the different decisions that result from them. But nobody can be ultimately responsible for any aspect of their character. Perhaps your deeper understanding of morality is due to your having taken an ethics course, and your friend's hedonism is part of her genetic inheritance. (Perhaps you "freely chose" to take the ethics course, but the hard determinist will simply trace the causal origins of this decision back to factors outside your control.) So, concludes the hard determinist, it makes no sense to praise you for your actions and blame your friend for theirs, since neither of you is ultimately responsible for your actions (Rosen et al. 598).

I must admit that this objection has some force. However, I maintain that the hard determinist errs in focusing exclusively on the big picture—that is, on the *ultimate* causes of our actions. While it is true that our ordinary notion of moral responsibility is tied up with the causes of actions, that notion also leads us to distinguish between causes of different types, as I argued above.

Moreover, our ordinary notion of moral responsibility implies that we are morally responsible for many of our actions. The hard compatibilist must deny that we are morally responsible for *any* of our actions, with devastating implications for our moral reasoning. (I have no space to discuss these implications here, but you might consider what such a view would imply for our criminal-justice system.) The kind of compatibilism I have defended here thus seems to fit better overall with our ordinary understanding of moral responsibility.

To summarize my argument: The hard determinist claims that because we have no control over the ultimate causes of our actions, we cannot be morally responsible for those actions. I argue that as long as an action follows from a normal process of rational deliberation it is free. A full defense of this thesis would require an account of rational deliberation, and this is worth pursuing since the compatibilist account of free actions accords better with our ordinary notion of moral responsibility than the hard determinist's denial of such freedom.[2]

Works Cited

Ayer, A. J. "Freedom and Necessity." *The Norton Introduction to Philosophy*, edited by Gideon Rosen et al., 2nd ed., W. W. Norton and Company, 2018, pp. 618-25.

Pereboom, Derk. *Free Will.* Cambridge University Press, 2022.

Rosen, Gideon, et al. "Do We Possess Free Will?" *The Norton Introduction to Philosophy*, edited by Gideon Rosen et al., 2nd ed., W. W. Norton and Company, 2018, pp. 595-600.

Strawson, Galen. "Free Will." *The Norton Introduction to Philosophy*, edited by Gideon Rosen et al., 2nd ed., W. W. Norton and Company, 2018, pp. 600-10.

Timpe, Kevin. "Free Will." *Internet Encyclopedia of Philosophy*, edited by James Fieser and Bradley Dowden, https://iep.utm.edu/freewill/. Accessed 12 June 2023.

[2] I thank my roommate, Pat, for helpful suggestions on a draft of this paper.

5

Appendix C
How to Study for, and Take, a Philosophy Exam

In addition to assigning papers, philosophy instructors commonly assess their students' philosophical knowledge and abilities by requiring them to take exams. Exams have a wide range of formats. In this appendix, we offer some advice based on our experiences of both grading exams and taking them ourselves when we were students. Much of this advice should be helpful for taking exams in other subjects. However, anything your instructor says about an exam in her own class should, of course, take precedence over our advice.

We have written this advice with timed, in-class exams primarily in mind, but most of it applies equally to, or can be easily adapted for, take-home exams, whether timed or untimed.

C.1 Studying for a Philosophy Exam

Start right away. This advice for working on your paper applies equally to studying for an exam. If you find yourself staying up late the night before the exam, trying to cram information into your brain, it's a sign that something has gone wrong with your studying. To do well on an exam, studying should be something that you do regularly throughout the semester, not something that happens just before the exam.

Philosophy is much more like a skill than a set of facts, so becoming proficient at it requires habits like those used to learn a language, a musical instrument, or a sport: You have to practice regularly. It is through *doing* philosophy that you will prepare most effectively for a philosophy exam. There are two main ways of doing philosophy: having philosophical discussions and writing philosophical prose. Despite what you might have expected, simply *thinking* about philosophical questions is of limited use in preparing for an exam. You will be assessed on your ability to *express* your thoughts, so that is what you must work on. Moreover, when you first try to express your thoughts, you will often discover that they are not as clear or easy to express as you had expected.

Philosophical discussions can give you a sense of how well you understand the material. It's most rewarding to have such discussions with people who know at least as much philosophy as you do. Other students in your class, students in other philosophy classes, and students who have taken philosophy in the past are thus all good candidates to have fruitful philosophical discussions with. Organize a meeting with other interested students where you can discuss a particular issue, and really try to hash it out: What is the main question in this area? What are the different views one can take? What are the best arguments for and against each view? Which view is the strongest overall? Take notes during the discussion, just as you would during class. (See §8.1.3.)

Another great resource for philosophical discussions is your instructor. You don't have to have a specific question in mind to go to office hours. You can simply try to articulate your views on a topic and let the discussion develop from there.

You should already be writing philosophy regularly in the form of notes taken while reading and in class. (See §8.1.) Rather than treating these notes as your study materials, which you read and reread, trying to memorize as much as possible, you should use them as draft materials that you re*write* over the course of the semester and as you study for the exam. The more you know about the format of the exam, the easier it will be to create customized study materials. For instance, if you know there will be short-answer questions requiring you to explain terms, theories, or arguments you have covered in class, you can draft a paragraph on each term, theory, or argument and then create flashcards to help test your recall of this material. You should get feedback on your study materials, if possible. Your instructor and other students in your course may be willing to look at your materials and make suggestions.

If the exam will include an essay, and you know (or have a pretty good idea) what the topic will be, you should prepare a draft essay on the topic. While no one expects an exam essay to be as polished as a paper, the more of our advice about writing philosophy papers you can follow, the better your exam essay will be. In particular, try to ensure that your essay clearly and accurately articulates the philosophical question or problem it aims to answer or solve, and a thesis that provides your answer or solution. Make sure, too, that you understand the particular function of each paragraph in your essay (explaining a theory, setting out an objection, etc.) and how those parts fit together to make a strong case for your thesis.

Once you have a draft essay that you are reasonably happy with, try rewriting it under exam conditions. That is, give yourself the amount of time you'll have in the exam to write the essay, and try to write the whole essay out, without looking at your notes. This will give you a sense of how securely the structure and content of the essay is fixed in your mind. Did you leave out any major parts of the essay? Did you get confused when explaining a particular concept, theory, or argument? Let these observations guide your further preparation for the exam. The more often you write your essay under exam conditions, the better you should get at this task.

Writing out the essay under exam conditions also lets you calculate how fast you write. Count how many words you wrote in the time available, and use this to guide you in editing your draft in preparation for the exam. This can also help you prepare for other exam essays. Calculate roughly how many words you can write in half an hour, say, and then use this information to figure out how long an essay you can write for a particular exam, given the amount of time you'll have.

C.2 Taking a Philosophy Exam

Make sure you know when and where the exam will take place. Just as you should schedule extra time to submit your paper, in case you encounter any last-minute obstacles, you should plan to arrive at the exam early, in case things do not go as planned. Make sure you know what materials you are required to bring (writing materials, notes, textbooks, etc.) and what materials are not allowed (phones, notes, textbooks, etc.)

Time management is an essential component of taking an exam successfully. You should spend time on the various parts of any exam in proportion to what each part is worth. For example, if an essay is worth 25% of the total points for the exam, you should spend 25% of the exam time on the essay. Any extra points you might get by spending more time on the essay will likely be outweighed by the points you will lose by not spending enough time on the other parts of the exam.

Though taking exams may not be your favorite activity, you should not leave the exam as soon as possible. Some instructors write their exams so that you have plenty of time to complete the required tasks; others design exams so that you have to work solidly throughout the allotted time in order to achieve a good grade. Either way, if you finish the exam early, you should review your answers. Try not to second-guess yourself, but consider whether you have omitted anything crucial from an answer, whether you could clarify your explanation of a term, and so on.

This is not to say that more words will result in a better grade. In all of your answers, you should aim for accuracy, clarity, and concision—in addition to completeness, given the time constraints you face. You should also be guided by the principle of charity; that is, you should express the ideas of others in their strongest form, even—perhaps especially—if you disagree with them. (See §§2.3 & 4.1.)

You should write all of your answers—including short answers—in full, grammatical sentences. As with any writing, the clearer your expression, the more likely you are to communicate your understanding of the material. (If you are writing your answers on loose-leaf paper or in an exam booklet, do not write in the margins—instructors often use these to write grades or comments.)

Make sure you read all instructions carefully, and follow them. For instance, some instructors will ask you to write on alternate lines, or to write the numbers of the questions you answer in a particular place. You may not know the reasons for such instructions, but flouting them probably isn't the best way to find out.

If you are given a choice, make it. For example, if you are asked to explain one term or another, *do not explain both*. Pick the option you think you can answer best. Answering the additional option will take time away from completing other parts of the exam, likely for no benefit. Only one answer may be graded, and it may not be your best one. Alternatively, one of your answers may contain an error that shows you don't understand what you're attempting to explain, in which case you may do worse than if you had followed the instructions.

There is a difference between *explaining* a term and *giving an example*. Though an example might be *part* of an explanation, it can't constitute a complete explanation. Sometimes you'll be asked for an explanation, sometimes an example, and sometimes both. Again, do what you're asked to do, and *only* what you're asked to do. If you're asked to give an example, you should give as clear, obvious, and uncontentious an example as possible. For instance, if you're asked to give an example of a valid argument, it's better to give a simple one about dogs being animals (for instance) than one about the existence of God.

You should also give *original* examples if you can. Repeating your instructor's examples shows you've taken good notes and have a good memory, but it doesn't show your understanding of a concept the way an original example does.

Works Cited

Barker-Plummer, Dave, Jon Barwise, and John Etchemendy. *Language, Proof, and Logic.* 2nd ed., CSLI Publications, 2011.

Boardman, Frank, Nancy M. Cavender, and Howard Kahane. *Logic and Contemporary Rhetoric: The Use of Reason in Everyday Life.* 13th ed., Wadsworth, Cengage Learning, 2018.

The Chicago Manual of Style. 17th ed., University of Chicago Press, 2017.

The Chicago Manual of Style Online. University of Chicago, https://www.chicagomanualofstyle.org/home.html. Accessed 30 June 2023.

Evans, Jonathan St. B. T. "Selective Processes in Reasoning." *Thinking and Reasoning: Psychological Approaches*, edited by Jonathan St. B. T. Evans, Routledge & Kegan Paul, 1983, pp. 135–63.

Garner, Bryan A. *The Chicago Guide to Grammar, Usage, and Punctuation.* University of Chicago Press, 2016.

Garner, Bryan A. *Garner's Modern English Usage: The Authority on Grammar, Usage, and Style.* 5th ed., Oxford University Press, 2022.

GMEU: See Garner, *Garner's Modern English Usage.*

Hacker, Diana and Nancy Sommers. *A Writer's Reference.* 10th ed., Bedford/St. Martin's, 2021.

hooks, bell. *Teaching to Transgress: Education as the Practice of Freedom.* Routledge, 1994.

Lorde, Audrey. "The Master's Tools Will Never Dismantle the Master's House." *Sister Outsider: Essays and Speeches*, The Crossing Press, 1984, pp. 110–13.

MLA Handbook. 9th ed., Modern Language Association of America, 2021.

Podell, Leslie. *The Sojourner Truth Project*, 28 June 2023, www.thesojournertruthproject.com.

Putnam, Hilary. "The Meaning of 'Meaning.'" *Mind, Language, and Reality: Philosophical Papers*, vol. 2, Oxford University Press, 1975, pp. 215–71.

Rosen, Gideon, et al., editors. *The Norton Introduction to Philosophy.* 2nd ed., W. W. Norton and Company, 2018.

Saul, Jennifer, Esa Diaz-Leon, and Samia Hesni. "Feminist Philosophy of Language." *The Stanford Encyclopedia of Philosophy*, edited by Edward N. Zalta and Uri Nodelman, fall 2022 ed., https://plato.stanford.edu/archives/fall2022/entries/feminism-language/.

Seech, Zachary. *Open Minds and Everyday Reasoning.* 2nd ed., Wadsworth, 2005.

Smith, Peter. *An Introduction to Formal Logic.* 2nd ed., Cambridge University Press, 2020. (Free download available at https://www.logicmatters.net/books/.)

Sober, Elliott. *Core Questions in Philosophy.* 8th ed., Routledge, 2021.

Wolf, Michael P. "Philosophy of Language." *Internet Encyclopedia of Philosophy*, edited by James Fieser and Bradley Dowden, https://iep.utm.edu/lang-phi/. Accessed 28 June 2023.

Index

Pages in *italics* refer to figures; pages followed by "n" refer to notes.